940.54 T
Two soldiers, two lost fronts
30049003031045

 MAR 2015

DISCARD

Piqua Public Library
116 West High Street
Piqua, Ohio 45356

TWO SOLDIERS, TWO LOST FRONTS

TWO SOLDIERS, TWO LOST FRONTS

German War Diaries of the Stalingrad and North Africa Campaigns

940.54 T
Two soldiers, two lost fronts
3004900303045

DON A. GREGORY
&
WILHELM R. GEHLEN

Piqua Public Library
116 West High Street
Piqua, Ohio 45356

CASEMATE
Philadelphia & Newbury

Published in the United States of America in 2009 by
CASEMATE
1016 Warrior Road, Drexel Hill, PA 19026

and in the United Kingdom by
CASEMATE
17 Cheap Street, Newbury RG20 5DD

Copyright © Don A. Gregory and Wilhelm R. Gehlen 2009

ISBN 978-1-935149-05-7

Cataloging-in-publication data is available from the Library of Congress
and the British Library.

All rights reserved. No part of this book may be reproduced or transmitted in
any form or by any means, electronic or mechanical including photocopying,
recording or by any information storage and retrieval system, without
permission from the Publisher in writing.

10 9 8 7 6 5 4 3 2 1

Printed and bound in the United States of America.

For a complete list of Casemate titles please contact:

CASEMATE PUBLISHERS
Telephone (610) 853-9131, Fax (610) 853-9146
E-mail: casemate@casematepublishing.com
or
CASEMATE UK
Telephone (01635) 231091, Fax (01635) 41619
E-mail: casemate-uk@casematepublishing.co.uk

Mixed Sources
Product group from well-managed
forests and other controlled sources
www.fsc.org Cert no. SW-COC-002283
© 1996 Forest Stewardship Council
FSC

CONTENTS

Preface   vii

PART I: TO STALINGRAD AND BACK   1

Introduction   3

1 / Departure from Paris and Arrival in Charkov   15
2 / The Battle for Charkov, 5–29 May 1942   17
3 / Forward to the Oskol River, 31 May–22 July 1942   31
4 / Toward the Don and Ssal, 23–30 July 1942   47
5 / Advance to the Caucasus, 1 August–24 November 1942   53
6 / Our Part at Stalingrad, 25 November–25 December 1942   73
7 / Our Retreat from Stalingrad, 26 December–19 March 1942   79

Historical Timeline   89

Part II: TO NORTH AFRICA AND BACK   109

Introduction   113

1 / Conscription and On to France ("Case Yellow"), 1939   135
2 / My North Africa Campaign, 1941   139
3 / Chase and Being Chased through the Desert, 1942   161
4 / Home to Germany 1943   187
5 / The End of the War, 1945   197
6 / After the End   201
Epilogue: The Fall of Berlin and the Airlift   205

Historical Timeline   215

Appendix 1: Biography of Ludwig Bloos   253
Appendix 2: Obituary of Rolf Krengel   258
Bibliography and Sources   261

MAR   2015

For
Judith and Barbara

PREFACE

These diaries allow a glimpse into the lives of two German soldiers. Neither was famous nor of especially high rank, and no books have been written on their military careers. Diaries and memoirs written by high-ranking military and political leaders of World War II abound, but the remembrances and diaries of those who were directly responsible for carrying out the orders given from on high are rare, and those that are available are often sketchy with little detail. This is certainly understandable since those actually involved in the battles did not have the time nor the inclination to examine the overview of what they were experiencing during combat, and they were not very interested in writing about it afterward.

The unique feature of both of these diaries is that they were written as the events occurred, not after the war when memories have faded and "historical revisions" have been encouraged for social or political reasons. These are the real stories, not written for a general audience, or really for any audience at all. Perhaps they illustrate just how the reach of Hitler exceeded his grasp when he opened and tried to maintain fronts in both Russia and North Africa. History records the "two front war" as being the Eastern and Western fronts; however, there was a third front in North Africa as well. These campaigns truly signaled the end of the beginning phase of the war and the beginning of the end of the Third Reich.

The first diary, initially attributed to Oberfeldwebel (Master Sergeant) Ludwig Bloos, was a printed copy with distribution limited to the German Wehrmacht. Bloos is mentioned in Franz Kurowski's book *Panzer Aces: German Tank Commanders in World War II* (Ballentine, 2002). Recent research on Knight's Cross winners has determined that the diary was not actually written by Bloos but merely signed by him. The assignment for keeping the diary was probably given to one of the members of the 201st Panzer Regiment by one of the commanding officers, and the author never saw fit to include his own name. It is obvious from the writing style and the subjects covered in the diary, however, that it was not written by a high-ranking officer but by someone closely in touch with day-to-day events. The 201st Panzer Regiment did cross paths with Bloos' outfit, the 11th Panzer Regiment, on at least one occasion near Stalingrad. That is perhaps where the author of the diary and others in the 201st became acquainted with Bloos. It is also conceivable that, some time later, the owner of the diary simply wanted the autograph of a Knight's Cross winner on his copy. We have included a short biography of Bloos at the end of the book.

The second diary's author is well known today. His name was Rolf Krengel and the diary is the original, handwritten copy, complete with some well-done drawings made by Krengel, and it includes a few photographs. A separate photo album, with Krengel named as the owner, accompanied this diary as well, and some of those photographs and drawings have been reproduced here. The diary is also signed by two of the notable figures of the war: General Erwin Rommel and Colonel Claus von Stauffenberg. It was in Africa that von Stauffenberg, who would later attempt to assassinate Hitler, was severely wounded on April 7, 1943.

Professor Krengel, as he was later to become, died in 2002, and economic scholars worldwide noted his passing. His obituary appears at the end of this book. He was best known for his work after the war, beginning in 1948 in assisting U.S. General Lucius Clay's organization of the Berlin Airlift. The final entry in the diary refers to his initial meeting with Clay's staff.

We can see the big picture now, given the historical accounts, but as the events unfolded in real time, only quick snapshots were available to the soldiers, and that is evident in reading the diaries. Rarely is anything mentioned about the eventual outcome of the battles they were involved in, because the diaries were written as the battles occurred and neither author saw fit to offer comments afterward. This is especially notable in the Krengel diary when, after his departure from North Africa, he declines to even mention the capitulation of the Axis forces he'd left behind, including his own 21st Panzer Division. It is understandable, however; individual soldiers are generally not given the overall goals or debriefed after the mission is completed. They are simply going about their jobs as soldiers, mostly oblivious to the political implications of the campaigns in which they are involved. Both diaries also show what every soldier knows about the drudgery of war, the hurry up and wait, the plans that don't work, and the loss of life of comrades. Perhaps this is the perspective that is gained by reading war diaries written not by the generals but by the soldiers on the ground.

We have devoted a considerable amount of effort toward translating the diaries accurately while also giving background to the story as told by the writer. To that end, we have not spent a great deal of time researching all of the "tongue breaking" (as one of the diarists calls them) names of the small towns encountered. We have reproduced the names exactly as they were given in the diaries. Many of them have changed names (and spellings) several times since the war, or they simply no longer exist. Some we could identify, others we just left as they were written in the diaries. A map was included in the Stalingrad diary with the route of the 23d Panzer Division marked, along with additional notations to clarify highlights. The major towns and landmarks are still there and the major roads are still in use.

Both diaries illustrate just how critical fuel shortages and supply routes were in each campaign. In many instances, opportunities were missed because of a lack of fuel for the tanks, and battles were definitely lost because in both Russia and Africa the vehicles could not maneuver. Reconnaissance missions were cancelled, and in some cases tanks were left behind because they had run out of fuel. Paulus in Stalingrad might have been rescued and all of North Africa might have been occupied for years if the fuel situation had been solved. In any case, it would have been a very different war.

Our purpose in writing this book is to present insight into the lives of two soldiers, not to explore or interpret the history itself. Nevertheless, we have added timelines and additional information about the campaigns and units in order to help the reader put the diaries in context. We have also chosen to make some translations more readable by converting German military ranks to their American or British equivalent, except when the German rank is popularly known, and we have made some conversions from the metric system to the English system when we felt they were warranted. Some paragraphs have been broken up for readability. Whenever possible, we have identified individual soldiers mentioned in the diaries and have given small details about them when they were available. We have limited the details to those pertinent to their service during or near the time covered by the diaries, so awards won later are generally not mentioned. Our comments and notes throughout the diaries are given in brackets [ ].

We chose to combine these two diaries into a single book because they are representative of those written by German soldiers involved in the largest and most decisive campaigns of the war. The two diaries are actually somewhat literally connected in an unusual way. The Stalingrad diary covers a portion of the German effort to rescue General Paulus, trapped in Stalingrad in late 1942. Earlier, in April 1941, Paulus had been sent by the German High Command to North Africa to restrain General Rommel and personally deliver orders for him to slow his ambition to quickly subdue all of Egypt. The High Command had a plan but Rommel was not eager to follow it, planning instead to submit a *fait accompli* to his superiors in a few months.

It is interesting to read the diary accounts after knowing the historical facts, and to see the very basic things that were important to the everyday soldier—sometimes it was a bath, sometimes it was a girl, and sometimes it was a beer. Very often, however, it was foremost to fight as well as possible against the enemy, while trying to stay alive.

Don A. Gregory, Huntsville, Alabama
Wilhelm R. Gehlen, Telford, Tennessee
March 2009

PART 1

To Stalingrad and Back

[Anonymous]

2d Battalion, 201st Panzer Regiment
23rd Panzer Division
LVII Panzer Corps
Army Group A

Insignia of the 23d Panzer Division

[Translation from the inside cover of "Feldzug in Russland"]

For Service Personnel Only!

This is a top secret item as designated by Paragraph 88 of the Reich Book of Laws (24 April 1934). Unauthorized use will be punished according to this and any other applicable laws.

This report can only be issued to soldiers, according to Heeres Division Order 99, and may only be used for service related matters. This item must be stored under lock and key.

If this publication is openly published at a later time as a War Diary (Eastern Front), then the affixture "For Service Personnel Only" can be omitted.

Panzer Armee

[Signed]

N. von Vormann
[Lt. General, Commander, 23d Panzer Division]

Introduction

CAMPAIGN IN RUSSIA
Diary of the II./Pz.Rgt. 201

The 201st Panzer Regiment was formed on December 16, 1940 from two battalions (Abteilungen) each having three Panzer companies of (mostly French) captured tanks. The regiment was initially assigned to Panzer Brigade 100 on March 1, 1941. II Abteilung (2d Battalion), with 4th and 6th Companies, was renamed Panzer Battalion 211 on March 7, 1941. The 2d Battalion (of this diary) was created from the renamed Panzer Battalion 301 on March 22, 1941. Panzer Regiment 201 was assigned to the 23d Panzer Division on December 11, 1941. The regiment was issued German tanks by the end of the year and eventually was renamed Panzer Regiment 23 (of 23d Panzer Division) on August 16, 1943. All this renaming was common throughout the war. Battalions were routinely moved from one regiment or division to another as the need arose and sometimes they were renamed, sometimes not.

Regimental Commanders were (in order):
Oberstleutnant Conze
Oberst Werner-Ehrenfeucht
Oberstleutnant Soltmann
Oberst Pochat
Oberstleutnant von Heydebreck
Oberstleutnant Soltmann
Oberst Burmeister

3

Oberst Werner-Ehrenfeucht
Major Illig
Oberstleutnant von Heydebreck
Oberst Sander
Major Fechner
Oberst Sander
Hauptmann Rebentisch
Oberstleutnant Bernau
Hauptmann Fischer
Major Rebentisch
Oberstleutnant Prinz zu Waldeck und Pyrmont
Major I.G. Jahns

Many of these names will be encountered in the diary to follow.

The organization of the German Wehrmacht was well defined, even when the required personnel were not available. Generally the important delineations from largest to smallest size were: Army Group (Herresgruppe), which could contain over a million men in two or more armies; Army (Armee), made up of Corps units (such as Army Corps, Panzer Corps, etc.), which could contain several hundred thousand men in two or more corps; Corps, with 20,000–60,000 men in two or more divisions, Division, with 6,000–20,000 men with no set number of divisions per corps; Regiment, with 3,000–5,000 men, generally two or three regiments per division; Battalion, with 800–1,000 men, generally three battalions per regiment; Company, with 100–150 men, generally eight companies per battalion. In addition, there were also Kampfgruppen (battle groups) which were ad hoc formations created for specific needs and could range from the size of a battalion to larger than a division. This was a common unit toward the end of the war or at the end of a major campaign when many casualties occurred and constant reorganization was required.

The 23d Panzer Division (nicknamed the Eiffelturm-Division) was formed on September 21, 1941 in Paris. The Eiffel Tower was a part of its official insignia. The division was built around the 101st Panzer Brigade and two infantry regiments. In April 1942, the division was transferred to the southern sector of the Eastern Front at Charkov (or Kharkov), and that is when this diary begins. It arrived just in time to meet a large Soviet offensive around that city, and then took part in the Germans' own spring offensive to the Caucasus oil fields. One of the most important assignments for the division came when it was ordered to take part in the attempt to relieve the surrounded German forces in Stalingrad. After the failure of this mission, the division was eventually forced to withdraw through the Ukraine and Poland, finally being sent to Hungary, where it fought alongside the I and II SS Panzer Corps at Lake Balaton. The 23d was involved in several "last ditch" battles in Hungary and Slovakia before being decimated by the Soviet Army near Tamsweg in Austria. What was left of the division surrendered to the Russians on May 8, 1945.

The battle of Stalingrad was not a single battle by any means, even though it is usually referred to as such. Although this diary only covers about a one year period, it does cover an important aspect of the battle: the attempted rescue of General Paulus and the Sixth Army. Scores of books have been written on the Stalingrad battle and movies have been made of the real and imagined characters involved, but little has been written on the major rescue attempt that von Manstein mounted. Most historians would have us believe that the German High Command simply abandoned Sixth Army after it was obvious the city would be lost, but that is not true. The diary tells another view of the story from the perspective of the individual soldier, and perhaps adds a bit to the historical record of the battle of Stalingrad.

The signature of Oberfeldwebel Ludwig Bloos, along with that of Lieutenant General Nikolaus von Vormann, appears on the inside cover of the diary. Von Vormann was the commander of the 23d Panzer Division from December 1942 to October 1943. It was during his command (on August 16, 1943) that the 201st Panzer was renamed the 23d Panzer Regiment, so von Vormann can legitimately be called the last commander of the 201st and the first commander of the 23d. Von Vormann received the Knight's Cross on August 22, 1943. A photograph of Bloos was also stuck inside the book. Bloos was born on March 7, 1915 in Oberweiler, France, and joined the 11th Armored Regiment on October 1, 1938. It is known that Bloos received the Knight's Cross on April 6, 1944, six months after this diary was finished, for destroying five Soviet T-34 tanks on February 15, 1944, while a platoon leader in the 11th Panzer Regiment, 8th

Panzer Division. The battle occurred near Kamenka, Russia. It is also known that Bloos was seriously wounded in the battle. The diary also mentions the meeting of the 11th and 201st Panzer Regiments on or about December 17, 1942. At this time the 11th Panzer Regiment was a part of the 6th Panzer Division.

The diary was published, without citing an author and in a limited printing, by the Wehrmachtformularien Verlag in Erlangen, which was the home base of the 201st Panzer Regiment. It is not known when the diary was printed, though we suspect it was soon after Bloos received the Knight's Cross award.

There were two Knight's Cross winners in the 201st Panzer Regiment: Hauptmann (Captain) Robert Alber, September 7, 1943 and Hauptmann (Captain) Rudolf Behr, January 25, 1943. The 201st Panzer Regiment was renamed the 23d Panzer Regiment in August 1943, but the award to Alber is still credited to the 201st. Both men are mentioned in the diary, as are several of the division commanders listed earlier. The diary also lists those of the 201st killed in action during the period of time covered. This is particularly useful because it provides a firsthand account of how some of them died and can be used to confirm other historical records that may exist.

The Stalingrad rescue attempt in which the 23d Panzer Division was involved was called Operation Wintergewitter, which is translated as "Winter Storm" or "Winter Tempest" in most popular writings. The original title of the diary was "Feldzug in Russland" ("Expedition in Russia"), with the following notice:

Herausgegeben: II./Pz.Rgt.201
[Published: 2d Battalion, Panzer Regiment 201]
Druck & Verlag: Richard Weissmann, Wehrmachtformularien Verlag Erlangen.
Alle Rechte bei der II./Pz Rgt. 201
[All rights retained by the 2d Battalion, Panzer Regiment 201]

AN HISTORICAL VIEW OF THE RESCUE ATTEMPT OF THE GERMAN SIXTH ARMY AT STALINGRAD

Adolf Hitler ordered Field Marshal Erich von Manstein to take command of the recently created Herresgruppe (Army Group) Don on November 21, 1942, for the purpose of leading the recently planned rescue of the German Sixth Army trapped in Stalingrad. Army Group Don, which wasn't really an army group in the strict German military definition, consisted of worn-out men and equipment scrounged from the remnants of other army groups. Hitler had an almost impossible task in mind. He ordered Manstein to lead Operation Winter Storm ("Unternehmen Wintergewitter"), the recently planned rescue effort begun by Hermann Hoth's Fourth Panzer Army and auxiliary Romanian troops to rescue the German Sixth Army commanded by General Friedrich Paulus. Sixth Army, which had been occupied during the fall with a siege of Red Army holdouts within Stalingrad, had itself been surrounded after a massive Soviet counteroffensive that commenced on November 19.

During the prolonged fight for the city, Stalingrad had been bombed into ruins but the city had not been fully captured. The failure of the German siege of Stalingrad has long been called the beginning of the end of the war, but perhaps it was the failure of the rescue that was the real beginning of the end. Manstein was no stranger to siege warfare, as the previous summer he had reduced the fortress-city of Sevastopol, and he had been involved in the siege of Leningrad just a few weeks before. His headquarters was actually located in Vitebsk, near the border between Russian and Latvia, some 810 miles [1,300 km] from Stalingrad.

The forces assembled to relieve Stalingrad included Army Group Hoth (the VI and VII Romanian Army Corps, LVII Panzer Corps and XLVIII Panzer Corps), the battered Third Romanian Army, and Army Detachment (General Karl) Hollidt, which consisted of one panzer division, one Romanian tank division, three German and four Romanian infantry divisions. Army Detachment Hollidt was at the time already tied up holding a strategic line on the Chir River, some 37 miles [60 km] from Stalingrad. General Hollidt's forces were nonetheless, the closest to Stalingrad, but he could do little to help the entrapped Sixth Army because there simply were not enough vehicles on hand to transport men and material, plus fuel was in short supply. In any case, Hollidt already had enemy forces trying to break through his lines south toward Rostov-on-Don. Manstein's only option was Army Group Hoth, which was some 62 miles [100 km] from Stalingrad. They would be his initial striking force, but he needed reinforcements for Hoth and time to organize them into a cohesive force. Three panzer divisions from other parts of the Eastern Front: the 17th, 23d, and 6th were sent to Hoth's LVII Panzer Corps, and the 11th Panzer Division was sent from Army Group Center to the XLVIII Panzer Corps.

There were some 250,000 of Paulus' Sixth Army trapped inside the "Stalingrad Pocket," as it came to be called. By the time the rescue attempt was organized, subsisting the German troops was becoming as difficult as fighting the Soviets. Rations were slim if any; the men began starving as resupply failed and many became mentally disoriented because of the constant shelling. The Soviet attacks were almost continuous and casualties reached critical levels. There were no replacements for those lost. Most of the wounded died, often because they could not be transported to suitable medical facilities. Paulus' army was not equipped for this sort of sustained siege warfare. However, morale among the men was still generally good because communication lines were still open so they knew that Manstein was now in charge of their rescue. "Der Manstein kommt" (Manstein is coming) was the mantra that kept them alive.

It took two weeks for Manstein to assemble his forces and finalize his plans. Paulus could probably have evacuated his army from Stalingrad relatively intact as late as the last week of November, and even requested Hitler to allow him to do so. It was the insistence of Reichsmarschall Hermann Göring who said he could use his Luftwaffe to resupply Stalingrad that convinced Hitler to issue orders to Paulus to remain there. The Luftwaffe, with substantial air superiority, had indeed been able to partially resupply troops engaged on the Leningrad front beginning in September 1941. Although Paulus didn't need further encouragement, on November 30th Hitler promoted him to Colonel General. Since Manstein was in constant communication with Paulus he knew the true seriousness of the situation in Stalingrad and the general size and location of Russian forces. The Russians had the city surrounded but their positions were not yet secure, and Manstein knew he had to get into action before the Russians could build and improve their defenses.

Manstein launched "Operation Winter Storm" from the southwest of Stalingrad on December 12, 1942. The plan specified that XIV Panzer Corps would fight its way through the Soviet encirclement and link up with a Sixth Army detachment that would simultaneously fight through the encirclement from the southwest of the Stalingrad pocket. Manstein sent Hoth's panzer divisions to break through the line held by infantry divisions attached to Soviet General Trufanov's Fifty-first Army. The weather in southern Russia was moderate; winter had not yet begun. Manstein took full advantage of this and directed air strikes on Soviet artillery to pave the way for Hoth's attack. Things went well initially for Manstein, and the propaganda back home in Germany praised every engagement as a brilliant move toward the rescue of Sixth Army.

Hitler had ordered the 17th Panzer Division to be held in reserve as the 6th and 23d Panzer divisions made surprisingly good progress without it, catching the Soviets somewhat unprepared for the assault. The 6th and 23rd were battle-hardened units with a critical mission and they knew the eyes of all Germany were on them. Soviet units were driven back to the northern bank of the Askai River, where they were ordered by Stalin to hold at all costs. This was more than a motivational speech, since retreating Soviet soldiers, and even officers, were often shot by their superiors if they retreated. General Yeremenko, the newly named commander of the Soviet Southeastern Front, asked Stalin for reinforcements because he knew that Hoth's panzers could breach the rear areas of General Tolbukhin's Fifty-seventh Army holding the southwest region of the pocket. This could then allow Paulus to attempt a breakout of his own, and possibly link up with the advancing German armor. Yeremenko's concerns were well founded. This was essentially Manstein's plan from the beginning.

Stalin responded to Yeremenko's request and ordered the Second Guards Army to his area but added that, until it arrived, everything was to be thrown into the fight. The Germans had to be stopped at any expense. Yeremenko used whatever reserves he had: the 235th Tank Brigade, the 87th Rifle Division, and an additional tank corps, to reinforce the Askai line, but the effort was too little and too late. The Germans had already established bridgeheads on the northern bank of the river. By the time Yeremenko was ready to counterattack, the Germans had a well running operation to transfer men and equipment across the Askai.

Desperate, almost nonstop fighting occurred in the hilly regions between the Askai and Mishkova rivers over the next five days, with the advantage changing hands several times, often within a single day. Soviet infantry companies, supported by their trademark half-buried T-34 tanks, were scattered all over the expansive countryside, waiting for the German panzers they knew were coming. Soviet artillery relentlessly bombarded the panzer divisions as they pushed forward toward Stalingrad. In one of the larger battles, which took place on December 14, Panzer Regiment 11 (Bloos' regiment) of the 6th Panzer Division fought off an attack of some 80 Soviet tanks, destroying half of them and forcing the rest to retreat.

On December 13 Hitler released the reserve 17th Panzer Division, which finally gave the Germans clear command of the battlefield. This made a total of three German armored divisions involved in the operation. The Soviet defenses gave way, and by December 18, Hoth's tanks were approaching the Mishkova River, although Russian attacks on their flanks continued. The 6th Panzer took the lead with the 23d Panzer covering the right flank and the 17th Panzer covering the left. They were a formidable force. On the morning of December 20, the 6th Panzer's armored group commanded by Col. Walther von Hünersdorff reached the Mishkova near the town of Gromoslavka. The lead forces of the Soviet Second Guards Army were arriving at the same location at about the same time. They had been ordered south two days earlier to stop the German attack.

Hünersdorff's tanks were very low on fuel by this time and couldn't wait for the supply trucks to arrive. The obvious choice was to retreat to a safe location and refuel, because without fuel they were sitting targets facing a force that substantially outnumbered them in tanks, personnel and guns. In a brilliant move, however, Hünersdorff stole the initiative by attacking. The German tanks led a Panzergrenadier battalion of Regiment 114 (and its commander Major Hauschildt) to the Mishkova River. They crossed and were able to secure a bridgehead in the middle of the battle. German infantry was sent across the river and expanded the bridgehead to a few kilometers. Stalingrad was now less than 31 miles [50 km] away.

For the Germans, crossing the Mishkova River was probably the high point of "Operation Winter Storm," but there were not enough infantry and heavy weapons across the river to sustain the bridgehead. The Russian Second Guards Army stopped the attack after only a small number of German panzers had crossed. The Germans were convinced that the Soviets would attack Army Group Hollidt and the XLVIII Panzer Corps to the south, which tenuously held the Chir River line. This theory kept the German commanders from committing more forces into holding the hard-earned Mishkova bridgehead. The momentum then swung back to the Soviets where it then remained.

From the beginning of "Operation Winter Storm," von Manstein believed that Hitler's intention was for the breakthrough to open the way for Sixth Army to break out and evacuate the city, but Paulus was given direct orders from Hitler to hold Stalingrad at all cost. The two commanders, Manstein and Paulus, had worked out a pre-arranged code word, "Donnerschlag" (Thunderbolt). Von Manstein's understanding was that the "Donnerschlag" order meant that Paulus would simultaneously drive for a link-up with von Manstein's force and begin evacuating the Sixth Army from Stalingrad. Paulus however refused to comply with "Donnerschlag" without direct orders from Hitler, and he knew very well that those orders would probably never be issued. There was an argument between von Manstein and Paulus, beginning even before the end of the war, about whether or not the "Donnerschlag" order was ever even issued.

Ultimately, complying with the "Donnerschlag" order would not have mattered much anyway. Sixth Army's fuel and ammunition supplies were so low that most of the heavy equipment, trucks and armor and such, as well as the wounded, would have had to be abandoned if the breakout had been attempted. Hitler refused to discuss the withdrawal of the Sixth Army from Stalingrad. This is generally looked upon by historians as an example of Hitler's fanaticism and lack of military leadership, but perhaps he realized that without transport and armor, such a retreat would be a massacre. It would be better if Sixth Army could be resupplied and hold out for future offensive operations, or at least tie up Soviet forces while German forces took up the offensive elsewhere.

As Christmas of 1942 approached, the situation for the Sixth Army in Stalingrad was not just serious, it was desperate. Manstein's relief column had been forced to retreat, and supplies arriving by air were scarce and mostly fell into Soviet occupied areas. Starvation and illness began to claim as many casualties as bullets. "Operation Winter Storm" was finished, but the Sixth Army still hung on for more than a month. Soviet artillery had by this time forced the LVII Panzer Corps completely out of the Mishkova bridgehead, and by the end of December all of the panzer divisions were driven back to their original "Winter Storm" mustering area. There would never be another ground-based attempt to free the German forces at Stalingrad.

General's Rokossovskiy and Yeremenko continued to tighten their stranglehold on the encircled Sixth Army. On January 8, 1943, Rokossovskiy ordered a message to be hand-delivered, asking Paulus to surrender. The German position was hopeless and both Rokossovskiy and Paulus knew it. It was just a matter of time before the battle would be over. The main German front was being pushed back further every day and the Russian's greatest ally, the winter weather, would soon decide the matter. Rokossovskiy claimed that food and medical assistance for all of Paulus' men would be guaranteed, and that they would allow all officers to retain their rank and decorations. On the other hand, he guaranteed the total destruction of Sixth Army if his offer was not accepted. Paulus did manage to get a radio message through to Hitler asking for permission to surrender, but Hitler refused and ordered Paulus to stand and fight where he was, "down to the last man and the last bullet." Paulus chose to follow Hitler's directives and not surrender his Army at this time.

Contrary to many historical accounts however, Hitler did not just abandon Paulus' army to destruction. He sent Luftwaffe Generalfeldmarschall Erhard Milch to the front to regenerate the airlift of supplies to Stalingrad, but not even Milch was able to summon the seemingly divine intervention that would be required to obey the Führer's orders to resupply Paulus. Milch was initially optimistic until he arrived at the airfields that were to be used for the resupply. There was nothing left. Generaloberst Wolfram von Richthofen's total air fleet was now down to 100 miscellaneous aircraft, and Soviet planes were bombing the runways and supply dumps required for the airlift. Milch returned to Germany where he did manage to put together an additional assortment of some 300 aircraft, but he could not match the winter and the dominance of the Red Air Force in the air over Stalingrad.

Hitler promoted Paulus to Field Marshal on January 30th, possibly with the thought that Paulus would not allow himself to be the first German Field Marshal to surrender to an enemy. Or, perhaps, it was because Paulus had survived this long, while preserving as many of his men as possible while obeying Hitler's orders in the process. Paulus surrendered most of the surviving Sixth Army on January 31, 1943, and two days later the final pocket of German resistance in Stalingrad was obliterated. About 110,000 German, Italian, and Romanian soldiers headed for a long Soviet captivity. Less than five percent of them would eventually return to Germany alive. The long and horribly destructive battle of Stalingrad was over.

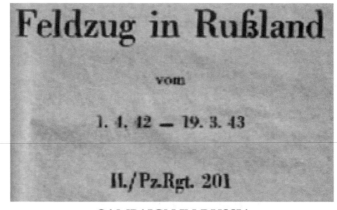

CAMPAIGN IN RUSSIA
from
April 1, 1942 to March 19, 1943
2nd Battalion/Panzer Regiment 201

ORIGINAL INTRODUCTION
(by the diary's author)

23d Panzer Division.
From Paris, 1 April 1942, to Stalingrad, Winter 1942
and Back to Nuremberg
19 March, 1943

This book is not supposed to be a suspense thriller. It is a sober and unaltered account of the day-to-day life of the 2d Battalion during our time at the Russian front. It should be viewed as a reminder of good and bad days, and of the struggles and victories of a proud Battalion.

May this diary serve as a reminder for the survivors and as an honor to our dead comrades.

Chapter 1

DEPARTURE FROM PARIS AND ARRIVAL IN CHARKOV

1 April, 1942: Paris, HQ and Air Ministry, our battalion [2nd] prepares for transport to the Russian front.

2:00 PM: Railroad Station Versailles–Matelot [France]. Loading of the Battalion in 6 trains starts with 8th Co. and HQ Co.

8:00 PM: Air raid, enemy planes over the railroad station at low level, no bombs; the loading continues.

3 April, 2:15 AM: Departure from railroad station, travel via Chalons-sur-Marne, Luneville, Mainz [Germany].

4 April: Darmstadt–Aschaffenburg–Schweinfurth–Hof–Reichenbach.

5 April: Zwickau–Chemnitz–Dresden–Bautzen–Hirschberg–Neisse–Ratibor–Oderburg–Cracow [Poland].

7 April: Jaroslaw–Przemysl–Lemberg [Lwow, Ukraine].

8 April: Tarnopol–Proskurow.

9 April: Rasatin–Sunla–Zerkow.

10 April: Snamenka–Krementschuk.

15

11 April: Poltawa–Charkov.

12 April, 3:00 AM: Arrive at railroad station Nowa Bavarija [Charkov, Ukraine], but we are not unloading until 5:00 AM because the ramp is occupied by another train.

8:00 AM: HQ Co. proceeds to their quarters at a tractor factory in the southeast part of the city of Charkov. The road is in bad shape and we are constantly under Russian air observation, so we march in companies with our vehicles dispersed between. We arrive at our new quarters without incident. Lt. Dittmann [Oberleutnant Günter Dittmann] has done a grand job finding us quarters. He was in the advance group tasked with finding quarters for all the men. In the next few hours, 5th and 6th Companies arrive with their trucks loaded with spare tank tracks.

13 April, 5:00 AM: The rest of the battalion, including the spare tank parts, reaches the tractor factory.

14 April: Tractor factory Charkov; we occupy our new quarters and service our armor and other vehicles.

14–24 April: Like the last 10 days, no enemy activity.

24 April–2 May: Battalion drill, all vehicles are serviced, no technical problems so far. Order from Division is that vehicles, including tanks or other tracked vehicles, must stay on hard surface roads because the incessant rain has made mud of everything else. Several times at night Russian aircraft fly over the city, but no attacks.

3–11 May, 1942: Division Commander [Generalleutnant Hans Freiherr von Boineburg-Lengsfeld] visits our Battalion and praises our work in keeping our equipment in top condition. Weather improves and we are permitted to leave the road to test our vehicles on cross-country driving. Several Russian bombers attack; bombs are dropped on Charkov but not in our area.

Russian fighter aircraft attack but our flak and Messerschmitts drive them off.

Chapter 2

THE BATTLE FOR CHARKOV, 5–29 MAY 1942

12 May, 3:00 AM, North of Charkov: We receive a radio message from the 201st Panzer Regiment headquarters that the whole division should be ready for deployment by 7:30 AM today. We are to stop a Russian breakthrough of our lines just north of Charkov. At noon we are still on readiness; at 2:00 PM another radio message saying that our battalion will be moving out shortly.

2:15 PM: Orders to move out from Regimental HQ. All companies take their places in the column.

4:15 PM: The point is taken by the 1st battle group of Major Heydebrand. We make good progress on march from Rogani to Jaruga. Near Jaruga we are attacked by 12 Ratas [Russian fighter aircraft] but their attack is uncoordinated and our mobile flak chases them off. We rest overnight in Jaruga; a few night attacks by Russian bombers but no casualties or damage.

13 May, 2:15 AM: Ready to move out toward Saroshnoje; our nonessential vehicles and supplies stay behind in Jaruga. The road is a bog; even the tanks get stuck in the mud, but we manage to extricate them. Air attacks by Russian fighter-bombers; we arrive at map coordinate 197.9. [For security reasons or the lack of a reconnaissance point like a forest or village, map coordinate points were often given.] We are attacked several times before dawn.

9:45 AM: Alarm given to all companies. Enemy tanks are report-

17

ed north of us. We assemble in attack line. Our target is the village of Pestschanoje. Our order of attack is: 1st Battle Group then 2nd Battle Group. We are to advance to the outskirts of Saroshnoje. We have to cross the small Tetlega River and the 3rd Panzer Engineer Battalion has difficulty in getting across. After crossing, we proceed through a ravine toward coordinate 188.4 and stop just south of that point.

10:30 AM: During our advance through the ravine we were attacked by fighter-bombers; no casualties, no damage.

11:30 AM: We form an attack wedge with 8th Co. in front of 1st Battle Group. On a slight rise we arrive at 206.2 and encounter the first Russian [lend-lease] tanks, Mk. II's ["Matilda," heavy British infantry tank] and light Christie's [J. Walter Christie, American born tank designer; Soviet BT (Bystrokhodny) tanks were called Christies.], in an attack position north of 206.2. Before we can commence firing, a Stuka squadron arrives and knocks out several of their tanks, the rest are destroyed by us. Our Panzer Grenadiers take care of any Russian infantry and take several prisoners.

We follow the retreating enemy but our 1st Battle Group ends up in a swamp and gets completely stuck 1.5 km north of 206.2.

The 2nd Battle Group tries to avoid the swamp but crosses the advance line of our infantry. Regiment radios them to circumvent a small forest and continue the attack.

500 meters east of Co. 6, at 203.1, our commander, out in front, sees 12 enemy tanks just south of Pestschanoje and we open fire. The distance is too great however and the muddy ground won't support a frontal attack.

An urgent radio message arrives: 2nd Battle Group has encountered the enemy west of a forest at 200.9 and near a farm at 188.4. The enemy is firing PaK [Panzerabwehrkanone, an anti-tank gun of caliber ranging from 37 mm to 75 mm (German version)]. Their point company is under heavy fire.

6th Co. 1st Tank Platoon goes to the rescue and, led by Lt. Dittmann, reaches the farm and destroys several PaK's and anti-tank rifles. Just north of 205.4 the commander of 6th Co. runs into a tank trap; he bails out with two of his men but all of them are killed. 1st Lt. Marquardt takes over 6th Co.

5th Co. reaches a fold in the terrain for cover, 6th Co. follows and both companies attack the forest on a small rise. Cover is given by Infantry Battalion Neubeck and a Panzer Pioneer Co. under Lt. Schäfer. Russian Artillery begins firing and 1st Lt. Völzke is seriously wounded.

After this fight we count captured Russian weapons:

5—75 mm PaK's
5—45 mm long barrel PaK's
4—Machine guns
12—AT [anti-tank] Rifles
15—Mortars

No enemy activity during the night.

16 May: Our hedgehog position in the forest at 205.4 gets supplies from Capt. Paetzold and 1st Lt. Schnewe; a job that took a lot of planning and hard driving. Ammunition and other supplies were brought up and a patrol was sent forward to reconnoiter the Russian positions, but the enemy had left, so more supplies were brought up to the hedgehog. Heavy Russian artillery harassed Capt. Paetzold's advance but the column reached cover in a ravine.

In the evening, a radio message arrives from Division HQ telling us to advance to a village called Ternowaja on special orders of the Führer. But we have already run out of gasoline and diesel fuel so the order cannot be executed until we refuel.

7:00 AM: We are finally ready for the attack on Ternowaja, but we are told not to get into a prolonged shootout there because the enemy has fortified the town.

Hill 207.2 was supposed to be occupied by the enemy but none was found – but attacks are expected from 218.6 and 226.3.

8:20 AM: Line of attack is formed with 6th Co. on the right, 5th Co. on the left and 8th Co. behind the two leading units. The rest of the battle group follows. We are reinforced by the 3rd Panzer's 128th Pioneer Battalion with a Battery of DO rocket launchers [DO was the code name for the Nebelwerfer rocket launchers, after its inventor, Walter Dornberger. Later, after World War II he was employed, along with Wernher von Braun, in the American space program.]

The DO-Werfers have orders to saturate the forest east of Ternowaja with salvos of 155mm rockets. The attack progresses well, the enemy north of 207.2 retreats to the east. We observe Russian infantry fleeing in panic; our fire follows them. Our Battle Group is targeted by several Russian artillery and PaK batteries from a forest southeast of Ternowaja. We exchange fire with the enemy PaK but the distance is too great, so we send a radio message to the 3rd Panzer Pioneers to send a few salvos of DO Rockets to the annoying enemy positions at 226.3, but the radio message does not get through. Finally, our Group Commander personally drives to the Panzer Pioneers with a spare Nebelwerfer hauled by an HT (Half Track) but enemy artillery fire probing the area scores a hit on the DO-Werfer and the HT, destroying both. The Panzer Pioneer Unit is under intense enemy fire, but their DO-Observation Post can direct the Nebelwerfer salvos and cover the rest of the battalion.

We roll forward, destroying PaK's, mortars and infantry foxholes by running our Panzer tracks over them. We turn toward the right as the enemy artillery in 226.3 fights back and even tries to get to us into close combat.

Our battle group reforms and breaks through to our encircled troops at Ternowaja. Heavy enemy artillery and mortar fire falls in the southwest part of the town.

Oberstleutnant [Lt. Col. Anton] Grünert [Knight's Cross, March 15, 1943], commander of the encircled group, is desperately short on ammo, so a few of our tanks take up a defensive position in the town. Reinforcements arrive; the 1st Battalion of the 126th Infantry Regiment and a platoon from the 3rd Panzer Pioneers with Nebelwerfers. Lt. Col. Schlutius [Oberstleutnant Kurt Schlutius, German Cross in Gold, awarded August 27, 1942] has orders to bring ammunition and other supplies at night into the town, especially DO Werfer Rockets. One Panzer Mk. III gets hit by a PaK but it can still move. But the relief column cannot reach the town; the Russians have sealed the breakthrough with PaK's and tanks. The enemy is busy digging themselves in outside town in areas 226.3, 218.6, and 219.7. We observe an enemy tank column 3 miles south east of Ternowaja.

17 May: Ternowaja. Our encircled troops are awaiting the relief convoy; gunfire was heard at night to the south; probably an attempt by the armored column to break through us. Early in the morning, an especially heavy artillery attack was launched by the enemy on the southern part of the town. Small Russian infantry infiltration is repulsed easily by Grunter's tanks which are dispersed around town. 9:00 AM: Orders came through to attack via 219.7 to Murawlewo but later a new order arrived: Attack to the west, to 200.9. Battle Group Schmitt-Ott [Ludwig (not Ernst Ludwig) Ott] has run out of ammunition, enemy tanks are approaching from the direction of Birak.

Another Panzer Platoon has also expended its ammunition, this time it is Lt. Schinner's platoon.

Artillery fire from the enemy becomes worrisome – then all of a sudden 40 T-34 tanks come in view west of the small forest at 226.3; another group of 6 T-34's is spotted with attack direction toward Ternowaja. Our Commander sets up a defensive firebase and attacks the enemy tanks with his 5th Co., supported now by 16th Co. The 6 T-34's now come under our flanking fire as 8th Co. takes on the 40 T-34's that have stopped on a hill across from our position.

Enemy PaK and artillery fire increases, probably supported by PaK's and tanks from a position behind the small forest. We cannot see.

5th Co. now is engaged in a Panzer battle and knocks out 3 of the 6 T-34's, but 2 of them manage to limp back into the forest, smoke billowing from their turrets. Minutes later the same T-34's reappear with guns blazing and machine guns rattling. It seems the T-34's had smoke dischargers that we thought were hits by our tanks. The 40 T-34's across from us now join the concerted fire onto our Battle Group, with help from PaK hidden in the forest.

Within a few minutes we lose 13 Panzers, either by direct hits or by hits in the tracks. Because of smoke and dust, we are unable to lay a precise fire onto the enemy tanks but soon we see the T-34's retreat over a hill. Obviously we too have scored – so we might have saved Platoon Schinner from destruction. Russian infantry can be seen coming after our tank crews that bailed out of their Panzers. Our Commander gives orders to retreat to Ternowaja. 5th and 8th Companies have lost their Commanders. 1st Lt. Schnewe takes command. Several Panzers return with the wounded, including our Regiment Adjutant, Freiherr von Colenden.

6th Co. is ordered to retreat to the town. They have sustained heavy losses. The rest of the battle group now has 23 Panzers left, 19 of them are combat-worthy. Our efforts to retrieve some of our disabled Panzers come to nothing. We could loose a few more tanks that way. Panzer crews without tanks are being formed into destroyer troops, armed with anti-tank mines to be dispersed around town.

Despite the hard battle we fought, the morale of our group is high, especially in the tank crews that lost Panzers. Those who escaped Hell, out of their burning armor, are elated, clinging to their allotted anti-tank mines in their fox holes. They jokingly declare, "Let the Russians come now, we'll give them Hell."

But Ivan does not come, not yet; but by late evening the enemy manages a small break into our lines, but not for long. Infantry of the 28th Regiment and Grünert's Panzers close the gap; the Russians that survived are taken prisoner.

Now we are truly surrounded, not knowing when our division can come to the rescue. We have to ration our food because we expect 5 days to pass before we are relieved. Each man gets a packet of Wasa hard tack, 6 men divide a 2-pound tin of vegetable soup; not much to fight a war on, but our Commander has the good fortune to find two stray cows; those are being slaughtered and the meat will be distributed equally.

18–19 May: Russian artillery and fighter bombers plus mortar attacks continue. At night, Russian patrols do get into town but are always either destroyed or they retreat under heavy losses. Because our infantry is now in a desperate state of fatigue, the Panzers have to do most of the fighting in town.

Three Panzers from 1st Lt. Cramer's Platoon, plus an Infantry Platoon from Grünert's group command set out during the night to clear the enemy from the suburb of Federowka. The Russians retreat but our infantry has to retreat as well because Russian artillery has zeroed in on the unit, and have scored many casualties. Telephone contact to the dispersed units in Ternojawa is hampered by constant enemy artillery fire.

Our Luftwaffe drops supply canisters 2 times a day but most fall into enemy lines. It took a tank platoon just to retrieve 2 canisters.

20 May: Our Stukas appear in the sky and attack the Russian lines around town and in the forest; immediately Russian artillery fire slacks off. We finally make radio contact with Division; their reply was: "Hold out, we'll break through with everything we've got," but Battle Group Schmitt-Ott of the 5th SS Panzer Division "Viking" was unable to break though on that night.

21 May: Early morning brings our Luftwaffe Ju-87 Stukas back into the melee; we rejoice, probably so does Battle Group Schmitt-Ott, stalled since last night several kilometers south of Ternowaja, but by 9:00 AM this Battle Group finally reaches the southern approaches to the town. The Group holds a corridor open so an ambulance convoy and supplies can come in.

Russian artillery answers with intense and accurate fire and we lose 2 ambulances and a HT by direct hits. The rest of the wounded, 450 of them, are ferried out by the HT's and ambulances. The enemy keeps up a constant barrage. Later that afternoon, Russian rocket launchers, Katyschkas [called "Stalin's Organs" by the Germans], join in and the few houses in town, that so far have stood up to the incessant attacks, burn down.

22 May: An order to evacuate the town arrives and in the early morning we march toward Wesseloje. 1st Lt. Salwey however, returns during the morning hours to Ternowaja with 4 HT's and manages to retrieve 3 of our 100mm artillery pieces. We assemble at Wesseloje and the battalion returns to our quarters at the tractor factory in Charkov by mid morning.

23 May, South of Charkov: After a day of rest, used for maintenance of our armor, 2nd Battle Group under command of Lt. Col. Soltmann, leaves the Charkov tractor factory at 2:10 PM. The advance goes via Tschugujew-Krakowo and encounters no enemy.

The group reaches a stopping point 5 km north of Andrejewka at 7:30 PM and goes into bivouac for the night.

Support vehicles for Panzer unit in southern Russia, Fall 1942

Small FW or Arado plane at a makeshift airstrip in southern Russia.

24 May: At 2:30 AM we are ready to set off, not much sleep; if we do not encounter enemy activity for the rest of the night, some of the men can sleep in the Panzers, but alas, not the driver or the spotter in the turret.

Via Tscherwonij on Don we reach Korana and go into the line 2 km north of 208.5. By 5:00 AM we are ready in our attack positions. Our infantry occupies a line along a forest at 208.5.

1st Tank reconnaissance platoon sets off, but 2 km in the direction of Schebelinke, they come under enemy artillery fire.

11:45 AM: The Battle Group assembles and at 12 noon the order for attack is given to capture 204.5, west of Schebelinke.

Order of attack: 5th Co. to the right, 6th Co. to the left, 8th Co in reserve.

Two minutes before attack commences, the sky opens up and a heavy rain comes down, but nevertheless, we proceed and we get engaged with Russian PaK and infantry. We observe Russians retreating far to our left; just east of 204.5 two Katyschka rocket launchers flee at full speed. Despite the distance we commence fire and our group stops 2 km further than our maps indicate. We got one of the "Stalin Organs" anyway.

We are ordered to a halt and secure our line; enemy artillery fire is a nuisance. Lt. Dittmann's reconnaissance unit advances up to a windmill in a small hamlet and takes several prisoners.

A motorcycle infantry unit takes over from us as we are ordered to secure a bridgehead at Melowoj Jar to the southwest of us. Cloudy skies and incessant rain hamper our advance.

An armored patrol led by 1st Lt. [Ernst] Rebentisch runs into an ambush of enemy PaK but they manage to extricate themselves without losses because the Russian PaK cannoneers can't see any better than us in this downpour. Finally all activity in this sector ends; Russia's rain and mud has won the day. We go into a night bivouac; a swamp covers our front. Sometimes here in Russia, swamp and mud are better covers than concrete; we love it.

25 May, 5:00 AM: We are ready to commence the attack in the same matter as yesterday but this time in a southerly direction to 176.2. 6th Co. got the job of reconnaissance patrol to determine if the river bridge is still standing; if not, to find a place to ford the river. Long Range 7.62 enemy PaK soon discovers this maneuver. Some of our armor get stuck in the mud and has to be recovered under enemy fire, but despite this upset, the patrol gets on with the job, only to see the bridge going up in a cloud of dust and debris. Ivan did an excellent job, and there is no other crossing or a low ford anywhere in sight. Concentrated fire from our cannons silences the enemy PaK, for a while at least, so 6th Co. extricates itself from the gluey mud. A short rest stop is required to refill the empty gas tanks, and then the attack commences and reaches 176.2. This is an elevated position with a good view all around. Several T-34's are seen in the distance and are fired upon by our AT 88mm guns but Ivan replies with artillery [and] one 88 mm sustains a direct hit; the entire crew is killed. A patrol sent out on foot returns with reports of more T-34's on the road to Michailowka. Another 9 Soviet tanks enter the fray but our own artillery takes care of them, destroying several.

Since our attack is blocked by T-34's, we turn toward Lipki, a small town, and we finally reach 175.3 with 5th, 6th, and 8th Co.

Just when we thought we had finally settled the issue, 12 T-34's and some KW-1 [heavy Russian] tanks are seen on the road from Michailowka. We concentrate our fire from 2 tank platoons onto the Russian armor. Three KW-1's take hits, 2 are burning to a useless iron shell, Ivan retreats. We settle down for the night.

26 May, 3:20 AM: Do we ever get a full night's rest? Our outposts report enemy activity on the road from Michailowka to Krotojarka moving south. Alarm! We assemble in pitch darkness. A messenger arrives and reports breathlessly that 9 T-34's have been sighted 2.5 km southwest of 175.3. We can't see our hands in front of our eyes; how did the patrol manage to identify 9 T-34's 3000 yards away?

Well, the messenger was right. We move out, hidden by a hedge from enemy view, which is just as limited as ours; nothing, but 500 meters further we see the T-34's in a line silhouetted against the faint horizon. We divide our forces, 5th Co. to right, 6th Co to the left. The T-34's are between us. We take out 4 of them with HE AT [high explosive, anti-tank] shells, turrets fly off; one is a KW-1. With its tracks shot to pieces, it explodes with a mighty roar. The rest of the enemy tanks retreat behind a hill at 165.2. We cannot follow them, we are out of ammo. Our last round in the breach is for emergency use. We stop and wait for our ammunition trucks to arrive.

6:15 AM: We form up for the next attack, orders are to take Michailowka and establish a bridgehead; 5th Co. on the right, 6th Co. on the left, 8th Co. is held in reserve. We roll forward but soon encounter a tank trap. With no way through, we turn north, no way there either. We turn south and run into the hedge we had encountered earlier that night. Two T-34's are well hidden only 100 yards away in the hedge. 8th Co. has a long barreled 75mm PaK on an HT and Corporal Greeme opens up first. The first shot is a bull's eye and the T-34 bursts into flames. The other tank has not moved or fired either. We send a patrol that returns with the news that the tank is empty, no crew; probably a breakdown and the crew took off when we attacked. A minute or two later we hear engine noises; our tank engines are running on low revolutions. We are loaded and ready for whatever is coming. A Russian truck full of Ivans with tools turns the corner, probably a work crew to recover the empty tank. One 50mm round sets the truck ablaze; those that are not killed disappear into the hedge.

Well directed enemy artillery fire covers 167.2 but we incur no casualties, so we use the hedge as cover to reach the assigned target.

5th Co. reports enemy infantry advancing on the road from Michailowka to Krutojarka. Covered by the hedge, we open fire. Most of the Ivan column consists of Panje [horse drawn] wagons. In a panic the Russian infantry tries to break out on foot to the northwest, but they run into the muzzles of our Infantry Regiment 126.

We return to our task, advancing in our ordered direction to the village. 6th Co. captures two 100mm AT cannons.

Meanwhile, 5th Co. searches the center and there the adjutant finds one 180mm artillery piece, three tanks and other war material, but all bridges have been blown by Ivan – just our luck. We reassemble on the southern side of the village.

12:30 PM: We are ordered to take Krotojarka, so half of our group will bypass the town to the left to seek cover in a depression. The other half, 6th Co., will enter the town from the southwest; the rest of the battle group will hold a line east of 176.5. Russian columns of infantry, mixed with AT guns and a few tanks are making a hasty retreat to the east; we open fire. Ivan replies with artillery, PaK and tanks. Some Russian AT rifles fire out of Krotojarka but despite their accurate fire, we did not take any casualties. Long lines of Russians come marching out of Krotojarka now with their hands held high. Here and there we see a dirty white bed sheet, a sign of surrender. 6th Co. has the unfortunate job of bringing some order to the stream of POW's. The rest of the regiment now takes the forward position toward the next town, Losowenjka. Here too, a stream of POW's marches toward our lines.

From the north we now get help in our attack. The 16th Panzer Division [later destroyed in the "Stalingrad Pocket"] and a Kradschutzen Battalion [Motorcycle Infantry] seal the northern escape route for Ivan. At one point, the 23d and the 16th Panzer Divisions both fire at the same targets; coordination is bad between the two divisions. In the end, 16th Panzer ceases firing. We destroyed three more T-34's. After this engagement, we take cover at 176.8 to refuel and take ammunition. The 88mm's are on their last rounds.

Toward evening, we receive orders to advance to a spot south of 171.8 and stay there for the night. 2nd platoon advances another 500 meters – it is crowded around here, but as soon as they arrive at 178.8, the platoon runs into well directed enemy PaK fire from the left flank. When it gets dark, the platoon retreats again to set up for the night 1.5 km northeast of point 178.8. Panzer Grenadiers take over guarding our tanks, but at 9:30 PM the Russians try to infiltrate our defensive position; 6th Co. soon beats Ivan back. The rest of the night is quiet.

27 May: Oh, why can't we make war in daylight so we can get a good night's sleep? We change position to the west of Losowenjka and here we wait over an hour in the dark. From the southwest over the crest of a hill, a stream of Russians marches toward us without weapons. They are POW's from the look of it; other groups of Ivans are milling around in a ravine behind the hill. A platoon from the 5th Co. with an interpreter borrow a Half Track and drive up to them. The interpreter sure knows his business and the Russians, after a minute of discussion between them, give up, hands above their heads.

5:30 AM: We search the area for more Russians. Without a fight, hundreds capitulate near Losowenjka; we run into our own friends from the 16th Panzer Division and take a break to refuel and stock up with ammunition. After some confusing orders, we go, we stop, we go, we stop – finally at 1:00 PM we set up camp 1 km west of Krotojarka.

28 May: No attacks, no marching orders; what a wonderful day, the motor pool engineers arrive to see to the tanks and the HT's, oil changes and track replacements. Meanwhile we clean our uniforms, have a cold dip in a creek to wash 2 weeks of grime off our bodies – we stink. Some engineers mutter; of course, they are 5 miles behind the front lines but they always manage to scrounge some water. The day is clear, no artillery, no Nahmaschienen [literally, Sewing Machines – Russian reconnaissance planes with a distinctive engine sound, at times used as fighter-bombers]

29 May, 3:30 PM: We saddle up with our panzers and Raupen-schleppers [halftracks with 88mm cannons in tow]. The route takes us via Trawki–Tscherwonyje on Don, Krakowo, Roganj, back to Charkov – but what a journey it is; no enemy encounters, but the heavens are against us and open up. In minutes the road turns into a sticky mud bath with the consistency of glue and the whole lot of wheeled vehicles gets stuck. HT's and tanks have to tow the unfortunate machines onto drier ground. Well, dry is misleading; in another 5 miles, the same thing happens again. We send two DEMAG [Duisburger Mechanical Engineering AG, heavy lift cranes] HT's with powerful engines up ahead to find a passable route and to radio back to us the best route to take.

One Nebelwerfer is completely submerged in the slimy mess and the Panzer Mk. III following it runs into it – a total loss of a good Werfer. Not until May 31st at 2:00 PM do we finally reach Charkov and our beloved camp at the tractor factory.

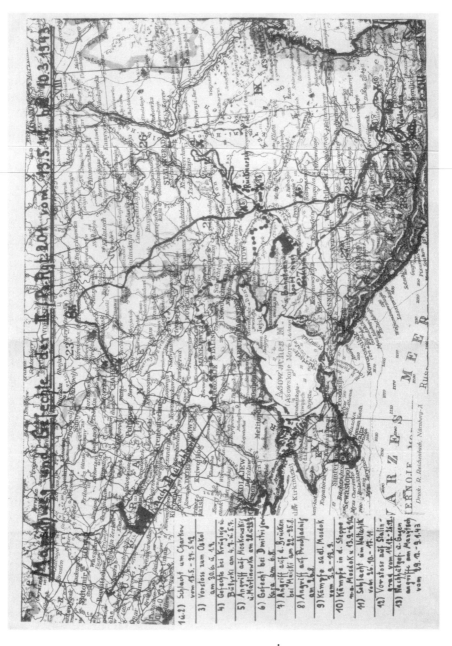

Original
map
showing
the route
of the
II.Pz.Rgt.
201 into
southern
Russia
and back.

Chapter 3

FORWARD TO THE OSKOL RIVER, 31 MAY–22 JULY 1942

---

31 May: Immediately after arriving in Charkov, we start on maintenance of our tanks and HT's, cleaning our uniforms, sewing lost buttons back on, scrounging for new boots, trying to find the Field Post Office to send letters home to our loved ones. Non-line officers (and there are many of them in Charkov) are again saluted with "Heil Hitler."

We get leave passes, but what is there to see or where is there to go in a city that has been in the front line for several months? A traveling stage opera group all the way from home has set up in the half destroyed opera house (yes, Ivan has opera houses, surprisingly) but most of the enlisted men avoid the big building, not because we don't like operas, but we don't feel safe in them. Russian bombers are a constant threat; nobody wants to be trapped in a building during an air raid. We beg the Quartermaster for playing cards, pencils, writing paper, and other thing, but like all good Quartermasters, they think the supplies are their personal property, so we swap a handful of Russian medals we took off the POW's at Krotojarka for a crate of Paulaner [beer].

1–16 June: We assemble in the yard of the tractor factory; "What is it now", some guy grumbles. Officers arrive and Lt. General von Vormann congratulates our Regiment for the conclusion of a victorious campaign, then we are introduced to the new Commander of the

31

201st Panzer Regiment, 23rd Panzer Division, Oberst [Colonel Karl-August] Pochat.

Several Iron Crosses 1st and 2nd Class are awarded. 1st Lt. [Gerhard] Fischer of 8th Panzer Company is the lucky recipient of the German Cross in Gold [awarded November 28, 1942]. He single handedly captured a complete 7.62 battery at Krotojarka, thus keeping the 8th Co. from running into a well concealed trap. With a grin all over his face and a smart "Heil Hitler, Thank you," and an about face, he steps back in line [and] we applaud. "Dismissed."

Now we are in for a break, an overhaul of equipment and other things. One day a truck enters the yard loaded with paint drums – that means our tanks and HT, including our own 88mm's, and other pieces of equipment will get a brand new camouflage makeover. Replacements for our KIA's and wounded arrive, mostly green men, fresh from the Panzer School at Erlangen – some have swapped their chairs at the Panzer Proving Ground at Kummersdorf for a place at the front. There are more heroes to be made here, more medals to earn. If they only knew what they were in for.

We work like beavers to be ready for redeployment at the front by June 15th.

During the night of June 14th to 15th orders arrive; we are now attached to Battle Group Bodenhausen [Hans Freiherr von Bodenhausen, German Cross in Gold awarded May 30, 1942] in the area of Woltschnsk. First 1st Lt. Grahn and 2nd Lt. Eisenlohr drive to the assigned area for a quick reconnaissance but are ordered back by radio. The weather has turned nasty again, and we might not be going. No point in going to the front when half of the Regiment is stuck in the mud south of Charkov.

16–21 June: Departure to the front has been postponed to June 26th; all vehicles not used or unsuitable for the coming offensive are parked in the tractor factory yard; incessant rain turns roads into quagmires. At 5:30 AM another reconnaissance patrol under the command of 1st Lt. Ott departs to view the area we are supposed to occupy before the attack near Woltschnsk. At 5:00 PM orders finally arrive; get ready to pack up, we are moving out.

9:30 PM: Get going, get moving, we're off. Not 5 miles have passed when a few ammo trucks skid off the muddy road into a drainage ditch, a Panzer follows, flips upside down and kills the tank commander – what a start.

22 June: At 6:30 AM we arrive at our allotted area, a few Sewing Machines try their best to bomb the Donetz Bridge at Woltschnsk but without luck. HQ Co. sets up at a point 1.5 km north of Burgrowatka; two days of rest in the beautiful forest camp are in for us. Supply trucks are searched for a brew or drinkable Schnapps; Field Post letters arrive. I tell everyone that today is a day to celebrate.

"Celebrate what?" Sgt. Grohn asks.

"Don't you know, I reply, today is the first anniversary of our glorious march into the Soviet Union; Ivan is on the run, we are more than half way to the Urals. Prost [German for "toast"]!"

25–26 June: Radio message from Division at 2:30 PM; we are to be ready to move out at 5:00 PM.

At 8:30 PM we reach the pontoon bridge of the Donetz River [a tributary of the Don River]. It's a Hell of a job to get across the narrow planked bridge in pitch darkness but we manage without losses. Now the moon comes up and at least we can see where we are. We arrive at the start-off point for the attacks.

8:00 AM: We are minus one Panzer platoon of the rear guard. A few bridging planks gave way and we lost one Pz.Mk. III and a command car but no loss in personnel. The rear guard arrives at 8:45 AM. A reconnaissance group reconnoiters ahead to find the best suitable route to commence our attack which is ordered for 4:00 PM, but an almighty thunderstorm with hail and rain sets in. With hatches closed, we sit in our damp, confined Panzers. The reconnaissance unit returns, there will be no attack today. It looks like it will be another night in our machines. As soon as darkness comes, 7 or 8 Sewing Machines arrive to bomb the area but no casualties are reported. Ivan, as usual, thinks he has better vision than us. If we can't see our command tank 50 meters ahead, how could Ivan see a tank from 200 meters up? Some lucky guys find a shed full of hay. They are the lucky ones.

27 June: We are still waiting. The Russians intensify their air activity during the morning but our 20mm and 3.7's [37mm guns] are on guard. We shoot one down. The pilot bails out, but at 150 meters he has no chance of surviving. He slams into the ground feet first, his normal height gets reduced by about 16 centimeters.

28 June: We are still waiting but now we share the hay shed with the other platoon. War seems to be a waiting game here in the south. Back in Charkov we dispersed the replacements so each Panzer has at least one newcomer. They have not seen any ground action yet and muse over it. "Has Ivan called it quits, they ask?" Are we going back to Erlangen and Kummersdorf without medals?" The guys look enviously at our EK's [Iron Crosses], KvK's [Kriegsverdienstkreuz, War Merit Cross], Panzer Battle, and Sonderabzeichen für das Niederkämpfen von Panzerkampfwagen durch Einzelkämpfer [Panzer Destruction Medals]. Some of us, those who had the guts to knock out a T-34 or KW-1 singlehandedly with a limpet charge, wear the Close Combat Clasp or the silver and black Tank Destroyer arm band.

Darkness brings the Sewing Machines back; this time they try machine-gunning our area but miss as usual.

3:00 AM: (Again 3:00 AM; do clocks stop here in Russia at 3:00 AM?) We are told to get ready to move out. Ivan has broken through our lines somewhere near an unpronounceable Russian kolchose [collective farm]. We start up, running our engines warm.

3:15 AM: We are ready; we can hear our own artillery fire a few km away. This probably is the area Ivan has chosen as a point of breakthrough.

Artillery HQ sends a coded message: Russian tanks and infantry are moving along the highway near Oktjabriskoje but a counterattack by the 126th Infantry supported by Panzers from the 5th SS Viking has re-established our positions. All day it's quiet but at 9:00 PM a lone twin-engine Soviet bomber approaches and drops 8 bombs in the area, 4 of them are duds, no casualties; only the kolchose gets a hit and goes up in smoke and flames. The farm was unoccupied by us because there was an infernal stink in the place.

29 June: No news of our proposed attack, we repair a few tracks. 6th

Co. has the idea of running a platoon of Mk. III's through a creek bed to get rid of tons of clinging mud but the Captain soon stops that operation. We have to conserve gas. We don't know how far in the rear our supplies are. Motorized patrols are going out to find a place for assembly prior to our attack.

30 June, 2:30 AM: Yes 2:30 AM, but it's early daylight around here and we know this is the day of our attack. Ju-87 Stukas are swooping down on Russian positions, artillery hammers the forward line, and by 2:45 AM the screeching sound of our DO-Nebelwerfer [literally, "Smoke Launchers," known for their loud screeching sound when launched; the Americans nicknamed it the "Screaming Meemie"] batteries chimes in. We are the second platoon in line to attack. Despite having been warned of a possible mine field in front of Nesternoje, one company wanders into the field and several of our tanks are disabled with broken tracks and Ivan fires artillery onto the sitting targets. A Panzer Pioneer Co. clears a path through the field, constantly harassed by Ivan's artillery. Finally the next platoon gets through the gap and others follow, staying in the tracks of the previous tanks. That way we get the group out of the mine field. One group reaches Nesternoje, slams through the town and collects its wits a few hundred meters north of the last dwellings. The 336th Infantry Division follows into the town and clears out the last Russians.

8th Co. meanwhile reaches the southern part of the town. Suddenly several T-34's appear from behind a hill in their flank. Company Commander 1st Lt. Ott's Panzer takes 2 direct hits and he and his crew die in the explosion.

The Battle Group has to retreat from the town and assembles north of it behind a covering hill, 1000 meters in front of the group. The T-34's have the high ground and are waiting for their next chance to get at our group. A flight of Ju-87 Stukas arrives and dives down onto the T-34's, bombing and strafing, but we are unable to see the results. We cannot attack as yet; several platoons run out of gas and ammunition and have to be resupplied. Despite this hold-up, 2nd Group attacks with 5th Co. in the lead; behind in loose formation follow 6th and 8th Co's. securing our flank. 5th Co. advanced about 1 km when a Russian PaK, hidden in a clump of bushes, suddenly opened up; two of our Panzers sustain hits and are disabled. The Ivan PaK ceases fire so that we can't make out its position. Group Command radios us to extricate ourselves from the position and move to the southeast of Krugloj.

1st Lt. Cramer of 5th Co. does not receive the radio call because his tank has sustained a hit – so he could not relay the message to move out toward the other Panzers of 5th Co. In the ensuing melee, 5th Co. loses another 7 Panzers. Finally a messenger arrives to clear up this mess. We reassemble north of the town to re-arm and gas up. A huge NAG [Nationale Automobil Gesellschaft] gas tanker has found its way through Russian artillery fire and bombing and arrives unharmed at our assembly area. Group Command decides to bypass this Russian nest of PaK's and T-34's.

336th Infantry Division meanwhile has bypassed Degtjarnoje; we ask regiment via radio whether we ought to go around the town on the southern side. The answer from regiment is "No" so our group commander decides to barrel into the town. We do just that but find no enemy present. We do however observe a large group of T-34's and KW-1's just north of us. These must be the tanks the Stukas attacked but didn't destroy. We decide to out-flank them at the northwest corner of the town. 6th Co. is in the lead but immediately a hidden PaK and a T-34 open fire and the leading Panzer of 6th Co. takes a hit; two more tanks from 8th Co. are also disabled. A platoon from 5th Co. finds the PaK and destroys it. The lone T-34 manages to reverse direction and move behind a hill.

6th Co. resumes its move forward but due to bad swampy ground, the tanks have to move to the left nearer the main road to Degtjarnoje to advance on both sides of the highway, and promptly run into a mine field and lose 7 Panzers. Another receives a hit by a PaK, hidden somewhere near 233.5. The group has to retreat back behind a hill. Meanwhile, 1st Lt. Grahn, whose Panzer had also run across a mine, collects all the wounded and the tank crews and makes his way, unopposed, back to the company. Only 12 Panzers are in fighting shape now.

To the left of us, Battle Group 3 under the command of Col. [Rudolf] Muller prepares to attack the Russian lines northwest of Teresowka but runs into T-34 and mortar fire near the highway. The mortar fire is very accurate and their position cannot be determined. Another group of T-34's, discovered by an infantry patrol on foot, opens fire. Col. Muller decides to retreat behind a hill. The infantry, on their return from the patrol, are unaware of the Panzer regiment password, "Dinkelsbuhl" and are unable to answer when challenged by Muller's tankers. Shots are fired, machine guns on tanks pierce the darkness with tracers but eventually the situation is sorted out. Col. Muller appears on the scene and screams, "Damn it, we're supposed to be fighting Ivan, not our own troops."

Only one infantryman took a bullet in the arm; the rest took cover.

Despite the darkness, Col. Muller decides to attack the hill just north of the town of Sirotino, but the Russians probably expected the 23rd Panzer Division to attack this part of the line. We take fire from unseen T-34's hidden in the dark at 222.1. Col. Muller orders a retreat to a ravine northeast of the highway. 3rd Group is left behind as a covering force and the rest of the Battle Group settles down for the night.

Ivan did foresee the move by 23rd Panzer and devised a cunning defense with two tank brigades. They are not attacking or defending en mass with their tanks. No, they occupy hills and other vantage points with a few T-34's or KW-1's, or hide in prepared tank holes, backing into the cover, then swing their guns toward us so that only the turret is visible above ground, making themselves hard to identify. Because of their commanding height on top of the hills, they can open fire at 2–3000 meters. A frontal attack on these positions by us would be an invitation to disaster. When one of the Ivans figures out that we are tying to bypass or encircle a fortified hill, the enemy tank driver rams his forward gears in and runs Hellbent toward the rear.

That night our Regimental Commander, Col. Pochat, turns up in his Hanomag command car, followed by two divisional HT's with food and rations – potato salad and each man gets a hard boiled egg. (Where do the cooks find eggs in this god-forsaken country? We have not seen a chicken since we left Poltava, 500 km in the rear). We also get Sondermischung cigarettes, 2 packs of 23 per man, tobacco for the pipe smokers, and above all, matches. The dampness in our tanks plays havoc with matches, and lighters are a rare commodity. We get no mail though; guess we can't have it all. We are satisfied with what we get and try to get some sleep.

1 July: At 2:00 AM the order goes out that we are moving to an adjacent covering fold in the ground. Three or four small Russian Christie tanks are seen on the right, firing a few annoying rounds onto the highway and into the assembly area of Battle Group 1. Despite this, the supply trucks are ordered forward again to make sure each platoon has its share of ammo and fuel. At 8:45 AM we change position to the southeast of Sirotino and prepare for an attack.

10:00 AM: We bypass the town to the north and arrive on ridges at 233.1 and 222.1. The Battle Groups receive fire from 8 T-34's and a few T-60's but they pull the usual Ivan trick. After firing a few rounds and pinpointing our position, they turn around and disappear into a fold. This time however, our turn to the right has outflanked them. We open fire and 4 T-60's are wrecked by our Panzers. We have to abandon this fight quickly because the heavier T-60's, with a longer range, have the highway under concentrated fire. We decide to chase the fleeing group of T-34's instead, but south of Lomowka, we meet up with 3rd Group and a halt is called to reform.

Observers report retreating Russian infantry north of Lomowka. A battalion of the 100th Croatian Infantry tries to bypass Lomowka but ends up in a crossfire between us and Ivan and has to retreat. Enemy tanks again have dug themselves in on hills 236.0 and 214.0. Two platoons try a frontal assault but to no avail. The range is too great and Ivan has the commanding hills. Our Ju-87 Stukas arrive to deal with this menace, and also target the retreating infantry on the main highway.

3:00 PM: The whole 201st Panzer Regiment performs a concerted panther leap into Lomowka and reaches 236.0 without any losses. We advance out of town to the left of the highway. Our Stukas busted the Russian tanks, but now the highway is pockmarked with bomb craters and the Panzer Pioneers, with the dozers, are far behind us. A lone T-34, northeast of Tschemerkin, tries his very best to retreat northeastward but our lead Panzer scores a direct hit with its first shot, at a range of 2000 meters. Good shooting we call that.

Tschemerkin is free of enemy troops. 5th Co. encounters a wooden bunker to the left of the highway out of Tschemerkin, and a few HE rounds sends logs and sandbags flying. 6th and 8th Co's. find their advance blocked by another bunker system on the right, but with guns blazing, our tanks break through that line, leaving the mopping up to the 100th Croatian Demi-Brigade. They hate Ivan more than we do and assure us that not one Russian will be left behind in our rear to cause mischief.

We reassemble with Group Command 1 km north of the town for a short breather and then we're on the highway again, no mines this time. Iwan has had no time to booby trap the road. We reach a cross-road, about 1 km east of Nowaja Grinew (I wish these Russian towns had simpler spellings). Reaching the crossroads, we are told to hold the line, form a hedgehog position with a company of Panzerjäger [tank hunters] for reinforcement. Armored patrols are sent out to the north and return with a few captured retreating enemy and 15–20 T-34's. This is an amazing catch for them. Supply trucks come up with food, ammunition, gas, and lubricating oil. Some of our Panzers are running dangerously low on oil pressure.

9:30 PM: Orders come in via radio. We are being taken off the present line to reinforce an established bridgehead across the Oskol River, along with the 3rd Panzer Division, to cut off retreating enemy groups east of the river.

2 July: After marching all night, assisted by bright moonlight, we reach Chutorischtsche at 6:00 AM and take quarters in an old school-house; our supplies arrive shortly thereafter and we have breakfast. With our last drop of lukewarm Ersatz [replacement] coffee down, alarm bells ring at 9:00 AM; enemy tanks have been sighted near the town of Werch. We see no enemy in sight, so on we drive; north until we're almost at Jutanowka, still no Ivan.

At point 205.3 just south of the town, we screech to a halt. We get a report that 20 T-34's southeast of us have tried to eliminate a bridge-head at Kosslowka. We turn our turrets to the south, waiting. A report comes in from 190.3 that a group of 8 T-34's is heading in our direction, probably to snatch Werch from under our noses. Before we get a confirmation report from our Panzer Spahwagen [eight-wheeled armored reconnaissance car] we're sent an alarm by our infantry occupying Werch. Eight or ten enemy tanks are heading for the town from the east. We send two Panzer Mk. IV's from 2nd Group to reinforce the infantry. We destroy 4 T-34's and advance outside town another few kilometers only to find no enemy between us and Lewkimow. At 7:00 PM we retreat to 205.3 to resupply.

3 July: We rest until 1:30 AM. We have sent our supply trucks to meet us later in a pre-determined area across the Oskol River, but not until 3:00 PM is the Battle Group able to cross to the other side. During the morning hours, a Panzer IV broke through the primitive wooden planking of the bridge and fell into the river. A pontoon bridge had to be thrown across to support the weight of our Panzers. We occupy an attack position 2 km northeast of Salomnoje, our Battle Group in front with Col. Muller's forces in reserve. As for today's target, we are supposed to advance along the Wolokonowka-Gutschenka highway, swing to the north and cut off the retreating enemy at the town of Oskol. During our river crossing we are attacked by enemy fighter-bombers but the crossing goes ahead without any losses.

10:35: The order arrives, "Man your Panzers." 6th Co. is in the lead, 8th and 5th Co. follow close up. We advance on both sides of the highway and reach Scharapowka without enemy action at 5:45 PM. Here we stop for supplies from our trucks. At 6:30 PM we get an alarm and climb back into our Panzers. After waiting 15 minutes for orders to move out, we are told it's too dark now to attack, so we stay put. We have Panzerjägers guarding our area in case of a surprise attack by Ivan.

4 July: During the night a Sewing Machine kept circling above town. Two bombs were dropped but no damage reports came in. At 3:45 AM we are ready to move out of Scharapowka with the 2nd group leading, followed by 6th, 8th, and 5th Co's., a battalion of the 126th Inf., and a unit of Panzer Pioneers. Our march goes via Besginka-Nowoselowka-Jaruschnyj.

At Besginka we encounter a blown bridge. Engineers busily erect a temporary metal structure that can hold the weight of our Panzer IV's, and we reach the highway to Jaruschnij. North of Wolotowo our Panzer Pioneers detect a mine field across the road. Some lighter Panzers leave the road to advance parallel to the highway and one of the Panzer II's promptly runs over a mine, damaging tracks and bogie wheels. The men are okay and jump onto a supply truck following us.

We stop 1 km east of Jaruschnij to refuel and have a hot meal from the field kitchen of the 126th infantry, bean soup with bacon; not fully cooked but nevertheless it goes down well. The hinges on the Panzer hatches have to be oiled because the farts created by half-cooked beans can suffocate a driver and bow gunner deep in the bowels of the iron monsters. The gunner-commander and loader can always open the turret hatch if no Ivan is in sight.

At 1:00 PM we are ready again to move out. The Command Panzer, in the lead, runs into another mine belt but the rest of the group bypasses this obstacle and Panzer Pioneers clear a path through the belt. At point 225.4 we encounter an anti-tank ditch, and from a ridge further along, we take PaK and machine gun fire. There is a bunker line atop the rise. We return fire and destroy 2 PaK's and several bunkers. Bypassing the line to the north with 126th Inf. in tow, we encounter more bunkers and PaK's. We stop at the anti-tank ditch while 2nd Group gives us protection. The infantry dismounts the tanks and crosses the ditch on foot and moves forward to the outskirts of the village of Krugloje. Panzer Pioneers meanwhile blow the rim of the AT ditch so we can cross.

5 July, 6:30 AM: We had a good and peaceful night in Krugloje. We parked our Panzers in an orchard, leaving two platoons as a security guard to cover the three roads that enter the village. There was not much battle damage to the town, so we found several houses fit enough to spend the night in. A well we found soon provided us with water to wash our grime off and we boiled some water from our own water tanker to make coffee or tea. One Corporal from the 6th Co. found a Quetsch Kommode [squeeze commode, German nickname for an accordion] in an empty house and soon we were singing the old songs we all knew. Even the Sewing Machines stayed away that night; only far off to the northeast was the rumble of artillery fire to be heard. By now, the 6th Army of General Paulus was probably on its way east toward the next objective, the Don River line.

We saddle up, next target Repiewka. No enemy contact as yet. A motorcycle infantry unit and platoons of the 2nd Group are in the lead; then we run into another bunker line and receive PaK and infantry fire. We send the rest of 2nd Group with a company of the

126th Infantry and a Panzer Pioneer Co. around the bunker line. A small village is ahead at point 170.7. The 26th Inf. with the Panzer Pioneers manages to enter the village and open the road for the motorcycle unit to drive right through. The platoons from the 2nd follow suit. Ahead now is the next town, Repiewka, covered by more bunkers to the north. To protect our motorcycle unit and platoons from this new menace, we order a battery of DO-Werfers forward that smothers the bunkers with their 150mm rockets. The village is surrounded by another anti-tank ditch. This means that probably Ivan has mined the road somewhere ahead. Our Pioneers blow the rim of the ditch to enable the Panzers to cross, then the Pioneers turn their attention to the road, but no mines are found. Ivan is slacking off in his defensive preparations. We decide to call a halt for today in the village to rearm and refuel.

6 July: A day of rest in the village, guns are cleaned and breaches oiled. A few tracks need adjusting and hydraulic fluid is checked. The field kitchen arrives, not beans again I hope. No, it's potato soup, kommis bread [a dark hard bread] and sausage, mineral water, and a bar of chocolate; we live like kings.

7 July: No disturbances during the night. At 7:45 AM we are ready to leave, but it's 10:00 AM before we start up our engines and move out. The target for today is Drakino. We arrive there by noon without being shot at by Ivan and we call a halt until 6:00 PM. Shortly thereafter we're off again, turning south and arrive at Sititsche at 9:30 PM.

8 July, 3:30 AM: All day we proceed to the south, the day is extremely hot. The Panzers are like bakery ovens inside; we leave all the hatches open but this means dust, and soon we are covered in it, but better dirty than suffocating. At 8:00 PM we finally reach a place called Olchowatka on our maps. The village is full of Russian soldiers who surrender without even firing a shot. We turn them over to the 126th. We are tankers and cannot guard POW's.

9 July, 2:15 AM: We advance to the south, through Coscharny, Kalinowaja-Balka, and Nowo-Belaja. 2nd Group is out front with

infantry of the 126th riding on our Panzers. Our reconnaissance, far out in front with Puma 8-wheelers, reports drawing enemy fire from north of Nowo-Belaja. We soon reach the town and find that the reconnaissance patrol has taken care of Ivan but outside town in the distance we can see retreating columns of the enemy, mostly on horse-drawn wagons, with small caliber AT guns dispersed among them. 6th Co. takes care of them and we find an undamaged bridge to cross a river. 3rd Co. of the motorcycle battalion and parts of the 126th cross the bridge and reach point 206.1. We stay put in Nowo-Belaja for now.

10 July, 2:00 AM: Now we are assigned to Battle Group Muller of the 126th Infantry and he is the Commanding Officer of today's operations. Our job is to reach the railroad at Markowka and an important crossroad near the town of Kantemirowka. We reach the crossroad at about 9:00 AM. Several of our trucks come under fire from retreating Russians with light AT guns. Just before Markowka, a single KW-1 comes out of a copse and attempts to cross the highway running at full throttle over destroyed weapons and abandoned staff cars. Our Panzerjäger unit opens up with all they have but the KW-1 manages to get away into a forest. We admire the audacity of that tanker crew.

At the appointed crossroad, we meet up with a Panzerjäger unit of the 29th Motorized Infantry Division that had been unable to hold a small village because of an enemy tank attack. We travel another 3 km further and wait for additional orders.

How it came about that we ran into the 29th was the fact that they had 1:300,000 scale maps and ours were 1:100,000, so we had better details. The 1:300,000 maps did not even show the crossroad.

11 July: We stay overnight in this small village, Bani or something similar sounding. We are still there at noon when the new commander of the 201st Panzer Regiment arrives, Col. [Arnold] Burmeister [from the 128th Panzer Grenadier Regiment, which was attached to 23rd Panzer Division, German Cross in Gold awarded September 9, 1943]. We're ready to move out at 5:30 PM with orders to assemble at Battle Group Headquarters in Prossjanij. We stop at the outskirts of the small town and a radio message arrives that says, "At noon the railroad station at

Schelestowka was attacked by 15 T-34's, our infantry had to retreat, T-34's turned to the northwest."

It seems from radio reports that another attack on the railroad station is imminent so we move around Prossjanij to reach the railroad station just south of Schelestowka. We drive into a fold to have some cover only to find a battalion of the 126th Infantry already there. It seems Ivan has given up taking the railroad station, so we hang around several hours, nothing. Then at 7:15 PM we get a new and urgent radio message: "15 T-34's sighted 2 km north west of Prossjanij." We do a 180-degree about face and go full-steam back toward our departure point, leaving a baffled battalion of the 126th Infantry sitting on their haunches to guard the railroad station.

Just as it gets dark, at point 213.0, we make out 6 T-34's on the highway to the north, but because by now it is useless to start a firefight, we stop just south of the town. Our artillery nevertheless keeps up a brisk fire in the forlorn hope of getting at least some of the T-34's, now on a retreating course to the northwest. Four of the T-34's seem to have sustained some damage however. 1.5 km north of Prossjanij one of our Panzer Mk. IV's is hit by our own artillery and explodes. Two comrades die. The T-34's attempt to break into town several times during the evening. Our Panzer Pioneers are unable to get anywhere near the tanks to place limpets because of Russian infantry covering them. We are not moving any further tonight.

12 July: We park in a plum tree orchard and several of the men pick the unripe fruit; but it's better than nothing. Our supply truck most probably got lost in the dark.

3:00 AM: We are ready again to take the left front, west of Prossjanij. We heard a lot of truck and motor rattling during the night, southeast of us. It sounded like a full Ivan tank brigade on the move – probably toward the same crossroad as us. Later, reconnaissance tells us that 20 T-34's are rolling along the highway to the south. We thought our supply truck was probably somewhere near there, but they got out of the way before the T-34's barreled through. By 10:30 AM we are on the highway south, searching for the T-34's. Battle Group Bodenhausen is somewhere in the vicinity of point 221.4. Col. Burmeister, our new Regimental Commander is in the lead. We have buttoned the tanks up tight now because of prowling fighter-bombers. We are making good time.

The PtP [tank to tank] radio cracks in, "Pz 23 [tank number] to Platoon Command."

"What is it?" the Lt. questioned.

"Permission to stop Sir," came the voice from Pz 23.

The Lt. yelled, "What the Hell for, and who is speaking?"

"Unteroffizier Moos, Pz 23 Sir, I need to go out, Sir."

"I said what for Sgt.?" the Lt. replied.

"You know those unripe plums we had last night Sir? I got the trots."

"You've just got to hold it Sergeant. No stopping, hear me, over?"

"I can't, Sir,"

"For Hell's sake Sergeant, crap in your pants or squeeze tight, over."

"As you say Sir, in my pants Sir, over and out."

"What was that all about Lieutenant?" Col. Burmeister's voice came over the radio.

"Sir, some of the men have diarrhea, eating bad fruit last night, Sir."

"Tell them to ... Hellfire Lieutenant, look alive, we have fighter-bombers on our left."

That ended the PtP conversation, but either this Ivan has run out of bombs or he's just doing a look-over, because soon he is gone. We reach Gorobowski about 1:00 PM, where [the] other battle group meets up with us. Their morning was more successful than ours, claiming 12 enemy tanks destroyed, but several got away with their infantry and we have been assigned the job of catching them.

13 July: A shake-up of command during the night put us under Capt. [Fritz] Fechner's command [German Cross in Gold, awarded November 5, 1942]. Major [Werner] Illig [German Cross in Gold, awarded December 24, 1942] will follow the enemy with Battle Group Bodenhausen. Capt. Fechner collects all trucks, Panzers and other vehicles including the AT and the 88mm and we proceed back to Manjkowo. We have the dirty job of establishing a gasoline and ammunition depot.

14–16 July: Three days of rest for our group.

17 July, 9:00 AM: The Russian overseer of the local kolchose reports to us that about 100 partisans, some in uniform, some in civilian clothes are hiding in the woods, 8 km southeast of the farm, and there might even be Commissars among them.

11:00 AM: We form a "clean up" commando group led by Lt. Eisenlohr and 2 Panzer Mk. II's and a company of the motorcycle infantry battalion. By 2:00 PM we get more news from the kolchose overseer, putting the total number of partisans, armed with hand grenades and rifles, at almost 200, and according to him, they will try to break out toward the south tonight.

During the afternoon, we surround the woods but only manage to capture 23 of the partisans; the rest must have scattered when they heard the Mk. II's coming. We hand the 23 over to a Feldpolizei [military police] unit.

18–20 July: Manjkowo, nothing to report; we rest.

21–22 July: Orders arrive for us to get ready for further deployment and the regiment sets off for Alexandrowka at 5:00 PM, camping for the night at Kudinowka.

Chapter 4

TOWARD THE DON AND SSAL,
23–30 JULY 1942

23 July: Our group arrives without incident to a spot 1 km west of Alexandrowka. A forest clearing is converted into a camp.

24–26 July: Time to see to the Panzers, half tracks, our weapons, and ourselves. Group Illig will be dissolved and their vehicles sent back to the other battle groups. A reconnaissance group and a battalion of armor have left and they reported via radio that a bridgehead across the mighty Don River has been established and that they are awaiting further orders from Division. Knowing that the bulk of General Paulus's 6th Army is in the vicinity and that some units have already crossed the Don in force, they are told to set up camp and await our arrival. Our gas supply has not arrived so we can't continue our advance. Finally, on the afternoon of the 26th, fuel tankers roll into camp, but we are told that due to a shortage of tanker transport, we are only allotted 75% of our requirement. This leaves us little room for sidestepping enemy concentrations that we may encounter on our way to the Don.

27 July, 4:00 AM: We move out via Alexandrowka–Bolschinka–Kolcoff toward Tjapkin, a distance of 180 km, and arrive at Tjapkin at 7:30 PM where our trucks await us to refuel.

28 July: We are supposed to attack today in a southeasterly direction, under the command of the XLth Army Corps, whose 29th Inf. Division is engaged in a battle at Zymlanskaja. We move out at 2:30 PM and reach the Don River at Nikolajewskaja at 4:00 PM. By 6:15 PM we are across the Don River and marching toward Piroshok. 8th Co. has been transferred as reinforcements to Battle Group Zedlik of the 126th Bolschowskaja [Russian volunteers].

We arrive in Piroshok at 8:00 AM to refuel and eat, cold rations; even the ersatz coffee is cold and goes down like Trinitrotoluene [TNT]. We set off again, minus 8th Co., at 3:15 PM. We cross the Ssal River at Nessmejanowka. Here, 2 km south of the town, we go into line with Battle Group Burmeister to capture Moskowskij. According to a reconnaissance report, a T-34 group is hiding in the town. Five T-34's come out of town, but even before our 75mm long barrel PaK guns arrive, our artillery destroys two of them; the other three retreat immediately back into the town.

4:00 PM: We get the command to attack in order from the south to west. Infantry Battle Group Bachmann, 2 companies of 3rd Panzer, and 2 companies of 2nd Panzer are involved. We are covered by Oberstleutnant Schlutius [Lt. Colonel Kurt Schlutius, German Cross in Gold, awarded August 27th, 1942] and his artillery whose job it is to lay covering fire onto a crossroad outside town to prevent T-34's from getting to our rear.

Before the attack by our motorized forces, a group of Messerschmitt Me-110's and Dornier Do-217's pummel the town with bombs and low level strafing. By 5:30 PM we are ready to move into Moskowskij. 3rd Panzer Group tries to get into the town by swinging their attack to the west and encircling the enemy. To the south we set up a fire front of DO-Werfers to keep enemy infantry in check. Nebelwerfers are not much good against well protected armor but the rockets play Hell amongst infantry in open terrain. At the start the attack goes quite well but 1 km from the first houses, we draw light PaK and tank fire, but have no casualties. It's the artillery's turn now and our guns fire HE and smoke grenades into the center of town. The infantry Battle Group, followed by 2 Panzer companies, manages to get in among the buildings. The rest of the Panzer Group is in a holding position just outside town. Then out of nowhere from the north-west a T-34 and a KW-1, with guns blazing, head full speed toward the town, but our 3rd Panzer Group opens a concentrated fire and both machines go up in flames. As it is getting dark, further advances into the town by our Panzers is out; the infantry, however, still attacks and reaches a crossroad north of Moskowskij and settles down for the night.

29 July, 4:30 AM: We are required to resume our advance toward Martinowka with the Burmeister Battle Group, Pz. Reg. 201, minus of course, 8th Co. Today we also have the 128th Artillery Regiment with us, plus a unit of infantry from the 126th. 5th Co. is in the lead, 2nd Platoon is on point; our job is to take two important crossroads near Martinowka. We are told there is only a rearguard of the enemy in the town. We advance from the south. A motorcycle infantry unit will attack from the west.

5:45 AM: Reports come in of enemy activity northeast of Martinowka. They are trying to flee with all speed to avoid being out-flanked by the motorcycle unit and 88mm's mounted on DEMAG HT's. Two T-70's race along the Russian infantry column trying to protect them. One is shot to pieces; the other stalls, and before the crew can collect their wits, it is captured intact.

Our battle group with 5th and 6th Co. bypasses the town almost 5 km to the east; we try to outflank the enemy. Sgt. Hoffman and his lone Panzer IV races far ahead and with heroic actions, manages to capture a battery of enemy PaK 7.62 caliber and an infantry support cannon. From the outskirts of a small village, we take fire from an unseen heavy PaK or tank cannon but no direct hits are scored; a few shells just scratch the armor up front. The incoming shell, because of the long distance, had a low velocity by the time it reached us. Inside town, between two groves of birch trees, we spot two T-34's but 5th Co. takes care of them. One is knocked out by a Panzer Pioneer's limpet mine. Battle Group Burmeister now has reached Martinowka and stops at the Ssal River; 2nd Group re-establishes communications with the main battle group at the MTS [Motor Tractor Station] near Martinowka.

Prisoners and deserters coming out of Martinowka report that the Russian Corps Command has its HQ in town. Along a road near the River Ssal, a stream of command cars and trucks is spotted and shelled by 2nd Battle Group. We capture 4 staff cars, and in one we find the corps commander, a general, sitting in the back seat smoking a Machorka cigarette. Our group now has control of the road along the river. Two T-34's appear across the river but are soon knocked out at a distance of only 200 meters by our PaK 75. Another T-70 falls to the concentrated fire of 6th Co. A motorcycle infantry unit has already crossed the Ssal but is unable to enter the town because of a mine belt, so they hide in a small wood for the time being until a Panzer Pioneer Co. can clear a path through the field. Part of 2nd Group crossed the undamaged bridge and is in town, advancing further to the outskirts. They take cover in a wooded area 800 meters further on and come under fire from PaK's to the west. The rest of 2nd Group, including a platoon of 88mm's on DEMAG HT's, decides to barrel right through the center of Martinowka.

About 100 meters from the church, all of a sudden, two T-70's appear out of a side street; now who will score the first hit? Well, our 88mm saves the day and both T-70's go up in flames. Slowly we roll forward, past a church's open square with a statue of Stalin on a pedestal. For the 88mm crew the temptation is too much to ignore, so one round of HE sends the dictator flying. We divide our group; 1st platoon turns into a side street on our right, slowly Lt. Fischer of the 2nd Platoon creeps forward; a T-34 appears from a garden but before his turret can turn toward us, Lt. Fischer knocks him out. The Command Panzer and another Panzer from 1st platoon meanwhile find a road running parallel to the street where Lt. Fischer knocked out the T-34. They encounter two more T-34's parked on a side street and open fire from a distance of just 65 meters. After four hits, both T-34's are burning. Three T-70's try their luck from another side street just past the square, but the Panzers of Lt. Zirr, SSgt. Arnold, and Lt. Bohme are on guard and knock both T-70's out from 120 meters.

The leading platoon reaches the northwestern edge of the town when another lone T-34 tries to run diagonal in front of us into the cover of a garden, but he too takes 3 hits from the platoon and burns. At 5:00 PM we finally all reach the edge of Martinowka where we stop and look back and see the onion shape dome of the church burning. A group of our 126th Infantry with Panzerbuchsen [AT rifles] marches toward us, but we can hear engine and track noises from somewhere very close. We only have a clear view forward; behind us is the town, to the left and right are the last few houses. Two T-34's break out of a garden and try to reach the main road. SSgt. Arnold knocks one out just 20 meters from our position. A Panzer Pioneer with a limpet leaps from behind an HT and slams it just below the turret, the most vulnerable part of the tank apart from the engine compartment, and pulls the fuse line. The top hatch opens and the enemy tank commander appears with a sub-machine gun in his hand, but before he can squeeze the trigger, the limpet goes off and blows the turret from its turning gear. It seems that was the last of the enemy armor, so we secure our perimeter and the 126th collects the enemy infantry, engineers and cavalry, but we find no horses. One man of the 5th Co. is wounded by a sniper before the clean-up is complete.

At 6:00 PM our motorcycle battalion arrives in town, and with our group, we all establish a safety zone so our supplies can enter the town. We are all low on ammo and fuel and a decent meal would be very much appreciated.

In the evening we count our tally for today, July 29th.

    8 T-34's
    6 T-70's
    2 42mm PaK's
    2 Infantry support guns
    Numerous trucks, staff cars, and wagons.

That's not counting the tally from the morning in our advance toward Martinowka: 10 T-34's, 8 T-70's, 4 PaK's and a battery of Flak. We also capture a General and a Regimental Adjutant. Not a bad day, no, not bad at all.

30 July: At 3:00 AM our last supply trucks finally roll in and we roll out of bed. 1st Lt. Salwey, the commander of supplies, immediately sets about to refuel and rearm us so that we are ready at 4:30 AM to move out. Today we are assigned to Burmeister's Battle Group to secure the eastern flank at Beketnij. As soon as the engines start to turn over, down comes the rain and within minutes the road is a mess. All our wheeled vehicles get stuck and we have to leave a much needed Panzer Platoon behind to extricate everyone out of the mire; only the tracked vehicles keep going.

5:30 AM: Traveling through the mud, 3 km north of Nikola-jewskaja [Nowo-Nikolajewskaja], we see a Russian truck column heading west but apparently stuck in the mire like our wheeled transport. We try our best to get nearer, even letting loose a few long range shots, but no luck. A swamp between us and them saves Ivan from destruction. Our AT guns, in tow by the half tracks, could easily reach them but after a few shots the gun crew gives up. The PaK sinks deeper into the mud after every recoil. It takes a Panzer Mk. IV to extricate the HT and AT guns; we are wasting precious time.

At 8:00 AM we reach our destination, 3 km north of Nemetzko [Nemetzko-Chaginskoe or Kronental], securing the highway there in case of Russian attack. We wait now for our trucks and the Panzer platoon we had to leave behind. 5th Co. advances on the right of the highway a few hundred yards further. A Russian PaK, nestled somewhere behind us, keeps up an annoying fire until SSgt. Pascke has enough and reconnoiters the area and sees the gun concealed in a hedge. He comes back and mounts an HT with a quad 20mm, an absolute deadly weapon in ground combat, and 4 streams of 20mm tracers find the PaK and ends the nuisance.

31 July: A day of rest. The commanding general arrives and awards medals to the 201st. Three Iron Crosses 1st Class, 35 2nd Class, 41 Tank Battle medals, 2 of them in silver. The Iron Crosses 1st Class go to 1st Lt. Grahn, 2nd Lt. Dittmann, and SSgt. Arnold. We rest until 6:30 PM before we move out toward Rebrischanskyj and arrive there at midnight.

Chapter 5

ADVANCE TO THE CAUCASUS,
1 AUGUST–24 NOVEMBER 1942

1 August: We are in Romanow now, waiting for new deployment and are now part of Battle Group Bachmann. Several enemy columns are reported to the south, heading toward the Don Bridge at Proletaskarja but they turn off to the east when Stukas appear in the sky looking for them.

2 August: All day and night we are in Romanow cleaning weapons and repairing our armor. At 5:00 PM we leave the town to meet up with our 201st Panzer regimental headquarters group at Jelmut.

3 August, 4:00 AM: We are off to Proletaskarja and arrive at 6:30 AM and report to Brigade HQ. Our orders to proceed to meet up with Battle Group Burmeister are cancelled because our gas supply is low and the tanker trucks have not arrived as yet. Nobody seems to know their whereabouts. We have just enough fuel to send 8th Co. toward Bolgarski to search for an enemy battle group that had earlier attacked our supply trucks and destroyed several of them. The area is typical of the Kalmuk Steppe: undulating hills, crisscrossed by deep balkas [valleys], ideal for concealing a whole battle group, but we find no enemy. We suspect Ivan to be hiding in one balka but darkness sets in, so we set up a hedgehog position to await daylight.

4 August, 6:00 AM: We search several balkas only to find a few

Russian 2-ton trucks and take about two dozen prisoners. Ivan has retreated during the night, so we start up the Russian trucks and take them with us as replacements for the ones we lost yesterday.

5 August: During the night, the rest of the tanker trucks arrive. We refuel and go back to sleep.

6 August: Early this morning, artillery and MG fire can be heard from the southeast. The commander gives the alarm and at 4:00 AM we are ready to move out; reports come in of a Russian attack near the main highway. This sounds big and 3rd and 23rd Panzer Divisions move out to the south. Distinct battle sounds come from that direction and we are told that Russians ambushed a column of our trucks belonging to a Luftwaffe unit and caused considerable damage. We send a motorcycle infantry group ahead, side cars occupied by Panzer Pioneers with AT rifles and heavy machine guns.

We reach a small town as enemy mortar and light artillery fire destroys the observation post of our own artillery. In the town, the order from Division arrives to cross a small river immediately, but we find that our engineers have blown the crossing prior to Ivan's attack, so two Panzers from 1st platoon, 7th Co. find a ford to get across. Several more ford crossings almost fail because of the muddy river bed but the two Panzers from 1st Platoon, with the help of a thick wire cable, pulls 5th, 6th, and 8th Co. across to the other side and we fall into immediate attack formation. Ivan's artillery ceases fire and the enemy crews, plus their infantry, can be seen running away in a northerly direction. 6th Co. goes into pursuit of the fleeing Russians, with motorcycle patrols covering the Panzer's flanks.

To the west we can make out enemy artillery columns marching eastward. We don't have a complete battle group now because we are dispersed and have only 1st platoon who pulled our group across the muddy ford. All we have to confront the enemy artillery column with is a Panzer II and a Panzer III but Lt. Fischer is a daredevil and with his 2 tanks he charges into the Russian line, throwing hand grenades, firing his small caliber guns and generally playing havoc for 6 km along the highway.

5th and 6th Companies now get orders to clear enemy resistance toward the highway and stay in touch with 3rd Panzer Division. 8th Co. meanwhile moves into a burning village and, finding no enemy, they proceed to a point 2 km from the village. Arriving there, our infantry dismounts the Panzers and clears the area to our west. The motorcycle unit searches the northern sector; both are told to capture all Panje horses and carts. Because of the muddy roads, this is about the only transport that can move our supplies forward.

6th Co. reaches the highway, takes many prisoners and finds a lake not marked on our maps. They proceed along the northern shore of the lake, capturing two heavy 178mm artillery pieces with supplies and ammunition and reach a kolchose marked on our maps as Liman. Russian PaK wounds 2 men of our infantry that were mounted on our tanks. We encircle the kolchose and a few rounds of our guns set the farm ablaze. We capture the PaK hidden there and our crew takes POW's.

Meanwhile 3rd Panzer Division now has possession of the main highway and advances in two columns while 8th Co. covers their flank. Soon an enemy truck convoy comes in sight. We race toward it and capture every vehicle, including the Luftwaffe trucks Iwan took from us earlier – plus their drivers. The Luftwaffe unit radios a big "thank you" and offers us some supplies, but we generously decline because our own supply is just beyond the horizon.

Our Battle Group in this action is credited with the capture or destruction of nine pieces of 105mm artillery, three pieces of 155mm artillery, two 178mm long barrel guns, seven 210mm guns, a huge 280mm siege gun, four Ratsch-Buns [7.62 mm high-velocity guns], several PaK's, 23 Prime Movers, five field kitchens with hot Kapustra soup, 100 Panje horses, various machine guns, machine pistols, and 300 POW's.

A close inspection of the brand new 105mm guns reveals they are made in the USA; so Roosevelt has finally accepted Stalin as a big bother in our fight against him and Bolshevism.

Six hundred more prisoners arrive shortly thereafter, taken by 8th Co. The captured artillery will be given to our own division units to reinforce their firepower and we found trucks full of ammunition for them too. We assemble our units and return to Filonenka. The enemy attack, made by two full regiments, has failed.

155mm field artillery piece being towed by a heavy DEMAG,
southern Russia, Fall 1942.

Unknown town in southern Russia, December 1942.

7 August: Nothing doing in the night. We repair a few breakdowns, clean our uniforms; rumor has it that we are about to advance to Woroschilowsk.

8 August, 6:30 AM: We depart in a southerly direction and at 11:00 AM we meet the rest of our division on a highway near Donskoje.

9 August, 4:00 AM: We set off and reach Woroschilowsk at 11:00 AM and take quarters in the southern part of the city. Here we are assigned to the 23rd Division as a flank guard to the main highway that leads to the Caucasus. The Kuban River is ahead and we already have heard that General von Manstein has captured the City of Kertch on the Crimea and is preparing to cross the narrow 30 mile channel of the Black Sea to the Caucasus. Patrols around the city and up to the Kuban River find no enemy and we all return to our camps.

13 August: About 100 Russian soldiers march into the city of Woroschilowsk with hands held high and surrender without any trouble.
14 August: The gasoline tankers and ammo trucks finally catch up with us. We load up and move further south, reaching the town of Kalngli by late afternoon. On our arrival there, we come under the command of the 128th Panzer Grenadier Regiment and camp for the night.

15 August, 6:30 AM: We continue our march south with no enemy contact and reach Marjinska at 4:00 PM. There we are returned to Battle Group Burmeister and the 128th Panzer Grenadiers reluctantly let us go.

16 August: Our group arrives at the Regimental HQ for new orders. We are told of enemy concentrations to the south of us and we assemble in battle formation to cross one of the many tributaries of the Kuban River; this one is called the Bakssan. However, Ivan has blown the dams further up the river and it's impossible to get across until the water subsides. Meanwhile the Russians make a clean getaway to the east and our battle group, just about ready to move out, is halted. At 10:00 AM we are again called to formation; this time we are supposed to capture a bridge across the swollen river at Maiskij. Enemy twin-engine bombers, with an escort of 10 fighters, appear but our light Flak is on alert and drives them off.

2:40 PM: 8th Co., traveling with an 8-wheel Puma, encounters another river not marked on our maps and that river puts a stop to our progress. There is no bridge and the water is too high for fording. Our attack on Maiskij is off for today, besides, we need to refuel and there are no tanker trucks anywhere in sight. 6 km from Maiskij we try to make camp but enemy air activity is hampering our search for suitable cover. Everyone seems to be searching for a bridge and we see tactical identification marks from many different units, but despite this gathering, the enemy bombers drop theirs eggs far from the milling point.

17 August: In the morning we again have enemy air activity; this time in cooperation with a bunch of fighter-bombers. Concentrated fire from our 20mm Quads brings two of them down; the rest scamper to the east. One pilot bails out unharmed and is taken prisoner. We have no one who speaks Russian to interrogate him so we hand him over to regiment. Ivan is firing long-range artillery, so our supply column has to saddle up and run Hellbent in search of cover. An exploding gasoline or diesel tanker is not an occurrence to take lightly in this confined area with hundreds of our vehicles waiting to cross the still swollen river.

18 August: Fighter-bomber attacks in the afternoon and one of the Panzer Grenadiers is wounded. We abandon the village of Karagatsch. Panzers in a confined space like the village have no room to maneuver, so we move to the highway as protection for our supply columns. 5th Co. gets caught in a Russian artillery attack and loses one Panzer Mk. III with a broken drive sprocket; no casualties among the crew.

20 August: Battle Group Burmeister receives reinforcements in tanks and men and reassembles. Battle Group Bachmann has already established a bridgehead across the next river, the Urwanj, and forms a flanking screen. At 12 noon we advance again, crossing the bridge and move 2 km further in the cover of a large cornfield. We are assigned to the Panzer Grenadier Battalion of Lt. Col. Unger to extend the bridgehead, then we are to turn left and try to capture the bridge at Maiskij.

21 August: The attack is scheduled to start at 4:30 AM and it goes off without a hitch. At 5:15 AM we encounter the first Russians, a reconnaissance patrol about 2 platoons strong, but without much ado they surrender. We motion them into the house of a kolchose to wait there for Military Police. We reach a railroad track and from the east we see 2 freight trains steaming toward us; one seems to be a Panzerzug, [anti-aircraft and anti-tank guns mounted on a railroad flat car]. A few rounds are fired from our 50mm's and both locomotives are destroyed. Panzer Pioneers meanwhile blow the track sky high. We then regroup back at the kolchose where the POW's are still waiting to be taken to the rear. Here we assemble with the 126th Infantry to capture the road bridge at Maiskij; but before we set off, a direct hit from a Russian PaK destroys our artillery observation point, killing all the men.

This kolchose, in peace time, is a large communal dairy farm, with a cheese factory about 1 km north in a copse of trees, and we think that the PaK fire is coming from there. Sure enough, a fast patrol by 5th Co. detects two 7.62 guns among the cow sheds and captures both of them before the crew has time to reload, but we are now without a proper artillery observer. We nevertheless move forward, receiving heavy Russian field artillery fire 600 meters from the bridge. We destroy several more 7.62's but with the concentrated enemy artillery fire, we have to retreat to the farm. About 4:00 PM, an almighty explosion tells us that Ivan has blown the bridge at Maiskij. Now we will try to get to the railroad bridge before it is destroyed as well. At 5:45 PM a motorcycle unit races toward the bridge, covered by our artillery and super heavy mortars, and they get to within 100 meters of the bridge when it explodes. Regiment HQ radio tells us to retreat again to the farm and to secure our position there.

22 August: 8:00 AM: A patrol of 8th Co. sets out to investigate if the road bridge can be repaired well enough for infantry to cross, but the 12 ton structure is beyond repair and crossing under enemy artillery fire is impossible, so 8th Co. returns to the farm. Enemy infantry, supported by medium artillery, is trying to force us out of the farm. Two platoons from 5th Co. and Captain Brandenburg's infantry company repel the first attack, but Ivan tries again, with a whole battalion. This time we get support from the 128th Infantry's own DO-Werfer Battery. The rockets play havoc with the enemy attack and they finally call it a day.

2:00 PM: 6th Co. counterattacks and tries to reach the railroad embankment 1.5 km away and succeeds. Ivan runs to the east, leaving behind a score of dead. 6th Co. returns to the farm without losses.

23 August: During the night we have sporadic enemy artillery fire. Capt. Brandenburg and his company retired to the village so we have no infantry cover to secure the highway.

4:00 AM: Again the enemy has nestled into the cheese factory. Their artillery intensifies; six men are wounded and one is killed. The farm receives mortar fire and 5th Co. again moves out, and with the help of our artillery, we push back the enemy. It seems Ivan is trying his very best to eliminate our precious bridgehead; time and time again he attacks but we repel each one with heavy losses to him.

24 August: All day Russian artillery fire hampers our traffic on the highway. This enemy artillery, using long range guns, cannot be eliminated without Panzer cannons. Our artillery cannot pinpoint the enemy because he is covered by a ridge. Finally, at 6:30 PM, we get orders to leave the farm and reassemble 1 km south of Altud and stay there for the night.

25 August: Before we set off toward the southeast, we are assigned to the 3rd Panzer Division.

5:30 AM: We move out and at noon we arrive in Ssoldatskaja. Yes, Ssoldatskaja. There are sure some tongue breaking names for towns around here. Supplies arrive and some warm food for a change. We rest for the day.

26 August: Orders for Battle Group Burmeister are to take the important railroad junction at Prochladny, leave a battalion of Panzer

Grenadiers, then proceed south along the Lenin Canal. A fast push brings 5th Co. into the town, and they barrel right through to the outskirts on the other side. From the north, a small battle group under Lt. Col. Mendel arrives too, but loses several men to enemy snipers. These snipers, we later hear, are students at a tractor school and were trained especially as snipers. The town has several mine belts and our Pioneers find 84 of them. We capture 300 enemy, including the sniper platoon.

27 August, 11:00 AM: We leave Prochladny; our target is Dementewski and we arrive there at 6:30 PM. No casualties on this move.

28 August: Nothing to report today. We rest.

29 August: According to reports from Russian civilians in town, a village a few kilometers east of us is occupied by the enemy. Lt. Eisenlohr sets out on a reconnaissance mission and returns at 2:00 PM but finds no Ivan.

30 August: We have reached the Terek River. Just south of us, the mighty range of the Caucasus Mountains is just discernable. We are now nearer the borders of Persia and Turkey than Charkov. 52nd Army Corps arrives today with 3 infantry divisions and part of the 5th SS Panzer Division "Viking," under the command of General Felix Steiner. 52nd Corps moves into the surrounding villages along the Terek. Battle Group Bodenhausen secures 52nd Corps' left flank, east along the river. 5th Co. has orders to join up with BG Bodenhausen, the rest of the BG is to follow at 1:00 PM.

There is supposed to be a ford somewhere nearby so we can cross the Terek and establish a bridgehead. 52nd Corps really wants to find a place to ford the river because building a temporary bridge is out of the question under these conditions. Ivan occupies the far side and any engineering attempt to build a bridge would come under their direct observation since they have settled in the Caucasus foothills. A patrol that pushed forward to the river embankment, however, finds a cable ferry still intact. The Terek is 15 feet deep there. The patrol has to return because of heavy enemy machine-gun fire from the far bank.

31 August: A day of rest. No enemy contact, apart from probing long-range artillery.

1 September: Still camping along the Terek. A Mountain Troop Regiment to the right of us is mentioned in dispatches to have climbed the highest mountain in the Caucasus range, Mount Elbruz, and raised our national flag on top of it.

2 September: Our regiment is now attached to the 40th Panzer Corps, 111th Infantry Division, and we will support the infantry in extending a bridgehead south of Mosdok. Under difficult circumstances, we cross the Terek on a cable ferry. 5th Co. manages to get across but the engineers stop further crossings because of darkness and heavy rain.

3 September: At daylight the rest of the group gets across and advances immediately to the south to a point 1.5 km from a small fishing village. 6th Co. is next across the Terek River and they meet heavy enemy resistance. A Sturmgeschutz Co. [tracked assault guns] led by Oberstleutnant [Karl] Dressler [German Cross in gold awarded February 3, 1943] has also crossed, and when they enter the fray, Ivan retreats. Now that the bridgehead is secure, engineers start on a proper bridge construction.

4 September, 8:00 AM: The 2nd Battalion of the 111th Infantry, attached to us, mounts the 23 tanks of our group and we proceed to the south. We are now in the foothills of the Caucasus. It is very difficult to maneuver a Panzer battalion with infantry hanging on the armor plating. We hope to capture a pass over the hills near Wosneskaja. We advance at a good pace but then enemy infantry, PaK's and AT guns, open a brisk fire. Our own infantry dismounts and we attack a line of enemy with our Panzer cannons. We destroy or capture three 7.62's, seven 40mm PaK's and 20 AT rifles, and 165 Ivans march to our rear as POW's. Further advancement is out. We need ammunition and fuel. Enemy artillery falls on the 111th infantry and causes many casualties. It seems Ivan has a well fortified line in those hills ahead of us and we radio for artillery support. Instead, a battery of super heavy Panzer Werfers, 210mm rocket throwing monsters on assault gun chassis arrive; each of them capable of sending a salvo of ten 210mm rockets against Ivan. 40 rockets every 5 minutes arc toward the Russian line and soon the fire from Ivan stops. But, all is not won; 18 T-34's appear from behind a hill and roll up our flank. 5th and 8th Co. set up a defensive line and 9 of the T-34's are destroyed. Ivan's infantry takes the full brunt of our "Stukas on foot" [nickname for the heavy Panzer Werfers].

5 September: Early morning at daybreak we just make out a group of T-34's to the south. The distance is too far for us to have any effect, since the heavy DO-Panzer Werfers have gone to the rear to re-arm. The bridge across the Terek was completed during the night and the rest of the 13th Regiment Panzer artillery, Panzer Regiment 4, and the 117th infantry are now across. Oberst [Colonel] Herfurth of the 117th Infantry Regiment assembles all units to form a battle group to capture Wonessenskaja the next day. We stay in line, on full alert, expecting an attack, and sleep inside our vehicles when we can.

6 September: The lineup for today's attack is: up front–Panzer Regiment 2, then a Group of 201st Regiment Infantry of the 117th, mounted on tanks; then support from the 13th Panzer artillery and their Panzer Werfer, finally Division artillery, 111th infantry. A Sturmgeschutz battery is lined up just in front of the 117th. The attack commences at 4:00 AM, but soon 2nd Battle Group runs into heavy AT fire from the flank and loses 4 Panzers. Communication with the 117th is lost for a while until the group reassembles.

After reassembly the 2nd Group goes forward again [and] reaches a hill with the battalion of the 117th. The enemy now fires with heavy artillery; Stalin's Organs and even fighter-bombers of a new type are being employed by Ivan. The battalion of the 117th is reduced to 80 battleworthy men. A company of the 4th Panzer Regiment has several tanks disabled by the enemy's long-range artillery. Our own guns cannot see the enemy artillery as they are behind a ridge and must have a well camouflaged observer to direct their fire. Attempts to pinpoint the observation post by a determined patrol of the 117th fail and a few more men are lost. Nevertheless, 2nd Group resumes the attack and manages to capture an elevated position southeast of the town.

The attack stalls in a mine belt and we lose several Panzers because of blown tracks. Enemy PaK picks off the disabled tanks one by one. There is no way to reach the town from this side. A company of the 4th Panzer tries to circle around from the west but also runs into a mine field and has to retreat into a fold, only to find enemy machine gun nests in this position and they have to fight their way through them.

4:00 PM: 2nd Battle Group of the 201st Panzer Regiment observes a large group of enemy tanks and AT guns heading for the bridgehead. Immediately a Panzer Company is sent forward to deal with this menace but the enemy tanks turn tail and run full speed toward the east. Unknown to the Panzer Company, the enemy left its heavy PaK and personnel behind. Two concealed Russian AT guns have the Panzer Company under heavy fire and cause a total loss of this company. All units in that area now retreat to the bridgehead to refuel, re-arm and rest. Five of the tanks of the Panzer Company are a total loss. Three more are retrieved during the night by Panzer Pioneers.

7 September: Early in the morning, Ivan attacks the bridgehead again with tanks and infantry. We build a defensive fire line within minutes and repel the Russians easily. 5th Co. accounts for 7 T-34's destroyed; our infantry hold the line superbly. With 4th and 201st Panzer Regiments assisting, the enemy infantry is destroyed by our heavy Panzer Werfer.

8 September: Again Ivan stages an attack with T-34's and manages to send our 50th Infantry regiment into full retreat. A fast battle group, formed from the 4th Panzer Regiment, sends Ivan packing once more. Lt. Fischer of one of the tank companies stays behind to watch for more enemy attacks. Suddenly, four T-34's appear out of a dense forest. Lt. Fischer is all on his own with one Panzer IV armed only with a 50mm "Stummel Kanone" [short barreled 50mm cannon]. He knocks out two of the T-34's and the others scramble to the east. Lt. Fischer has singlehandedly saved us a great loss. [Lt. Fischer later received the Knight's Cross for this daring feat.]

9 September: Today we extended the bridgehead and 6th, 4th, and

201st Panzer Regiment, with an infantry battalion, go forward. A small group under Col. Liebenstein [Oberstleutnant Kurt Freiherr von Liebenstein, German Cross in Gold, January 26, 1942, and later served in the Afrikakorps] covers the 111th infantry still at the bridgehead.

10 September: Today, Battle Group Liebenstein sent out strong patrols and they returned with several prisoners. 6th Panzer Regiment meanwhile makes a sweep to the east; enemy air attacks occur but no casualties are sustained. They return with 200 prisoners. Our group recrosses the Terek to do a reconnaissance to the east along the river bank. No enemy contact and we return to our position to replenish our ammunition and fuel. We also take a few days rest; sleep, eat and see to our Field Post letters.

13 September: Today we are attached to Battle Group [Franz] Westhoven of the 3rd Panzer Division. We are to cross the Terek at 6:00 AM at Mosdok. 85 km and 9 hours later we reach Naurskaja, a godforsaken place in the foothills. Rumors are that our opponents consist of the 10th Guard Corps, with the 4th, 6th, and 7th Guard Brigades and the 92nd Artillery Regiment in support. As the situation is now, we will have to attack immediately with our Panzer groups and try to push Ivan to the east into the waiting machine guns of our motorcycle battalion. Enemy artillery, in fixed positions, is able to pinpoint our advance because of the huge dust clouds our tracked vehicles create. We lost one HT and several trucks, and the field kitchen, far in the rear, sustained a direct hit from a long-range stray shell, so our evening food is shot to Hell. There is no other choice but to retreat, along with Battle Group Westhoven. This we do in the night but lose one Panzer that got stuck in a ditch with a track broken. We dismantle the machineguns and take the cannon breach with us, and retreat 20 km to the north.

14 September: By noon we are back on the attack. This time we are reinforced by a light Flak company on four HT's carrying 37 and 20mm cannons. We don't see any enemy fighter-bombers so we use the Flak unit to break up Russian infantry groups. We encounter stubborn resistance in a 2 km-long potato field. Ivan has a remarkable ability to hide even among potatoes. They are well trained in anti-tank warfare; 2 Panzers are knocked out by Molotov Cocktails, burning the crew to death. Another Panzer was on fire but 1st Sgt. Lauterbach grabbed a fire extinguisher from an HT and put out the flames; all this under heavy small arms fire.

Panzer crews bale out of their machines to clean out enemy fox-holes one by one with their sub-machine guns. We then hold the line for the night at a village and take a rest in houses built from blocks of sod, one room; no beds. We wonder at times how the natives manage in peace time.

15 September: Another battle group from the 7th Panzer Regiment joins us. It's a clean-up operation with 2 battle groups like the day before, but this time Ivan has brought PaK forward, and artillery is hiding in the foothills. One Panzer of 6th Co. took a direct hit; 1st Lt. Schnewe was the only survivor, and he is badly wounded. We take about 80 to 100 prisoners, several infantry support guns and a few AT rifles.

17 September: Today Battle Group Burmeister has joined us and before noon we are on the attack again. We lose 2 of our officers, Lt. Viereck and Lt. von Weise, both killed. We are ordered to reassemble at Schefatoff where we are greeted by the commander of the 3rd Panzer Division, Lt. General [Hermann] Breith; medals are awarded: Iron Cross 1st Class to Lt. Strebel and Lt. Graber, 15 awards of 2nd Class to various members of the Battle Group. Our tally in booty is 16 T-34's, 45 AT rifles, 21 machine guns, 8 PaK's, several mortars, and 650 prisoners including 2 political commissars.

18–19 September: Two days of just cleaning our own gear, no drills, and we have had warm meals and real coffee. Where in Hell did the cook find all that? Our Panzers are all under scrutiny by mechanics, some gunsights have to be changed, armor plate welded, boogie wheels and sprockets replaced.

20 September: We move to another rest area, a horse breeding farm at

Konsowod, 8 km north of Awalow. We have air raids during the night with some bombs dropping nearby.

21 September–2 October: A mixed battle group was formed today to eliminate enemy infiltration into the area. For the first time, a mounted Don Cossack Regiment, under the command of Col. [Joachim] von Jungschulz, is attached to the battle group. They are fierce looking men on great horses, armed to the teeth, including sabers, but no helmets; instead they wear fur caps, even in hot weather. God help them if they run into a battalion of T-34's but God help the enemy infantry if they have no tanks. The rest of the group consists of a company of Panzer Pioneers, 2 companies of Panzer Grenadiers mounted on HT's, half an artillery battery, 1 Panzer company and a Field Police Unit. The spearhead is our old friend, the motorcycle unit under Lt. Dittmann and 1st Lt. Grahn.

3 October: Today the first snow flakes fall and a cold wind blows from out of Siberia to the northeast. Father Frost, Russia's other brother in arms, will soon be upon us. Reconnaissance has figured that about 2 regiments of enemy infantry are in the area. We search around Tak-Tak and Tuku Mekteb but find not a soul, not even the odd Babushka [Russian woman].

4 October: We leave at 6:00 AM in 3 columns. The southern column is the Don Cossack Unit under von Jungschulz. We encounter a few enemy outposts that soon take to their heels seeing the Cossacks coming at them in a gallop. At Sowchose we run into enemy resistance; Pioneers and infantry bypass Sowchose to get to their rear. Panzer Co. Grahn attacks the small village and takes 200 prisoners. The Cossacks take none but kill about 150. These guys show no mercy. We stay for the night in Sowchose and set up a defensive perimeter, but all is quiet.

5 October: Patrols during the day find no enemy near us so we return to the horse farm and look for warm winter quarters. We stay there until October 19th.

20 October: Orders arrive to be ready for a sweep operation west of

Mosdok. 5th Co. moves out with 52nd Corps to reinforce the 111th infantry regiment at Terskaja. 7th and 8th Co., under the command of 1st Lt. [Joachim] Gleim, move into a forest west of Mosdok. The other battle groups stay at the horse farm.

21 October: At 4:15 AM we are in line for attack with 8 Panzer Mk. III's under the command of Capt. Arnold. We are to surround an enemy concentration near Terskaja. To our left a group from 23rd Panzer Division, on the right, the 117th infantry is to stop any attempt by Ivan to scramble to the east. Our group makes good progress to 3 km east of Terskaja. We take a few prisoners and proceed to the south in a wide arc. The 23rd is not so lucky and runs into a mine belt, loses 4 Panzers with track and boogie wheel damage. Pioneers clear a path in the mine field and we recover all 4 Panzers. On our way back, an urgent cry via radio reaches us. The 117th infantry ran into trouble; we turn around but the enemy, on hearing our armor coming, disappears to the east. The 117th had 3 dead and 7 wounded.

22–23 October: No orders for us. We stay in the forest of Lukowskaja.

24 October: At 5:00 PM we assemble to move out. Our Panzer regiment returns under the command of 3rd Panzer Corps. All our tanks, half tracks and supply trucks, gasoline tankers and field kitchens are being transferred to Prischibiskaja and we arrive there at 11:00 PM. We are occupying the eastern part of the town. Soon after we arrive, we have air raids and enemy bombers drop a series of 500 pound bombs but they do no real damage. Our own light Flak was caught with their pants down, being in the middle of setting up shop, when Ivan's bombers arrived.

25 October: Minor repairs are made to our equipment; then at 11:00 PM we get assigned to our attack positions. Ours is in a large orchard to the east of Katjawarewska. 13th Panzer Division crosses the Terek and takes their place in line to our right. All night, enemy railroad guns keep up a brisk interdiction fire on the town, but because of the darkness they cannot pinpoint our assembly area – casualties are light.

26 October, 4:30 AM: The whole of 3rd Panzer Corps sets off for an attack in the direction of Naltschik. First is Battle Group Burmeister, with 2 assault gun companies, then to the right, Battle Group Bruckner and Battle Group Stegmann, with 1st Co. of the 12th Schwere Panzer Werfer [heavy Nebelwerfer] bringing up the rear. No enemy resistance so far. 51st Battalion Panzer Pioneers have cleared a path through the mine field in front of Katjawarewska; enemy activity has been seen to the north of our attack line. This smells of an outflanking movement, so Ju-87 Stukas are brought in to break up any Russian concentrations. Battle Group Bruckner captures the town of Argudan.

13th Panzer Division is hampered in its advance by difficult terrain, swamps, and mine belts, so they swing southward and reach a defendable position at 1:00 PM. Burmeister's group has encountered Ivan's 275th Infantry Division and is engaged in a firefight. Most of the 275th manages to break away, including a cavalry unit. We take the little town of Orsek and capture a 155mm artillery piece. We reassemble at the center of the village by the church and settle in for the night.

8:30 PM: Russian infantry filters into the town but 6th Co. is on guard and, in a firefight lasting about an hour, Ivan retreats with heavy losses. Sadly, one of our best commanders, 1st Lt. Gleim, recently decorated for bravery, is killed in this action. We close up and set up a strong security screen; there are still Russian sharpshooters in the vicinity and we are not taking any chances.

27 October: We spend the day clearing the town of any remaining enemy. Three Mk. III Panzers and a Pioneer Co. get detached to Battle Group Stegmann. Our supply trucks arrive. Booty in the last few days: 155 POW's, 8 AT rifles, 1 PaK 7.62 caliber, 1 Howitzer and 10 trucks. We tighten our security perimeter; enemy columns have been reported in the vicinity of Argudan, to the northeast of us.

28 October: Nothing to report today. We repair equipment.

29 October, 1:00 AM: An order from HQ Regiment arrives to form a company of heavy Panzers and proceeds to Argudan. 5th Co., with 8

Panzer Mk. III's, leaves at 4:00 AM and sets out for Argudan. The rest of the battle group is staying behind and is attached to the 128th Panzerjäger Battalion. 5th Co. now is in attack position with the 2nd Panzer Grenadier Battalion of the 126th, and in a valley on their way toward Argudan, they capture two villages, cross a 750 meter high mountain pass, and snatch 3 road bridges from Ivan. But before capturing the town of Chasnidon, the group's command vehicle, an armored car, sets off a road mine and all members of the crew are wounded. Nevertheless, Chasnidon is captured by our tanks, with the 128th Panzerjägers lagging far behind.

Eight Panzers cross the bridge over the river Uruh. Our infantry and the 128th are still out of sight and our Panzer company waits by a factory in town. It turns out to be the local creamery and cheese factory. The next small village is only 2 miles ahead and the 8 Panzers, with 1st Lt. Cramer in command, proceed without infantry or AT support. One mile on, the company runs into heavy fire, from concealed T-34's buried up to their turrets in an orchard. Three of our tanks are knocked out. 1st Lt. Cramer and his crew die in the explosion of their Mk. III. The other 5 Panzers retreat back to the creamery.

At noon, the rest of the Battle Group arrives in Chasnidon and attacks the orchard and the surrounding hills. Enemy light bombers interfere but are unable to stop the operation. The group finally reaches an east-west highway flanked by cornfields; the stalks are all dried and shriveled by now but they make excellent cover for enemy infantry with AT rifles and mortars. The fields are finally cleared of Ivan and, in the process, a T-34, lingering 500 yards away, is destroyed. Another bridge is captured, but soon darkness sets in, so we stop 400 meters from the bridge for the night. No supplies reach us and our gas tanks are almost empty.

2 November: A town by the name of Alagir is our target for today. 2nd Battle Group and the 126th Infantry Regiment have the job of capturing it. Short of the outskirts, near a railroad embankment, we have to stop. One of our HT's has hit a mine; the machine is a wreck, but the crew is all right. They join the 126th. Then suddenly, an armored train comes out of town toward us, stops, and commences firing on us. We reply with all we've got. A flight of Stukas comes to our help and destroys the train. 5th and 8th Co. then drive into town along the main street.

Near the Market Square, 2 enemy tanks open fire. At first our tank gunners are a bit perplexed seeing this type of tank, but soon knock both of them out. A close inspection reveals they are American-made Sherman tanks with Russian markings. 8th Co. accounts for 5 more tanks, T-34's and KW-1's. Just outside the town we see 2 bridges across a river; in fact, the river has two branches, and both are spanned by separate bridges. 8th Co. manages to cross both and secures a bridgehead. 5th Co. is pinned down by enemy PaK and loses 2 Mk. II Panzers on the first bridge. The 2 Panzers are effectively blocking the road now so that the rest of 5th Co. has to sit it out until our Panzer Pioneers clear the obstacles out of the way. We call a halt for the night and Panzer Grenadiers secure our bridgehead perimeter. A few explosive charges are found by the pioneers under one span and are defused. We settle in for the night.

2 November, 6:30 AM: The attack units assemble by the Ardon Bridge. The target today is another bridgehead at Dsuarikau, across the River Fiagdon. This is now the main highway to the south, to Armenia, Aserbeidschan [Azerbaijan], and to the border with Persia.

At our assembly point, the 126th Infantry Regiment mounts our Panzers in droves. The men are loaded with hand grenades, AT rifles, carbines, machine pistols and a few with parts of light mortars. They are clinging to every handle or piece of armor plate they can grip. Off we go. Small enemy pockets are brushed aside; 3 enemy tanks appear but retreat when they see our column. One tank has stalled and we capture it immediately; the crew is sent to the rear, guarded by a Field Policeman. We turn the captured tank around; two spare crew members take it, a driver and a gunner-commander, and we now have additional firepower. Basically, all tanks work on the same principles, whether German, Russian, or the new American tanks we have seen.

A mile further we capture a battery of field artillery. We leave the guns behind for the mopping up units; then we have to slow down; a bridge over a creek has been blown. We also encounter a mine belt. Despite all this, we reach the Fiagdon River Bridge and, with full speed, firing our cannons, 5th Co. races across; the bridge is ours.

Mortar fire from the enemy across the river injured our Group Commander, so Major Wulf takes command. Three batteries of the 128th Panzer artillery come up and take positions; Ivan is on the run to the east. A crossroad near Dsuarikau is the next target, but for now we settle down for the night. Security is provided by the 126th. Our supply convoy arrives to see to our needs in gas, ammunition, and stomachs.

3 November, 4:45 PM: We move out and secure the crossroads. We then do an armored sweep with the 126th infantry toward Dsuarikau, but many of the Russian infantry get away in the bushy and hilly countryside. We reassemble 4 km south of Fiagdon to clear any enemy out of the area, including T-34's that have been reported. Just then, heavy PaK targets our assembly area and we lose 2 Mk. III Panzers. We are ordered to retreat to the crossroads.

11:00 AM: We try our luck again. This time we swing north and fall into the rear of Ivan, but the fight develops into a major engagement and we lose another tank, a total wreck. We stop short of Kibaka with our Panzerjägers and settle down for the night.

4 November: Our supply convoy arrives at 6:00 AM then we move to a kolchose south of Fiagdon.

5 November: We are told to return to the assembly area at Chatalon. Our 2nd Group has only 10 battleworthy Panzers left; these are distributed to the 1st Group. All we keep is our wheeled armor, HT's, Pumas and scout cars.

6–24 November: Now we are without tanks. Our group services our trucks and wheeled vehicles. Ivan attacks several nights with low flying bombers, fast twin-engine YAK's. [Probably YAK (Yakolev) 6's that were new in June, 1942]. One bomb hits a sleeping quarters killing and wounding 7 of our men, including Commander Fechtner. We receive 37 replacement men and on November 24th, a new Group Commander, Lt. Col. Tilemann [Oberstleutnant Burchhard Tilemann, German Cross in Gold, November 27, 1941]. We move into Alagir and into a rest camp.

Chapter 6

OUR PART AT STALINGRAD, 25 NOVEMBER–25 DECEMBER 1942

25 November: In the middle of a cold night, a motorcycle messenger arrives. Regimental Adjutant 1st Lt. Strebel has received from Regimental HQ the order for our Battle Group to withdraw and prepare for a new assignment with 2nd Group. All Panzers of 1st and 3rd Groups are being transferred to 2nd Group. 6th Co. is dissolved and their complete vehicle stock and all their equipment is being given to 2nd Group. As dusk descends on the steppe, the group moves out with tracked vehicles (tanks and HT's) in the lead, wheeled vehicles close behind; destination Prischibiskaja.

26 November: We are waiting for railroad transport. 22 Panzer crews are being transported by trucks to the railhead at Niwinkaja to take possession of new Panzer Mk. IV's, but on arrival, they find that the new tanks are in Ssalsk. 1st Lt. Stocker (in command), boards a train with his men and travels directly to Ssalsk to look for his tanks.

We begin loading special flatbed tank transport railroad cars at 5:00 PM, interrupted occasionally by Sewing Machines. The rest of the group, including the wheeled transports, arrives the same night and are loaded onto the train as well. The train leaves at 5:00 AM on November 27th.

29 November: All day we are on a train to an unknown destination.

30 November: We arrive in Gaschun [Gashun], a forlorn railroad station southwest of Stalingrad on the Ssal River. We unload two trains, including our 22 new Panzer Mk. IV's. We re-group our available forces; 1st Co. is now HQ-Co. 5th and 8th Co.'s each have 21 Panzers, 9 of them are Panzer Mk. III's, 12 are Mk. IV's.

4 December: The new battle group is ready and the commander arrives with the rest of the regiment, Panzer Pioneers, Grenadiers, etc. We also get an unexpected present of 11 NCO's and 60 men of Motorized Infantry Division 29/1, who were supposed to be in Stalingrad by now but, because the Russians have closed the ring around the city, the men were left stranded and so get detailed to our battle group.

6 December, 5:00 AM: We are on our way; ordered to keep a gap open at the Ssal River line for 4th Panzer Army to break through to Stalingrad. 6th Co. advances to Gurejew to secure the area. No enemy contact but reports come in that Ivan now has done a turn to the north, most probably to reach the Don crossings and attempt to cut off our forces in the Kalmyk Steppe.

9–12 December: Snow is falling now. We are supposed to cross the River Ssal, but because of the impossible weather condition and no bridge, we are only able to get our wheeled transport across and that required the help of a powerful winch on a 14-ton crane. To reach the area around Gurejew, our Panzers would have to head south to find a bridge crossing but because no gas supplies are available, they stay in Kryloff [Krylov]. We are not the only ones; two more Panzer groups are disabled for lack of gasoline and diesel fuel. We therefore set up a defensive arc near Gurejew with a Romanian Regiment as security.

Now the typical meddling of other commands starts. First, we are required to give our Panzer Mk. IV's to another group; we in turn get Panzer Mk. III's that have just come from the repair shops, and some of them break down after only a few miles. All reconnaissance is out; we are so low on fuel that half the Panzer crews now have no tanks. 1st Lt. Fischer takes these crewmen to Gaschun to the Panzer repair facility to await new equipment. Kryloff is being turned into a fortified town now with one Romanian infantry battalion, two batteries of Romanian artillery, and a 20mm flak battery. Fortunately, the enemy has no inkling of our pitiful situation here in Kryloff. Finally a supply convoy arrives with fuel and ammunition so we send 3 Panzer Mk. III's out for a reconnaissance but they return without making enemy contact.

The whole of 57th Panzer Corps is now ready to attack to the north, break through to our surrounded comrades at Stalingrad, and contribute to a victorious end of the Battle of Stalingrad. Our orders are to push along Panzer Highway 1 toward Pimen to protect the right flank of the 5th Panzer Corps.

12 December, 5:30 AM: Departure of 7th Co. and the supply convoy from Kryloff, followed at 5:45 AM by 5th and 8th Co's. We arrive at Pimen-Tscherni at 3:00 PM and call a stop for the night. A patrol of 3 Panzers is sent forward to find the best road for our early morning departure and they return without enemy contact.

13 December: 2nd Group, Heydebreck [Georg-Hennig von Heydebreck, German Cross in Gold, awarded October 23rd, 1942] departs at 7:00 AM with orders to reach Nebykowo and reinforce 3rd Group. Our commander, Lt. Col. Tilemann, falls sick and is transported to the Military Field Hospital in Kotelnikowo. 1st Lt. Stocker takes over as group commander. At 11:00 AM, our column arrives in Nebykowo only to be told by Division HQ to stop for the rest of the day and night.

14 December, 5:00 AM: We move out, along the railroad line from Kruljakov [Kruglyakov] to Stalingrad. North of Kruljakov, 2nd Group finds a railroad bridge and a road bridge across a small river. Russian engineers are busy preparing both bridges for demolition but we capture the engineers. 1st Lt. Cornelius is wounded in a fire exchange with the engineers but we take both bridges intact and call a halt to reassemble.

15 December: During the night, several enemy demolition commandos tried their best to get at the two crossings but we captured the lot, including their trucks loaded with explosives.

2:00 PM: We are relieved by the 128th Panzer Grenadier Regiment and we move on to Romaschkin, arriving there at 3:15 PM.

17 December: We establish contact with the 11th Panzer Regiment [Ludwig Bloos' regiment] 1 km from Kryloff, then swing to the northeast to search for a reported enemy tank column coming out of Stalingrad. We encounter no Ivan and return to Kryloff.

17 December, 5:30 AM: Alarm. Enemy tanks are approaching Kryloff and we immediately engage in a firefight; 4 T-34's and 10 T-70's are destroyed. We move forward to search for the enemy infantry and finally find them in a balka near a crossroad but they retreat into Kumskij. We are unable to take the village because of fuel and ammo shortages – plus the fact that the village is heavily fortified with PaK's and T-34's. We return to Kryloff.

18 December: The main enemy assembly area seems to be east of the Stalingrad to Kamenka railway. Therefore, 23rd Panzer Division attacks in that direction to capture Kamenka and get into the flank of the enemy, but the town bristles with AT guns, PaK's, tanks, and Stalin's organs. On top of all this, a typical Russian blizzard starts with temperatures falling to minus 40 degrees. Diesel turns to wax and blocks fuel pumps in engines, water-cooled vehicles have to keep their engines running. The battle group turns 180 degrees and heads back to Kryloff.

19 December: Despite the blizzard, Ivan attacks, but by mid-morning the weather clears and our Luftwaffe appears to attack enemy positions. By 10:00 AM we are southwest of Stalingrad at Hill 800 where the 201st Panzer Regiment arrives just in time to stop an enemy tank attack. But more tanks are heading toward us and even with the strongest determination in the world our small battle group won't be able to stop this large formation of Russian armor. We turn around and head for a nearby balka.

Here we have the luck of the day; we find two Sturmgeschutz companies and 4 DEMAG HT's with 88mm's in tow under command of

Col. Hassel-Bach. He had moved into the balka to await the end of the snowstorm and lost all contact with Division. The Col. immediately offers his small battle group to repel the Russian tank attack. The men know their business and within 5 minutes, the whole battle group is on the march. One kilometer to the north, Col. Hassel-Bach sets up his defense: 4 88mm's, 8 assault guns, and 75 long-barrel AT guns; our Panzers cover the flanks. Ivan is spotted 2000 meters away coming toward the battle line. The 88's hold their fire until the T-34's and T-70's are only 1000 meters away and then open up. Within minutes 16 T-34's and 9 T-70's are knocked out of the enemy formation; the rest scuttle back into the balka. Being low on fuel and ammunition, we have to run back. We all shake hands with the Colonel and he heads west with his group. We return to Kryloff.

20 December: A railroad crossing is our target for today and we encounter more T-34's. Even lacking our long-barrel AT guns and 88's, we still reach the crossing in a heavy snowstorm, but further advance is stopped by enemy tanks and a halt is called near Hill 162.

21 December, early morning: Our battle group is now under the command of Captain Schnewe and reinforced by a company of Panzer Grenadiers. With HT's we attack Hill 162 and surprise the Russians in a heavy snowstorm. Parts of the 6th and 17th Panzer Divisions meanwhile take Wassiljewka, but we have to abandon further attacks because of the blizzard conditions.

22 December: Battle Group Schnewe advances again. The terrain becomes hilly and, because we still run our tanks on summer tracks, the hillsides are like an ice skating rink and our tracked vehicles slither all over the ground. Nevertheless we take a hill marked on our maps as 106. One Panzer Mk. III runs into an icy ditch; enemy PaK soon finds him and put him out of the fight. Russian salvo cannonfire finds no targets because we retreat back to Hill 162.

23 December: No enemy contact. Half of our battle group moves out to Antonov far behind our lines to celebrate Christmas in quiet surroundings.

24 December, 3:00 AM: We move out to the west and reach a balka at 10:00 AM where we meet up with Lt. Col. Tilemann who has recovered from his illness. Our Command HQ on Hill 162 is moved to the rear at Moisejew. An enemy spearhead of T-34's along the railroad line from Antonov to Stalingrad is repulsed with the loss of 2 of our Mk. III Panzers. Because of the atrocious weather conditions, 100 km/hr winds and blizzard snowstorms, we are ordered to retreat to Antonov. 1st Lt. Stocker has been taken to a field hospital with suspected frostbite on his feet. The temperature has fallen to -45 C.

25 December, Christmas Day: There is nothing like Christmas. I don't think anyone knows it's the 25th. All still drivable Panzers and a few from the repair shop are driven to Schwstakoff [Shestakov]. Two kilometers northeast of the town, other Panzers from Capt. [Alfred] Wolf [Iron Cross, 1st Class, awarded January 18th, 1943] and 1st Lt. [Robert] Alber [German Cross in Gold, awarded September 7th, 1943] join us, but no enemy in sight.

As darkness falls, we all retreat into the town. Divisional orders are to hold Schwstakoff at all costs. We now have Pioneers and an infantry battalion under Lt. Col. Bucher attached to us. A company of tankers that have had their Panzers destroyed also arrives on foot. Hand grenades and pistols are all they have; using them as infantry would be useless. These men have never been trained for this type of warfare but they defend the town as best they can. 1st Lt. [Günther] Korte is killed in this action by an enemy sharpshooter. We do manage to get all our drivable Panzers across the bridge to Romaschkin [Romashkin]; all other Panzers and vehicles that we cannot take with us are blown up. We hold Romaschkin during the night but early in the morning we set off westward. A lone Pioneer Battalion has to stay behind to cover our retreat.

Chapter 7

OUR RETREAT FROM STALINGRAD, 26 DECEMBER–19 MARCH 1942

26 December: We are now trying to disengage our Battle Group and support vehicles from the Russians. Our limited supplies prevent any attacks by us. Captain [Joseph?] Stiewe, with 3 Panzers and a motorcycle unit, has the job of escorting our supply train to the west. The rest of the group defends the town of Schwstakoff, but Ivan manages to get a foothold despite our long-barrel PaK's accounting for 7 T-34's killed. We lose 2 Panzer Mk. III's but the rest get away across a river bridge. Our Pioneers blow the crossing and we retreat toward Tschilekoff where the enemy has found a ford in the river and established a bridgehead that we try to eliminate. Captain Wolf and a small company of 4 Panzers throw the enemy back across the river. At 7:30 PM the order arrives to retreat from Tschilekoff. All the PaK's and other equipment we cannot bring with us have been destroyed. The road bridge over the Akssai River is blown by our Pioneers. A Russian patrol on horses is taken prisoner. Two enemy scout cars and a group of infantry, trying to get into the town before the bridge is destroyed, comes under fire from our 20mm flak and turn back.

27 December: Kotelnikowo; we have a restless night. Tank and artillery fire is constantly disturbing the night. We retreat across another river using the railroad bridge because the road bridge has already been destroyed. Our rear guard arrives at 4:00 PM. The 16th Motorized Infantry Division is holding a corridor open for us to get away to the west but we are still under enemy long-range artillery fire.

28 December, 5:00 AM: The enemy artillery fire intensifies; Stalin's Organ rockets now rain on our position and a panic occurs. The supply trucks, gasoline tankers, horses, field kitchens, and non-essential personnel stampede out of town to the west. Only with pistols and carbines do we stop this hysterical retreat. When Lt. Col. Tilemann arrives with his last tanks, we manage to establish some order and fix a defensive line, but orders arrive to disengage and use the main highway to march to the west. Lt. Col. Tilemann makes certain that the traffic on the highway keeps flowing – and that any enemy advance will be opposed.

29 December: The battle group retreats to Nagolnij but the town is already occupied by a small detachment of enemy infantry. We chase them out with the rest of our Panzers. Group Tilemann brings up the rear and has a firefight with Russian advance elements. In Nagolnij we take stock; not much is left. We are assigned as Divisional Reserve to Battle Group Heydebreck. As best as we can, we fortify the town for the night.

30 December: In the morning we see endless columns of enemy armor and infantry marching along a north-south road. Several T-34's that attempt to break into the town are destroyed.

31 December: From POW's we are informed that today Iwan will attack our position with 2 brigades of infantry and a tank regiment. 5:00 PM brings a hail of rockets from Stalin's Organs into the town. Most explode in the center square where a Nebelwerfer Co. has set up shop; there are dozens of casualties. The commander of the DO-Werfer unit, Adjutant Reinicke, is killed.

The attack by Ivan that follows is repulsed by concentrated fire from all our heavy weapons. Our Panzer Werfer was parked in another section of town and thus escaped the Stalin's Organs attack. They chime in now with their super heavy Werfer rockets. Ivan's attack stalls but soon about 20 T-34's appear between the first houses; but again our heavy weapons stop the tanks. 15 T-34's are either destroyed or disabled, the rest have had enough and turn tail. Now Stalin's Organ rockets rain down on us again. The enemy is trying to soften us up this time. PaK and medium artillery fire increases. At 3:00 PM we get the order to abandon the town. Lt. Col. Tilemann has the unpleasant job again, it seems, to form the rear guard with 3 Panzer Mk. III's and 2 Flak Vierlinge [20mm Quads on HT's]. The Russians cautiously and slowly enter the town on the heels of Tilemann's rear guard and take it without any more casualties on our side.

1 January, 1943: The battle group arrives in Andrianoff. We have exactly 11 Panzers left and so are assigned as divisional reserve. We are reinforced when we get 9 Panzer Mk. IV's from Company Kromer; that brings us up to 19 battleworthy tanks.

2–3 January: No enemy contact on the 2nd. On the 3rd, two Panzers are sent out for a reconnaissance and return with reports that the enemy is trying to get into the rear of us by using unmapped forest roads. Because the ground is frozen solid, the tanks have no problem with getting stuck. The enemy uses an engineering battalion to blast trees out of the way to clear a path for their tanks. Today we either retreat further or we might get cut off by Ivan, who is reported to have passed our flank. We set camp in Kumorjarskij.

4 January: More enemy activity is being reported from our flanks. We resupply our few remaining tanks and half-tracks and send a few reconnaissance cars out. They return without encountering the enemy.

5 January: We are in Sundroff for the night and have had no enemy contact. To the north and south, heavy artillery fire can be heard. Things are remarkably quiet around us and we have a good night's sleep in a pile of blankets the Quartermaster left behind.

6 January: We are told that we have Ivan now in our rear so at 5:00 AM we have to be ready to break out. Heavy snow is coming down, visibility is almost zero, but nevertheless, by 9:30 we have broken through. Amazingly the Russians flee in droves back east, taking their armor with them. We soon find out the reason for the retreat; from the west a Grenadier Regiment under Col. Bachmann, reinforced by a company of brand new monstrous Tiger Panzers is sending Ivan back in droves. This is the first time we see these new battle wagons from our armory. Stavropol is ours for the time at least, but further advance is not possible because the Panzers have run out of supplies and need refueling. We set up for the night. Meanwhile a Stuka squadron and another Tiger group play havoc among the retreating enemy and almost reach Lenia, but stop short of the town. They have to wait for supplies as well.

7 January, 6:15AM: The battle group, minus the Tiger Company, which has been ordered to another enemy concentration to the south, attack Lenia with 12 Panzers, 1st Co. of DO-Werfer Battalion 128, 2nd battery of Light Flak, and a company of Grenadiers.

Panzer Pioneers of the 123rd search for a mine belt. Our left wing under 1st Lt. Kramer captures the first two houses in Lenia but further advance is hampered by a long narrow balka that extends all the way along the perimeter of the town. There is no way around; the bridges are out and there is no bridging equipment to be found. Holding the position is also out of the question. Ivan has the high ground and can see every movement. One company tries its luck from the south but draws heavy PaK fire from the town and stops 1 km short of the first houses. Behind the small town is also a low ridge where Ivan has heavy PaK and tanks in position to repel any attacks from us. Therefore, at 3:15PM, we are ordered to retreat. The enemy senses our movement and heavy fire covers our positions. 1st Lt. Kramer's group loses one Panzer Mk. IV, hit by heavy PaK which totally destroys the track; the crew manages to bale out. At 5:00 PM we arrive in Wessely and set up for the night.

8 January: No supplies have reached Wessely. We are extremely short of armor-piercing shells, so in the night a truck is sent to Orlowskaja with a message to bring urgently needed supplies today. Heavy blowing snow hampers any movements. Just before 8:00 AM the co-driver of the truck returns on foot; the supply convoy with AP ammunition has been ambushed by the enemy, who shot and killed all the others.

We nevertheless, assemble for attack. Heavy fire can be heard near the town and a patrol estimates the enemy to be 2 battalions strong. At 8:00 AM our group, attached to the 51st Pioneer Battalion with only about 150 men, moves up to the end of town and encounters enemy armor and PaK. An urgent radio message to Division brings the Tiger Company who breaks up Ivan's assembly. Ivan retreats for the time being.

Now we have a free run toward Ostrowanskij, but Ivan has occupied the village and has set up a defense line of 3 T-34's and 8 heavy PaK's. Despite being short of AP ammunition and fuel, we break into the town and at 7:00 PM we radio Division that the town is in our hands. Our losses are 1 Panzer Mk. III, 2 men killed and 12 wounded. We take stock of our available fuel and ammunition to find that we have only 20 AP shells left. We are very low on machine gun ammo, and fuel only for 25 miles driving. We therefore abandon Wessely and Orlowskaja. Wessely is taken by the enemy in the afternoon. We settle for the night 3 km west of Wessely.

9 January: Heavy firing during the night from the direction of Orlowskaja. A battalion of the Panzer Grenadier Regiment Germania of the 5th Waffen SS Division "Viking" recaptures Orlowskaja at noon. Plans of the Division are to retake Wessely with the Tiger Panzer Company. The Grenadier Regiment is under Bachmann and Tilemann's battle groups. Because Tilemann's battle group has run out of ammunition and fuel, the other units cannot execute this order on their own; the enemy is too strong. Without Tilemann's group, our unit has only 7 Panzers, hardly any ammunition or fuel, and the Pioneer detachment has shrunk to 96 men. A supply column that arrives during the afternoon brings fuel but no ammunition.

10 January: Just after midnight we have to retreat and at 3:30 AM we reach Orlowskaja.

An urgent radio message orders us, shortly after we arrive, to advance to a kolchose 10 km east of Proletaskarja; but 10 minutes later the first message is cancelled and the new order is to go with all speed to Romanoff and connect with the 128th Grenadier Regiment. At noon Lt. Tilemann is ordered to Division HQ and is promoted to be the new commander of the Regiment. His former group is taken over by 1st Lt. Kromer.

Since the beginning of the Russian attack around Stalingrad, our supply depots have had to be moved far to the rear at Ternowy. A massive enemy attack by tanks and twin-engine long-range fighter-bombers caught the supply base by surprise and much material was lost. Getting out of this trap is a fiasco because truck engines would not start in the intense cold; only a small column of Panje horse drawn wagons gets away. The rest were captured by the enemy. What is left of our supply depot was ordered to Kalinina – 50 km behind lines.

On January 5th, Major [Hans-Egon] von Einem formed a small security group with the rest of the supply depot, some stray 88mm's and a few badly repaired Panzers. This group was assigned to stop the enemy from crossing the Manytsch River. A Selbstschutz battalion [Russian volunteers fighting with Germany in Russia] was sent out to look for enemy infiltration but returned without seeing anything.

On January 8th von Einem requested (from Division), 2 Panzer companies from the 201st Regiment, and 1st Lt. Marquardt took command of the group. The same day, Russian advance units managed to capture an intact bridge near Wessely and get across the river. Just by luck, a train with 15 Panzer Mk. IV's arrived at the ramp in Ssalsk and was quickly unloaded. Immediately after refueling and taking ammunition, these 15 Panzers, with an infantry support unit, attacked the bridgehead. The Russians retreated across the bridge and we retook Wessely. All supplies were taken back to Krassny Manytsch.

15 January: 201st Panzer Regiment occupies a new defense line and we are again under Battle Group Burmeister.

16 January: All wheeled transport is ordered to retreat to Shuralewska; the 2 Panzer companies stay put. Because of enemy concentrations near Shuralewska, a Panzer infantry company is formed from tank crews minus tanks. One SSgt and 36 ex-Panzer men form this company, but drivers are not included in this small force. We are extremely short on tank drivers. This company is also attached to Battle Group Burmeister.

17 January: Divisional HQ has been set up in Shuralewska; the Battle

Group moves to Kalinina. The Panzer Infantry Company is detailed to provide security for Division HQ and control movement between both towns.

18 January: A new supply unit has to be formed; we only have 8 Panzers left in our group. Apart from that, there is only our field kitchen left on wheels. We scrounge every available and drivable truck. We need at least a capacity of 8 tons for our supplies. All material not used to keep our tanks in battle is unloaded.

19 January: A rearrangement of our depleted 201st Regiment is now necessary.

1st Group: Staff HQ, Battle Platoons 1, 2 and 3, three Panzer Infantry Companies, a supply company, plus Burmeister's repair company with 1 heavy tractor unit.

2nd Group: Commander, 1st Lt. Walther; Fuel, ammunition, food, 1 Panzer repair platoon and a small company of ex-Panzer crews.

Because there are no trucks left to transport 165 foot soldiers, they leave on a forced march at dusk toward Rostov on Don under Lt. Schmidt.

21 January, 6:00 AM: The tracked and wheeled vehicles move out to a new position but we are unable to reach the city of Rostov because of a heavy blizzard.

22 January: Today we reach the city. It was a harrowing retreat, blizzards and endless columns of westward heading troops and vehicles slowed our march to a snail's pace, burning precious fuel.

23–25 January: Here we have to call a halt. We don't have a drop of fuel left in our tanks. Our 2nd group under Lt. Walther finally catches up with us, bringing a precious HT with spares for our remaining Panzers.

26 January: We take quarters in an old schoolhouse at Nowo Iwanowka near the city. All 201st Panzer regiment units are temporarily under the command of Major Draffehn [Commander 4th

(Flak) Panzer Artillery Regiment 128]. It is his job to make sure all vehicles and tanks are repaired, collect our lost men in the city, re-enforce discipline, and form new crews for the remaining tanks and HT's. The rest of 2nd Group finally finds us as well.

27 January: More men of the Panzer infantry, dead tired from their retreat on foot, arrive but at least they bring a few Panje wagons with much needed spare parts.

28 January: We are still in Nowo Iwanowka and we stay here until February 11th to bring our equipment and tanks into a reasonable state of battle worthiness.

12 February: Early in the morning the command is given for us to march on foot to Stalino. At noon the wheeled and tracked vehicles follow, and after a 50 km march, we reach Stalino and finally stop in Balojarowka.

14–18 February: We stay 5 days here. All our companies are now with us.

19 February: We move out today. The trucks take all spares and ammunition. The rest of the battle group is transported by train to Saporoshje.

20 February: A train journey taking 20 hours, part of it in open freight cars.

22 February: We reach new quarters, our trucks have already arrived. We are staying in a factory at Saporoshje to recover from our battles and retreats. We are almost up to full strength now. Personnel that were reported MIA have finally caught up with us.

3 March: Twelve of our men receive the KvK with swords for out-standing performance in battle. What is left of our battle group is repaired as best we can.

4 March: Rumors abound; one is that our whole Battle Group is supposed to return to Germany – and it's true. On March the 5th, 2nd Group gets dissolved.

8 March: Today we hold a parade. 201st Panzer is inspected by the commander. Captain [Rudolf] Behr receives the Knight's Cross, finally, that he won on January 25th. [Behr was later KIA in Russia as a Battalion leader of Panzer Regiment 4.]

10 March: We are loaded onto a train at Dnieperostoij [on the Dnieper River near Zaporizhzhya]. All our remaining tanks and weapons are distributed to another battle group; we only take our personal things and HQ's paperwork. The transport manager is 1st Lt. Pollmann. At 6:30 PM the train starts off.

We travel via Nikopol-Snamenka-Kasatin.

At Pzemysl on March 15th we cross into the Reich. Cheers all round, de-lousing for sure here. We are mad with emotion.

On the train again which takes us to: Krakau-Gorlitz-Dresden-Nuremberg.

After a long 9 days on the train, we finally reach Erlangen at 10:00 PM on the 19th of March 1943. We are quartered in the Mihiel Barracks and will form a future Panther Tank Destroyer Battle Group.

Our campaign has cost the regiment 122 dead and 211 MIA. May we never forget them.

155mm field artillery battery being set up in the Stalingrad area, December 1942.

Artillery barrage in the snow near Stalingrad, December 1942.

HISTORICAL TIMELINE
"To Stalingrad and Back"

April 5, 1942: Adolf Hitler signs Directive 41 for Case Blau (Operation Blue), the German summer campaign of 1942 on the Eastern Front. It calls for a full-scale offensive toward Stalingrad on the Volga River and the capture of the Caucasus oil fields. German Army Group South is to be divided into Army Group A, whose orders are to cross the lower Don River and capture the Caucasus oil fields; and Army Group B, with orders to cross the upper Don River and capture Stalingrad. The offensive is scheduled to begin in late June.

Army Group A is assigned the Eleventh and Seventeenth Armies, First Panzer Army (to which the 23d Panzer Division is assigned) and armies supplied by Germany's allies, Romania, Italy and Hungary. Army Group B is assigned the Second Army and Fourth Panzer from Army Group Center and Sixth Army, part of the original Army Group South.

April 9: On the Kerch Peninsula, separating the Sea of Azov and the Black Sea in the Crimea, the Soviet Fifty-first Army begins an offensive against the German Eleventh Army under Erich von Manstein to attempt a breakout. Trapped on the peninsula with their backs to the Kerch Strait, Soviet units are fighting for their survival.

April 11: The Soviet offensive on the Kerch Peninsula is stopped by Eleventh Army.

April 22: German forces totaling over 100,000 men are encircled by Soviet forces in the "Demyansk Pocket" south of Leningrad in northern Russia. They break out with a loss of more than 3,000 men and much of their equipment.

April 26: Hitler asks the Reichstag for, and receives, authority to fire or demote any civilian or general for any reason, thus taking direct control of all military operations and starting the long road to eventual German military defeat.

April 28: Soviet forces launch an offensive against the German XIX Mountain Corps (Generalfeldmarschall Ferdinand Schorner) southwest of Murmansk, a city in the far northwestern portion of Russia.

May 2, 1942: On the southern tip of the Crimea lies the city of Sevastopol which as been under siege by the German Eleventh Army since late October. Manstein's siege of the strategically important fortress intensifies as he prepares for a massive assault to capture it.

May 8: The Eleventh Army begins a major assault against Sevastopol and the three Soviet armies on the Kerch Peninsula. Within hours the Soviet lines in front of the city of Kerch collapse.

May 9: The German offense against Sevastopol and Kerch gains momentum and destroys the Soviet Fifty-first Army, which surrenders outside of Kerch.

May 12: Soviet forces launch a two-front attack toward Kharkov on the Donets River. The northern offensive is launched from Volchansk by the Twenty-first, Twenty-eighth and Fifty-seventh Armies and the southern attack from the Barvenkovo salient by the Sixth and Ninth Armies. The German Sixth Army and First Panzer Army, (Generalfeldmarshall Paul von Kleist), repels the attack, inflicting heavy damage on Soviet forces.

May 14: German troops enter the city of Kerch where severe street fighting erupts.

May 17: South of Kharkov, the Germans begin Operation Frederikus, a counteroffensive against Soviet forces east of the city with the intent to encircle the five Soviet Armies in the Kharkov area.

May 19: The German counteroffensive has almost completed the encirclement of the Soviet forces around Kharkov.

May 19–20: The German Eleventh Army declares Kerch secure after causing almost total destruction of the remaining elements of the Soviet Forty-fourth, Forty-seventh and Fifty-first Armies and forcing them to either surrender or withdraw across the straits into the Taman peninsula. Some 170,000 Russian prisoners are taken while fewer than 40,000 escape across the strait to Taman. Over 28,000 Russians die while total German losses are about 3,400. Some Soviet forces refuse to surrender and will fight on for many months from the caves in the area. With Kerch secured, Eleventh Army turns its full attention on Sevastopol.

May 22: Encirclement of Soviet forces to the east of Kharkov is completed. The Soviet Ninth and Fifty-seventh Armies are completely destroyed and over 240,000 Russian prisoners are taken, along with more than a thousand tanks. The rest of the Soviet troops minus most of their equipment escape the trap and join other forces further east of Kharkov.

June 1, 1942: Adolf Hitler visits the headquarters of Army Group South at the town of Poltava in the Ukraine. It is one of his very rare appearances at the front.

June 2: Manstein begins a five-day ground and aerial bombardment of the fortress of Sevastopol.

June 10: German Sixth Army chases the remainder of the Soviet Sixth and Ninth Armies from the Kharkov area and continues to capture the towns of Volchansk and Kupyansk, incurring only light casualties.
June 18: German XXX and LIV Corps (General Erik Hansen) of the Eleventh Army breaks the outer defenses of Sevastopol.

June 28: "Case Blue," the German summer offense in Russia begins. The German Fourth Panzer Army and Second Army arrive from Kursk and launch an assault on the Soviet Bryansk and Southwestern Fronts, and then continue on toward Voronezh on the upper Don River.

June 30: The Soviet High Command orders Sevastopol to be evacuated. About the only military personal who manage to do so are the officers commanding the defense of the city. Meanwhile, the German Sixth Army begins a fast moving offensive toward the Don River.

July 4: The campaign in the Crimea is a resounding German success as the remaining Russians in Sevastopol are forced to surrender. The Eleventh Army takes almost 100,000 prisoners. Manstein is promoted to Generalfeldmarschall and transferred to Army Group North along with elements of the Eleventh Army to assist with the reduction of Leningrad. The rest of Eleventh Army is disbanded and its units sent elsewhere.

July 6: 24th Panzer Division captures Voronezh on the Don River 370 miles [600 km] northwest of Stalingrad.

July 8: Fourth Panzer Army begins an offensive southeast along the west bank of the Don River to meet up with the Sixth Army (Generalfeldmarshall Friedrich Paulus), which is advancing eastward toward the Don from Kharkov. First Panzer Division crosses the Donets River.

July 10: Fourth Panzer Army and Sixth Army panzer units meet north of Kalach on the Don River northwest of Stalingrad. Seventeenth Army (Generaloberst Richard Ruoff) and First Panzer Army advance from Artemovsk toward Rostov-on-Don, east of the Sea of Azov.

July 12: A new Soviet Stalingrad Front consisting of four armies is created under Soviet Marshal Semyon Timoshenko. Elements of the former German Eleventh Army take 30,000 Russian prisoners in the "Volkhov Pocket", one of the battles around Leningrad.

July 13: Hitler replaces von Bock as commander of Army Group B with Generalfeldmarschall Maximilian von Weichs.

July 15: Fourth Panzer Army captures Kamensk on the Donets River, west of Kalach.

July 18: German Seventeenth Army captures Voroshilovgrad, north of Rostov-on-Don in the Donets industrial area. German Army Group B is now ordered to capture Stalingrad.

July 22: Units of First Panzer Army advance to the northern perimeter of Rostov-on-Don.

July 23: Rostov-on-Don is captured by First Panzer Army, creating an unobstructed passage for the bulk of Army Group A into the Caucasus. Hitler orders Army Group A to move south of Rostov and Army Group B to move east on Stalingrad. This sets up the ultimate failure of the summer campaign by having the two army groups diverge, causing an ever-widening gap between them. Meanwhile, elements of the Sixth Army attack defensive positions of the Soviet Sixty-second and Sixth-fourth Armies along the Chir River northwest of Stalingrad.

July 26: Army Group A begins to advance into the Caucasus region in southern Russia. Soviet First and Fourth Tank Armies launch unsuccessful counterattacks north of Stalingrad.

July 27: Army Group A captures Bataysk in southern Ukraine. German Sixth Army units attack a Soviet bridgehead at Kalach, west of Stalingrad.

July 28: Stalin issues Order Number 227 to every Soviet military unit: "Not one step back."

July 29: Units of the First Panzer Army capture Proletarskaya and German Pioneers build a bridgehead over the Manych River in the

Caucasus. Army Group A and Fourth Panzer Army are 75 miles [120 km] from the Caspian Sea. German troops cut the last Soviet rail line into the Caucasus.

July 30: Soviets begin a counteroffensive at Rzhev, north of Moscow, and surrounds six German divisions. Army Group A reinforces its bridgehead over the Manych River and Army Group B continues the attack on the Soviet bridgehead at Kalach on the Don River.

August 1, 1942: Army Group A continues to expand into the Caucasus region. Meanwhile, Hitler orders Fourth Panzer Army to change direction 180 degrees and move on Stalingrad from the south.

August 4: Advance units of Fourth Panzer Army cross the Aksai River south of Stalingrad.

August 6: First Panzer Army crosses the Kuban River at Armavir in the Caucasus.

August 7: Units of the German Sixth Army cross the Don River at Kalach, west of Stalingrad.

August 9: First Panzer Army reaches the oilfields at Maikop, near the Black Sea in the Caucasus. Departing Soviet troops have destroyed the oil fields.

August 12: First Panzer Army captures Elista en-route to the oil fields at Grozny in the Caucasus. Units of the Seventeenth Army reach Krasnodar, south of Rostov-on-Don.

August 14: In the Caucasus, Seventeenth Army units cross the upper Kuban River at Krasnodar.

August 20: A counteroffensive is begun by the Soviet Twenty-first and Sixth-third Armies against the Italian Eighth Army, which results in the Soviet units gaining a bridgehead on the Don River at Serafimovich, northwest of Stalingrad. The Soviet First Guards Army accomplishes the same at Kremenskaia, north of Stalingrad.

August 21: LI Corps (General Walter von Seydlitz-Kurzbach) of the German Sixth Army crosses the Don River and builds up two bridgeheads at Luchinsky and at Vertyachy northwest of Stalingrad.

August 22: German Seventeenth Army units, moving toward the Black Sea, start to bog down because of fuel shortages. Meanwhile, the First Mountain Division raises the German flag on the peak of Mt. Elbrus (Elbruz), the highest point in the Caucasus.

August 23: The Luftwaffe launches a series of attacks on Stalingrad that reduces the city to ruins. Sixteenth Panzer Division units reach the west bank of the Volga at Rynok, just north of Stalingrad.

August 25: First Panzer Army captures Mosdok, west of Grozny in the Caucasus.

August 27: Soviet forces begin a counterattack against the German Eighteenth Army south of Lake Ladoga, part of the battles around Leningrad.

September 1, 1942: First Panzer Army creates a bridgehead across the Terek River at Mosdok in the Caucasus.

September 2: LI Corps of Sixth Army meets with advance units of the Fourth Panzer Army advancing from the south, completing the junction of the two armies on the outskirts of Stalingrad. This completes the land encirclement of Stalingrad, The Volga River is still in Soviet hands and provides a tenuous lifeline for soldiers trapped in the city.

September 3: German troops begin an assault on Mamai Hill [Mamayev Kurgan], the high ground controlling most of the northwest portion of Stalingrad.

September 6: Seventeenth Army captures the port of Novorossisk on the Black Sea.

September 8: German headquarters reports that manpower shortages will result in the Army being 18 percent understrength by November 1.

September 9: Soviet forces launch a series of attacks in an attempt to eject the German Ninth Army (General Walter Model) from the Rzhev salient on the Volga River northwest of Moscow.

September 10: The German 29th Motorized Division of Fourth Panzer Army reaches the Volga River between the Soviet Sixty-second and Sixty-fourth Armies, effectively dividing Stalingrad into two pockets.

September 13: Having finally secured a portion of Mamai Hill, German forces begin the attack on the city of Stalingrad itself. The LI Corps drives toward the city's main rail station, initiating a bloody struggle where the combatants share the same buildings and often the same floor.

September 17–26: XLVIII Panzer Corps breaks into the southern pocket of Stalingrad. After nine days of desperate combat, Paulus declares the pocket secure and has the Nazi flag raised over Red Square. Focus now shifts toward the larger and more heavily defended northern pocket.

September 24: General Franz Halder, chief of staff of OKH, complains once too often about Hitler having ordered inappropriate troop movements. Hitler decides Halder's nerves are shot and forces him to retire into the "Fuhrer Reserve," a place, usually home, where disgraced generals go. Halder is replaced by General Kurt Zeitzler, who is completely surprised by the move. Meanwhile, First Panzer Army attacks the port of Tuapse on the northern shore of the Black Sea.

September 30: the Soviet Don Front (the former Stalingrad Front) commanded by General Konstantin Rokossovskiy, attacks the German XIV Panzer Corps north of the city in one of a series of major offenses designed to find and fix German positions.

October 3: Although incurring heavy losses, German Sixth Army units drive the Soviet Sixty-second Army back toward the Volga at Pitomnik, a suburb of Stalingrad.

October 6: III SS Panzer Corps (SS-Obergruppenführer Paul Hausser) captures Malgobek on the Terek River in the Caucasus. Hitler stakes his reputation and makes the capture of Stalingrad the singular priority of Army Group B. Paulus temporarily halts attacks around Stalingrad due to rapidly declining strength. Infantry battalions are down to less than 100 men.

October 14: Paulus renews attack on a strategic tractor factory in the northern pocket at Stalingrad.

October 15: German Sixth Army units capture the tractor factory and reach the Volga. The Soviet Sixty-second Army by this time has been almost completely destroyed and the northern pocket is now divided into two parts.

October 18: Army Group A units advance toward Tuapse on the Black Sea to support First Panzer Army, but are held up by difficult terrain and Soviet flanking attacks.

October 22: In Stalingrad, Sixth Army captures most of the Red October factory.

October 25: Although unknown at the time, the last German offensive in the Caucasus begins.

October 27: The Soviet Thirty-seventh Army is defeated in the Caucasus and retreats.

October 29: German forces capture Nalchik in the Caucasus, some 50 miles [80 km] from the Grozny oil fields. The Soviet Southwest Front is created between the Voronezh and Don Fronts.

November 1: III SS Panzer Corps captures Alagir on the upper Terek River, southwest of Grozny.

Command vehicles ready to move out in southern Russia, December 1942.

DEMAG Sd.Kfz.10 medium-weight transporter outside Stalingrad.

November 2: 13th Panzer Division (III SS Panzer Corps) stops its advance five miles short of Ordzhonikidze (southwest of Grozny) because of supply issues and the onset of winter. This becomes the southeastern most point in Russia reached by the German Army during the war.

November 6: 13th Panzer Division struggles to prevent being out-flanked by Soviet forces on both flanks and rear. Stalin declares that "the aim of the (Allied) coalition is to save mankind from reversion to savagery and medieval brutality."

November 11: Sixth Army begins what turns out to be its last major attack trying to capture the rest of Stalingrad. Units make it to the Volga River but can't neutralize the two Soviet pockets in the city. Outside Ordzhonikidze, 13th Panzer begins a retreat to avoid being cut off by the Soviet counterattack.

November 19: Hitler has anticipated a massive Russian counteroffensive to regain Stalingrad, but thought it would not start until mid-December. Consequently, many of the reinforcements needed to bolster the flanks of Sixth Army are not yet in position. The Soviet Operation Uranus begins with the goal of encircling Stalingrad and Sixth Army. Several breakthroughs are gained by the Russian Fifth Tank Army and Twenty-first Army as they punch through the weak Romanian Third Army 90 miles [150 km] northwest of Stalingrad and advance more than 12 miles [20 km] toward the German rear. Nearer Stalingrad, the Soviet Sixty-fifth Army is also on the move, but makes little progress against the German Sixth Army. South of Stalingrad, the Fifty-seventh and Fifty-first Armies break through the Romanian Fourth Army and advance west and north to affect a link up with Soviet forces coming south behind Stalingrad.

November 20: Romanian Third Army disintegrates so fast nothing can be done to stop or even slow down the Soviet offensive. The Soviets make rapid progress toward Kalach on the Don River, 50 miles [80 km] west of Stalingrad. The Sixth Army and Fourth Panzer Armies try to reinforce Romanian defenses west and south of the Don. The

Romanian Fourth Army now collapses as the Soviet's pour through the gap between the German Fourth Panzer Army and Sixth Army south of Stalingrad. All Soviet armies are headed for a link up at Kalach. Army Group B orders Paulus to stop efforts in Stalingrad and use four divisions to try to shore up his left flank. Now that things also seem to be starting to fall apart for Army Group A in the Caucasus, Hitler relinquishes command and turns it over to Kleist.

November 23: The Soviet IV Mechanized Corps from the south and the XXVI Tank Corps from the north meet at Kalach on the Don. The German Sixth Army is trapped in the carefully constructed "Stalingrad Pocket."

November 24: Reichsmarshall Hermann Göring boasts that his Luftwaffe can supply Sixth Army from the air.

November 25: A Soviet offensive called Operation Mars begins. It is a major thrust against the Rzhev salient northwest of Moscow with units from the Western and Kalinin Fronts.

November 26: The Soviets consolidate their positions along the Don River west of Stalingrad. Hitler orders the Sixth Army to hold its ground and wait for supplies to be delivered by the Luftwaffe.

November 27: The newly created Army Group Don, commanded by Manstein, is ordered to open a corridor to Paulus' Sixth Army, now trapped in Stalingrad.

November 28: In the Leningrad region in northern Russia, the Soviet Eleventh, Twenty-seventh, and First Shock Armies begin an offensive with the goal of destroying the Demyansk salient.

November 30: Operation Mars against the Rzhev salient begins to bog down as strong German resistance and poor weather conditions slow advancing Soviet troops.

December 1, 1942: Relief of the trapped German Sixth Army in

Stalingrad begins. Called Operation Wintergewitter (Winter Storm), it will be the Fourth Panzer Army's LVII Panzer Corps leading the attempt to break through the Soviet lines to create a corridor south-west of Stalingrad. Two German panzer divisions (6th and 23d) and two Romanian Corps (VI and VII) will make the attempt. An assault on Kalach by XLVIII Panzer Corps is designed to draw Soviet attention away from Fourth Panzer Army's assault. General Paulus is ordered to concentrate all his panzer units to be ready to break out toward LVII Corps and if ordered, to strike toward Kalach. The planned date for the assault is December 8 but later is moved to December 12.

December 2: The Soviet Don and Stalingrad Fronts begin a major effort to crush the German pocket within Stalingrad. It will last for two weeks and tie down most of the German panzer units that are supposed to lead the breakout toward LVII Corps.

December 3: Soviet advances across the Don River around Kalach crush the remainder of the Romanian Third Army. Manstein has to commit most of the XLVIII Panzer Corps to blunt the attack, shore up the German lines and maintain a bridgehead across the Chir River. This removes most of the rest of the units Fourth Panzer Army's LVII Corps was planning to use to create the corridor into Stalingrad.

December 10: The Soviet Fifth Tank Army attacks along the Chir River, pinning down the XLVIII Panzer Corps at its bridgehead.

December 11: Far north of Stalingrad on Army Group Don's left flank, the Soviet Sixty-third Army attacks the Italian Eighth Army in an operation called Little Saturn. The Italians are driven back but manage to contain the Soviet troops.

December 12: Fourth Panzer Army's LVII Panzer Corps, now reduced to just two panzer divisions (6th and 23d), begins Operation Winter Storm with an attempt to break through the Soviet encirclement of Stalingrad. The strength of the defending Soviet forces is at least equal to LVII Panzer Corps, but German units make steady progress.

December 13: LVII Panzer Corps crosses the Aksai River in its attempt to break through to Stalingrad. At the Chir River bridgehead, XLVIII Panzer Corps is having trouble holding off the Fifth Tank Army and Fifth Shock Army, completely eliminating any ability of XLVIII Panzer Corps to support Fourth Panzer Army's movement to open the corridor into Stalingrad.

December 14: In the Stalingrad corridor, LVII Panzer Corps is reinforced by the 17th Panzer Division while German troops continue their slow progress toward Stalingrad. Meanwhile, Luftwaffe aircraft are only able to deliver 25 percent of the supplies needed inside the Stalingrad pocket.

December 15: Stalin calls off Operation Mars, the massive assault against German Army Group Center in the Rzhev salient northwest of Moscow after huge losses are incurred.

December 16: Northwest of Stalingrad, while the Soviet Sixty-third Army pins down the Italian Eighth Army, the Soviet Twenty-first Army and Fifth Tank Army begin massive attacks against the somewhat reconstructed Romanian Third Army to the right of the Italian Army. At the same time, the Soviet Third Tank Army attacks the Hungarian Second Army along the Don River to the left of the Italian Army. Within a few days, the assault punches a 125 mile [200 km] hole in the German lines, surrounds most of the Italian Eighth and Romanian Third Armies, and heads south toward Rostov-on-Don, far south of Stalingrad. This puts Soviet troops further west of Stalingrad and is the beginning of a potential encirclement within an encirclement of Army Group Don itself, which is still trying to relieve Sixth Army in Stalingrad. Southwest of Stalingrad, the Soviet Twenty-eighth Army begins an offensive toward Rostov-on-Don in an attempt to cut off Army Group A in the Caucasus.

December 19: Inside the corridor south of Stalingrad, LVII Panzer Corps crosses the Aksai River, turns north and captures Mishkova, 30 miles [50 km] from the Stalingrad lines. The Luftwaffe delivers about 200 tons of supplies to Stalingrad, its largest daily load ever, but still far short of the 550 tons a day required by the Sixth Army to survive.

December 23: With Soviet armies moving south behind Army Group Don and the operation against Rostov-on-Don, concern about the pending encirclement of Army Group Don forces Manstein to notify Hitler that the troops from LVII Corps involved in Operation Winter Storm are needed to reinforce the Italian and Romanian Armies to prevent the encirclement. Fourth Panzer Army is forced to withdraw in the direction of Kotelnikovo (its initial starting point). The Germans are also forced out of Tatsinskaya by the Soviet XXIV Tank Corps and lose one of the few airfields available for landing supplies inside Stalingrad.

December 24: Operation Winter Storm comes to an end. German LVII Corps is not able to create a corridor into Stalingrad and the only possible way the Sixth Army can escape is to attempt a breakout. Manstein removes the 11th Panzer Division from Fourth Panzer Army and creates a command under General Karl Hollidt with responsibility to hold the far left of the German lines against the Soviet Southwest Front. The Soviet Second Guards Army pushes LVII Corps back across the Aksai River while attempting to encircle Fourth Panzer Army by trapping it against the Twenty-eighth Army coming up from the south.

December 25: It is not a very merry Christmas for the millions of men and women on both sides who are fighting and dying or being injured on the frozen steppes of Russia. There are massive attacks by Soviets along the perimeter of and inside Stalingrad. The final rations are distributed to the soldiers of the Sixth Army as the remainder of the 12,000 horses inside the pocket are slaughtered for meat.

December 26: Paulus reports that hunger and -15°C temperature has weakened his army to the extent it cannot attempt a breakout without a supply corridor created by Fourth Panzer Army.

December 28: Hitler orders Army Group A to withdraw First Panzer Army from the Caucasus because of the Soviet offensive heading in the direction of Rostov-on-Don.

January 1, 1943: First Panzer Army begins its withdrawal to Rostov to avoid being cut off by Soviet forces.

January 3: The balance of Army Group A begins a withdrawal from the Caucasus region.

January 4: South of Leningrad, the German LIX Corps and Army Group Wohler mount an attack against the Soviet Third Shock Army to relieve German forces trapped in Velikie Luki.

January 5: Soviet units are now streaming into the rear areas of Army Group Don. Third Guards Army captures the German airfield at Morozovsk, further crippling the Luftwaffe's resupply route into Stalingrad.

January 8: General Konstantin Rokossovskiy, commander of the Soviet Don Front, issues an ultimatum to the encircled Sixth Army. For their surrender, he promises their lives, medical treatment, and safety. The offer is refused by General Paulus.

January 10: Soviet Operation Ring begins with a bombardment by thousands of artillery pieces and rockets coming from a total of seven armies against the Stalingrad pocket. The final destruction of the trapped Sixth Army begins.

January 12: In an attempt open a supply route into Leningrad, the Soviets begin Operation Iskra, designed to push back the German Eighteenth Army. German armies continue to abandon the Caucasus, most toward Rostov and some toward the Kuban bridgehead.

January 13: The German XXVI and XXVIII Corps at Leningrad suffer heavy losses at the hands of the Soviet Eighth Army in Operation Iskra. A Soviet assault along a 300 mile [480km] front northwest of Stalingrad in the area of Voronezh begins.

January 15: Velikie Luki is captured by units of the Soviet Third Shock Army.

January 16: Soviets units capture Pitomnik airfield inside the Stalingrad Pocket. Hitler puts Generalfeldmarschall Erhard Milch in charge of airlifting supplies to Paulus.

January 18: Outside Leningrad, Soviet forces drive a narrow corridor through German lines south of Lake Ladoga so the city can be resupplied. Soviet advances continue in the Caucasus to a point 250 miles [400km] southeast of Rostov-on-Don.

January 19: Soviet forces on the Voronezh area drive 75 miles [120 km] toward Kharkov. The Hungarian Second Army surrenders at Ostrogozh.

January 23: The last German airfield (Gumrak) in Stalingrad is captured by the Soviet Twenty-first Army. The Sixth Army is now completely cut off by ground and air.

January 24: Soviets capture Starobelskiy on the Donets River in the eastern Ukraine. Sixtieth Army takes Voronezh on the Don River. In the Caucasus, German forces stop the Soviet offensive aimed at the Kuban bridgehead at Novorossiysk and Krasnodar.

January 26: The German 297th Infantry Division in Stalingrad surrenders to the Soviet Thirty-eighth Guards Rifle Division. The Sixth Army is now surrounded in two small pockets within Stalingrad.

January 31: Knowing that a German Field Marshal had never surrendered, Hitler promotes General Paulus to Generalfeldmarschall, thinking Paulus would fight on or commit suicide. The southern pocket of the Sixth Army in Stalingrad surrenders to the Soviets after running out of food and ammunition. Field Marshal Paulus and 16 generals are captured.

February 1, 1943: The German X and II Corps retreat from the "Demyansk Pocket" south of Leningrad. Soviet units move southeast of Kharkov, east of the Donets River.

February 2: Survivors of XI Corps, the last German forces in Stalingrad, surrender. Over 160,000 of the 280,000 Germans in the pocket had already died in battle, starvation or because of the weather. Only about 40,000, mostly wounded, had been evacuated. About 100,000 Germans were taken prisoner and only 5,000 survived subsequent Russian captivity, returning home in 1955.

February 3: Hitler orders four days of national mourning for the Sixth Army. He declares that their bravery will not have been in vain.

February 4: In the Caucasus, Seventeenth Army fends off attempted Soviet amphibious landings at Novorossisk on the Black Sea.

February 5: The Soviet First Guards Army captures Izyum east of the Donets River and south of Kharkov in central Russia. The Third Tank Army reaches the frozen Donets River, but is stopped by the newly arrived 1st SS Panzer Division, Leibstandarte Adolf Hitler.

February 6: In the Caucasus, the Soviet Fifty-first Army captures Bataysk south of Rostov-on-Don. The First Guards Army crosses the Donets in the Ukraine.

February 7: Kursk, 95 miles [150 km] west of Voronezh in Army Group Center, is captured by the Soviet Sixtieth Army.

February 8: Finland asks the United States government to initiate peace talks on its behalf with the Soviet Union.

February 9: Belgorod, north of Kharkov and south of Kursk is occupied by units of the Soviet Sixty-fourth Army.

February 10: South of Kharkov on the Donets River, the Soviet Third Tank Army captures a river crossing.

February 11: The SS Leibstandarte Division, supported by the Das Reich and Totenkopf SS Panzer Divisions (together, II SS Panzer Corps), attacks Soviet forces outside of Kharkov.

February 12: In the Caucasus, the Soviet Fifty-sixth Army forces the Seventeenth Army into a pocket on the Taman peninsula.

February 14: Voroshilovgrad, north of Rostov-on-Don, is captured by Third Guards Army while Second Guards and Twenty-eighth Armies occupy Rostov-on-Don, forcing the Germans across the Kerch Strait into the Crimean Peninsula. (The reverse of the Soviets having been driven across the Kerch Strait on May 20, nine months before.)

February 16: SS General Hauser disobeys Hitler's orders to hold Kharkov at all costs, and orders II SS Panzer Corps to abandon it to avoid being overrun by the Soviet Third Tank Army and Fortieth Army.

February 17: Manstein proposes a plan to Hitler for a counteroffensive against the severely overextended Russian advances.

February 18: A counterattack by the XL Panzer Corps, while not part of Manstein's plan, is repelled by the Soviet First Guards Army.

February 19: General Hauser's II SS Panzer Corps attacks the Soviet Sixth Army south of Kharkov.

February 22: Manstein's forces destroy the flanks of the Soviet Sixth Army at Zmiyev, taking 9,000 prisoners. As Manstein moves north toward Kharkov, he outflanks the Soviet "Popov Group" further south, creating the beginning of a Soviet pocket. Manstein orders First and Fourth Panzer Armies to surround "Popov Group," which contains at least six Soviet tank corps.

February 23: Manstein continues and the German XLVIII Panzer Corps captures Barvenkovo, south of Kharkov. Meanwhile, the Soviet Fifty-seventh Army captures Sumy and Lebedin to the northeast.

February 24: The surrounded "Popov Group" disintegrates as the First and Fourth Panzer Armies continue to squeeze the pocket.

February 25: Army Group Center begins to withdraw from the Rzhev salient and is pursued by units of the Central and Bryansk Fronts.

February 26: "Popov Group" fights to the end before two-thirds of its survivors surrender.

February 27: Manstein's counteroffensive continues to gain territory in southern Russia. The Germans now control much of what they had lost in the previous month.

March 1, 1943: German Fourth and Ninth Armies begin a withdrawal from the Rzhev Salient.

March 4–6: General Hoth's Fourth Panzer Army attacks the Soviet Third Tank Army on the Voronezh front near Kharkov, inflicting heavy damage.

++++++++++++++++++++++++++++

The diary of the 201st Panzer Regiment, 23d Panzer Division ends on March 6, 1943. On March 5, the 201st was disbanded and its remaining equipment and personnel were transferred to other units. In August the disbanded unit was reconstituted and renamed Panzer Regiment 23 (though still a part of 23d Panzer Division).

Tactically, the German summer offensive in 1942 was a near success in that German units had captured most of the Caucasus and had conquered nearly all of Stalingrad on the Volga River. Strategically, it was a failure because German troops could not retain what they had taken. By the beginning of the summer of 1943, the armies occupied lines similar to those they had held a year before. The major difference was a large Soviet salient around the city of Kursk, which would be the object of the Germans' next, this time limited, offensive.

Following the Battle of Kursk, the majority of the offensive operations on the Eastern Front would now revert to the Soviets. Germany would continue to counterpunch, but relentless Soviet onslaughts will consistently hammer at the Germans until the Red Army arrives in Berlin in the spring of 1945.

PART 2

To North Africa and Back

THE KRENGEL DIARY

3d Reconnaissance Battalion
5th Light Division / 21st Panzer Division
German Africa Corps /
Panzer Army Africa

Insignia of the Deutsches Afrikakorps (DAK).

3rd Panzer Division insignia, also
seen on 5th Light "Afrika" Division.

21st Panzer Division insignia (one
variant).

15th Panzer Division insignia.

German soldiers demonstrating how the DAK found its insignia.

The first page of Krengel's War Diary. At bottom is a drawing of a Puma.

Introduction

THE KRENGEL DIARY

Rolf Krengel was one of many German soldiers conscripted prior to the invasion of Poland who found themselves serving in the Wehrmacht for nearly six years, on a number of fronts, until Germany's final surrender. After seeing no action in the Polish campaign, Krengel experienced his baptism of fire during the invasions of Belgium and France, as his unit pursued the retreating French army. It was not until the beginning of 1941, after half a year of inactivity, that he served as part of the spearhead of one of history's most renowned units: Rommel's Africa Corps.

"Operation Sonnenblume" ("Operation Sunflower") was the initial OKW order of February 6, 1941 for the deployment of German troops to North Africa. The first units departed Naples, Italy almost immediately and arrived in Tripoli, Libya, on February 11. On February 14, the first components of what would become the 5th Light Africa Division arrived in Tripoli. That is where the main part of this diary begins.

Rolf Krengel was on one of the first ships to arrive in Africa. His division was composed of the 3d Reconnaissance Reserve Battalion and a Panzerjäger (tank hunter) unit. Upon arrival they were issued desert uniforms and immediately ordered to the front at Sirte, Libya. The first commanding officer of the 3d Reconnaissance Battalion was Oberst (Major) Infried von Wechmar, who would earn the Knight's Cross for his leadership in the capture of Agedabia, El Aghelia,

113

Solluch and Benghazi. The Deutsches Afrikakorps (German Africa Corps, or the DAK) was the overall designation given to the initial German military forces to arrive in Libya, and the name would forever be associated with the German army in Africa. The DAK remained a recognizable formation even after much larger command structures were created. Panzer Group Africa was created in August 1941 with General Erwin Rommel in command. The Panzer Group was re-designated Panzer Army Africa in late January 1942, and eventually became the German-Italian Panzer Army (Deutsch-Italienische Panzerarmee) in October 1942. All of Germany's Panzer Groups were eventually re-designated as Panzer Armies. The combined Axis forces were finally upgraded to Army Group Africa in February 1943. The DAK became so well known by Allied and Axis news correspondents and thus the general public, that almost everyone equated all German units (and General Rommel himself) with the DAK, ignoring the fact that the DAK was actually just one part of the larger German presence in North Africa. The DAK was in fact never in command of all Axis forces in North Africa, and Rommel himself was technically under the command of the Italian military when he arrived.

Rommel was initially ordered by Adolf Hitler to command the DAK to provide support to Italian forces in North Africa. In mid-September 1940, five Italian divisions advanced 50 miles [80 km] into Egypt as far as Sidi Barrani, and then entrenched to await a British counteroffensive. The British Western Desert Force (WDF), commanded by Major General Richard O'Connor, chased the Italians out of Sidi Barrani in December 1940. In early January 1941, the WDF captured Bardia, followed by Tobruk in mid-month, and finally El Agheilia, Libya on February 9. O'Connor advanced over 800 miles [1300 km], destroyed eight Italian divisions and captured over 130,000 prisoners and 400 tanks.

Upon his arrival in Africa on February 12, 1941, Rommel discovered that he did not have much in the way of resources. When the Italians lost Cyrenaica (the eastern coastal region of Libya), they lost several major supply depots and the only available seaports, Benghazi and Tobruk. Since both the Axis and Allied forces needed the ports, this area would change hands several times during the campaign for North Africa.

A German "blocking force" was quickly created to slow the British advance. It consisted of the 5th Light Africa Division (which was previously the 2d Regiment of the 3d Panzer Division) and various other small support units. The 3d Panzer Division was the primary force designated for North Africa in mid-1940. This is why the insignia of the 3d Panzer Division was used by the 5th Light Division even after it was formally combined with, and re-designated, the 21st Panzer Division months after its arrival in Africa. All of the units that arrived in Africa around February 10 were organized by Rommel into what was named the 5th Light Division (or 5th Light Africa Division). In April and May the 5th Light Division was augmented by a substantial portion of the 15th Panzer Division from Italy, but this was after Rommel had already begun and completed a counteroffensive and retaken most of Cyrenaica. The DAK consisted of two divisions (the 5th Light Division and the 15th Panzer Division) plus smaller support units, and was officially subordinated to the Italian chain of command in Africa. Rommel had, however, conducted his Cyrenaica offensive without any authorization from the Italians. This was to become general practice throughout his campaign in North Africa, usually with the consent, or at least non-interference, of the Italians. Rommel was actually in charge, regardless of the organizational charts constructed in Berlin and Rome.

Additional forces were eventually brought to Africa and became components of the larger Panzer Army Africa. One of the units was the 164th Light Africa Division, which at first was little more than a motorized infantry division, consisting only of armored cars and reconnaissance vehicles. German divisions, regiments, and battalions in Africa were occasionally reorganized or re-equipped without a change of name, or conversely were re-designated with a new name without any substantial reorganization. Some divisions kept their identities even after being reorganized or absorbed into a larger command and some did not. This often makes it difficult to follow the timeline of any single unit. Throughout its tenure in the desert, DAK units were nearly always understrength and made up of whatever men and equipment that were available. None of the German forces actually fielded for service in North Africa completely met the German military's specifications for their composition. This was primarily due to battle losses, losses in the Mediterranean while in transit due to ships being sunk, and the tremendous wear-and-tear on the vehicles once they arrived and the difficulty in obtaining replacement parts.

In August 1941, the German 5th Light Africa Division was officially re-designated the 21st Panzer Division, but was still attached to the DAK. After the re-designation, the 21st Panzer was still often referred to by its previous name.

A CHRONOLOGICAL HISTORY OF THE 5TH LIGHT AFRICA DIVISION

The designation "Light" in reference to a German division did not have a specific meaning, and the term's usage seems to have increased as the war progressed. There were specific requirements for German military units, and they were organized according to the Kriegsstärkenachweisungen or "KStN" (organization and equipment specifications list, similar to the U.S. Army's TO&E, or Table of Organization and Equipment). It was standard procedure for each unit in the German Army to be assembled according to these specifications, and every unit had a corresponding KStN number and a date that designated when the specifications were met. "Light" seems to have been used when the division was missing one or more components. The 5th Light Africa Division had an organizational structure that was actually missing several components that kept it from being a complete Panzer Division. Many other divisions that arrived later in Africa were also designated as "Light." Specifically, the 5th Light Africa did not have the KStN-required number of tanks for its deployment. It only had 150 of all types – and not all of those were actually combat ready. The rest of the vehicles were an assortment of command vehicles and unarmed observer transports. The 15th Panzer Division was one of the few complete divisions, having all elements attached when it entered the North African theater.

The 39th Panzerjäger (anti-tank) Battalion was the first unit of the 5th Light Africa Division to arrive in Africa in February 1941. It was a motorized unit consisting of halftracks and trucks for towing PaK 37mm and 50mm guns. Joining the 39th were the infantry battalions from the 200th Rifle Regiment and a single artillery battalion from the 75th Artillery Regiment. The 5th Light Africa Division's offensive power came from the 5th Panzer Regiment (from the 3d Panzer Division) that contained 150 panzers of the MK. I, II, III and IV types, or a sampling of just about every type of armor in the German arsenal at the time.

Over time, other units joining with the 5th Light Africa Division included the 15th Panzer Division, the 21st Panzer Division (which was combined with the 5th Light and re-named), the Africa Special Purpose Division, later renamed the 90th Light Africa Division, the 164th Light Africa Division, the 999th Light Africa Division, the 334th Infantry Division, and the Fallschirmjäger-Ramcke Brigade. Later in the campaign, there were also eight Italian divisions (two armored, two motorized, three infantry and a parachute division) under Rommel's command in the Panzer Army Africa.

The British Western Desert Force, renamed XIII Corps in early January and commanded by General Richard O'Connor, captured El Agheila on February 9, 1941. O'Connor was in great position to encircle and eliminate all of the Italian Forces and their supply bases in the whole of Cyrenaica and perhaps as far as Tripoli. This loss would quite likely have meant defeat for all Axis military forces in North Africa, ending the campaign before it really began. However, once he arrived in El Agheila, O'Connor had to release most of his troops since they were needed in Greece. Because he had also outrun his supply lines, O'Connor's troops remained in El Agheila under the command of General Philip Neame while O'Connor returned to Cairo, Egypt. After its arrival in El Agheila, XIII Corps was deactivated and reverted to Western Desert Force.

The 5th Light Africa Division was officially activated on February 18, 1941, and its first commander was Generalmajor Johannes Streich [Knight's Cross]. He was an experienced commander who had excelled during the French campaign of 1940. Most of the divisional units had arrived in Tripoli by mid-February, but the last panzer elements were not deployed until after mid-March.

Rommel was initially ordered to establish defensive lines around Sirte, Libya, 150 miles [240 km] west of El Agheila, and hold there until May. His orders were then to pursue offensive action to capture

the port of Benghazi and to create a heavy defensive position to protect it from future British assault. Rommel did not believe this possible as long as the British held most of Cyrenaica. He also knew that at
this time there weren't enough Italian forces available to assist in
maintaining any sort of defensive position, since most of them and
their equipment had been captured by O'Connor. Consequently,
Rommel felt that he had to do something, so instead of waiting until
May he decided to take action immediately.

On March 24, 1941, Rommel began an offensive with the 5th
Light Africa Division and two Italian divisions. This was supposed to
be a limited operation, but British positions collapsed so fast Rommel
decided to push them as far as Mersa el Brega, Libya.

Once it was determined that Rommel's offensive was going to
overrun the frontier, the British, in an effort to protect their forces,
withdrew to Mersa el Brega and began building defensive positions.
Rommel, surprised by the quick withdrawal, decided to take advantage of whatever had prompted the British to retreat and continue his
advance. The British were overrun at Mersa el Brega before defenses
could be set up. Although Rommel had been instructed to begin action
against Benghazi no earlier than May, he could see the opportunites
before him and so he pressed the advance. British General Archibald
Wavell, Commander-in-Chief of the Middle East Command, greatly
overestimated the size of the Axis forces and ordered a withdrawal
from Benghazi in early April.

By now, Rommel was more than a month ahead of schedule and
was still on the move, so he set his sights on control of the whole of
Cyrenaica. Despite being severely understrength, he felt the British
were not yet ready to fight a major battle and that a quick, bold move
would eliminate the British forces. Rommel ordered the Italian Ariete
Armored Division to pursue the British retreating from Benghazi,
while the 5th Light Africa Division was to move into and occupy
Benghazi. By April 8, Cyrenaica (as far as the town of Gazala, 50 miles
[80 km] west of Tobruk) was under Axis control, all accomplished
with light losses. Now, Italian general-in-chief General Italo Gariboldi
tried desperately to contact Rommel to order him to halt due to supply issues, but Rommel was always conveniently out of communication. General Streich, the 5th Light Division's commander, also tried

to get Rommel to slow down because his vehicles were breaking down at an alarming rate, but Rommel refused to let a unique opportunity slip by.

Rommel received orders from OKW in Berlin that he was not to advance past Benghazi, but he chose to ignore them when he saw the opportunity to completely destroy the Allied presence in North Africa and probably capture Egypt in the process. He knew this window of opportunity would not last long, for the British would send reinforcements to the region. Rommel kept up the pursuit of the retreating British in the direction of Tobruk. Capture of Tobruk would give him a port to use for resupply and while removing it as a port for the British. During this time, the Germans managed to capture the Western Desert Force commander, General O'Connor, and the commander of British forces in Libya, General Philip Neame. This was an unexpected bonus and Rommel felt that with all this success, he could justify his unilateral actions with Berlin if the need arose. As long as he was making progress, he knew he could ignore most of his orders from OKW.

The assault on Tobruk began with Italian forces attacking along the coast, with the 5th Light Africa Division sweeping around to the south and attacking the harbor from the southeast. The initial assaults failed because Rommel had outrun his supply lines, but by April 11, Tobruk was surrounded and could be attacked from several directions. The remaining Axis forces continued pushing eastward and by April 15, Bardia was taken and Halfaya Pass in Egypt captured. German forces had now captured all of Libya and pushed the British almost back to where the British offensive had started in Sidi Barrani in early December. It appeared that nothing could stop Rommel, for it was expected that Tobruk would be occupied within a week and the battle for Africa won – with Rommel's methods vindicated.

It was not to be. The siege of Tobruk lasted eight months and tied up a substantial portion of Rommel's assets. The important port city was defended by the Australian 9th Division under Lieutenant General Leslie Morshead and included most of the British troops that had escaped Rommel's advance. There were about 25,000 entrenched Allied personnel who were well supplied, for Axis forces were unable to prevent Allied ships from entering the port to deliver supplies and reinforcements. Rommel hoped to capture Tobruk quickly because he was well aware that a lengthy siege would not work in his favor. Rommel launched a dozen small assaults using mainly his Italian forces, which were easily repelled by the Allies at great loss to the Axis. The Italian High Command was furious with Rommel over the losses, but the feeling was mutual as Rommel did not place much faith in the fighting abilities of his Italian allies.

Nevertheless, for months Rommel was certain that Tobruk would be taken and that its loss would spell the end for the British Army in North Africa. He requested reinforcements from Berlin but the German High Command was busy completing preparations for Operation Barbarossa, the invasion of Russia, and had none to spare. Rommel was essentially on his own with what he had, as he had been warned that a large force in Africa could not (and would not) be sustained for a protracted operation. Additionally, Berlin was not pleased that the order to stay in Benghazi had been ignored. If the British had conducted a well-planned counterattack from within Tobruk, they might have succeeded in breaking the siege. However, that was not going to happen because Allied intelligence convinced General Morshead that the German forces around Tobruk were much larger than they actually were. Both the British and Rommel tended to overestimate their enemy's strength throughout the campaign.

Generalleutnant Friedrich Paulus of future Stalingrad fame was sent to Africa to assess Rommel for he was gaining a reputation as a renegade by both the German and Italian High Commands. Paulus arrived at Tobruk on April 27, and the persuasive Rommel convinced him that a major attack was the appropriate action. Paulus agreed, but when the assault on May 4 started going badly, he halted it and ordered Rommel not to plan any further attacks without express High Command approval. Rommel knew that such permission would not be granted, and blamed the May 4 disaster on his commanders and the Italian forces. Rommel had to agree to abide by Paulus' orders and would hold off conducting any major offensives against the city until the 15th Panzer Division could be brought up to support the attack. Rommel, meanwhile, built strong defensive positions around Tobruk manned by his Italian forces. This way he could contain the siege with limited forces, allowing him to conduct other operations with his

German units. Mobile German and Italian forces were assigned to repel any British attacks that might come from Egypt, primarily in the area around Halfaya Pass which was the major access route from Egypt into Libya.

The British made two unsuccessful attempts to relieve the siege of Tobruk. General Wavell ordered General Noel Beresford-Pierse, commander of the Western Desert Force after O'Connor's capture, to make the attacks, codenamed Operation Brevity (May 15) and Operation Battleaxe (June 15). Although both assaults met with limited success, neither was a serious threat to the Axis' control of the area. However, during Operation Brevity, Halfaya Pass was briefly recaptured by the British. Axis forces recaptured the important pass on May 27 and reinforced their positions there. Operation Battleaxe culminated in a three-day tank battle, with the British losing more than 80 tanks and the Germans losing 25, and the Germans retained Halfaya Pass. Although the British losses were much larger than the Germans, neither side could long sustain this rate of attrition.

Operation Barbarossa, the invasion of Russia, began on June 22, 1941, with four million German troops along an 1800 mile [2900 km] front. There were going to be no additional units sent to Rommel and few individual replacements for those lost in battle. North Africa had become a very low priority concern for the German High Command.

In August, 1941, Rommel was made commander of the recently formed Panzer Group Africa, and the DAK was put under the command of Generalleutnant Ludwig Crüwell. The 5th Light Africa Division was re-designated the 21st Panzer Division in September, 1941, and was a component of the new Panzer Group Africa. In addition, Rommel commanded the DAK (with its many units), the 90th Light Division and six Italian divisions, the Ariete and Trieste Divisions (forming the 20th Motorized Corps), three divisions committed at Tobruk, and one division holding Bardia.

General Wavell was replaced by the Commander-in-Chief in India, General Claude Auchinleck, who became the new Commander-in-Chief, Middle East Command after the failure of "Operation Battleaxe." Also in September, Allied units in the Western Desert Force were formed into a new Eighth Army and were reorganized as the XXX and the XIII Corps. They were substantially increased in strength and

First kill: a British Matilda tank.

A Kubelwagen (German jeep).

placed under the command of General Alan Cunningham. Auchinleck and Eighth Army, with 770 tanks and 1,000 aircraft, launched Operation Crusader on November 18, a major offensive to relieve Tobruk. Rommel had the 15th and 21st Panzer Divisions with a combined total of about 250 tanks, along with the 90th Light Infantry. He also had five Italian infantry divisions and one armored division with about 150 tanks. The ensuing battle would be one of the largest tank battles of the war in North Africa.

The Eighth Army slipped by the German and Italian defenses along the Egyptian frontier south of Halfaya Pass and circled behind them to set up positions within range of the German positions around Tobruk along the coastal road to Bardia. General Cunningham planned to strike the DAK with an armored division while XXX Corps attacked the Italian positions at Bardia. Rommel had a plan of his own, however, and confused the British by attacking the southern spear of the British thrust at Sidi Rezegh. The British drives were repelled by well manned antitank positions around Tobruk and the mobile German and Italian panzer units. At Bir el Gobi, the Italian Ariete Armored Division engaged in a fierce fighting retreat that caused far more British losses than Italian. The 21st Panzer Division repulsed the attack aimed at them and counterattacked at Gabr Saleh. The British strategy of matching their forces in individual battles against those of the Axis instead of overpowering them in numbers, was not working against the fast moving forces of the Germans. Rommel, meanwhile, launched a concentrated attack with all of his armor on November 23. The 21st Panzer held Sidi Rezegh as the Italian Ariete Division attacked the British flanks, encircling and tying up most of the British armor. Overall, the Axis forces destroyed two-thirds of the British armor and the rest retreated south to Gabr Saleh.

Rommel saw an opportunity to take advantage of British losses and inferior tactics, and on November 24 he counterattacked deep into British supply lines, called the "dash to the wire," the wire being the frontier between Libya and Egypt. Rommel was also trying to cut off Eighth Army and relieve his garrison at Halfaya Pass. Rommel ignored the British forces in Tobruk and Bardia because he believed they would abandon those positions and pursue him, allowing him to capture Tobruk once the British forces had evacuated it. On

November 26, General Cunningham ordered a withdrawal of British forces in Tobruk, but that order was immediately countermanded by General Auchinleck, who then relieved Cunningham and replaced him with General Neil Ritchie. Rommel's plan had almost worked. The German attack, however, began to slow down because of a lack of supplies. As usual, Rommel had outrun his supply lines, and again he was roundly criticized by the German High Command for wasteful use of his resources and for disobeying orders. The strategy had nearly succeeded and would have dealt a serious blow to British forces, not to mention British pride.

During Rommel's counterattack on the British, Allied forces in Tobruk threatened to breach the weak Axis lines there. Rommel ordered the 21st Panzer Division withdrawn from Sidi Rezegh and sent back to Tobruk as reinforcements; however, British forces sent to relieve Tobruk and the defenders inside finally were able to join forces on November 27. Rommel could do little about this because his 90th Light Division was in danger of being overrun after their dash to the wire, and he had to rescue them. This was accomplished by December 6, but the next day Rommel felt it necessary to fall back to the defenses at Gazala and regroup. This left the Italians at Bardia cut off from the retreating German forces.

The British, Australian and New Zealand Allies pressed their attacks but with little enthusiasm. They were just as disoriented, tired, and unorganized as Rommel's men. The Allied pressure however was enough to force Rommel to retreat back to El Agheila, arriving on December 30, exactly where he had begun in March. The Italians surrounded in Bardia were forced to surrender on January 2, 1942. Rommel lost one of his most competent commanders as well. General Johann von Ravenstein, commander of the 21st Panzer Division, was captured by New Zealand troops on November 29. He was the first German General captured in the war. He was replaced by Lt. Col. General Gustav-Georg Knabe.

The DAK received much needed supplies on January 5, 1942, including some 50 new tanks. This was a surprise, considering the German Army at the time was withdrawing from Moscow and all equipment was being sent there. Rommel immediately started planning a counterattack which began on January 21. The attack badly damaged the Allied forces; more than 100 British tanks were destroyed. The DAK recaptured Benghazi on January 29, forcing the British and Australians to withdraw back to Gazala. For the next four months both sides rested, gathering their strength. On January 30, 1942 Panzer Group Africa was re-designated Panzer Army Africa (PAA) with Rommel still in command.

In April, 1942, the Germans gained air parity in a substantial part of North Africa. This led to an increase in supplies reaching Panzer Army Africa and the planning of a major offensive for the summer. The British line at Gazala was the goal. The Allies however were planning offensives of their own and they were in a much better position, equipment wise, to carry them out. The British had 900 tanks in the area to Rommel's combined German and Italian tanks numbering about 550. The Germans had demonstrated what they were capable of when facing a numerically superior enemy; however, many of the British tanks were the very latest United States designed M3 Grant model while most of Rommel's were the older Panzer Mk. II. Rommel's great equalizer was his 88mm anti-aircraft guns that could destroy the heavily armored British tanks, but these guns were in short supply and not very mobile. Rommel was substantially outnumbered and out-gunned in just about every other category.

The Panzer Army attacked Gazala on May 26, 1942, in a classic Rommel outflanking maneuver, while his Italian infantry and the DAK stormed the Gazala defenses in a direct frontal assault. Rommel wanted the British to believe that this was the main assault and that he had put all of his forces into it. In truth, Rommel's fast motorized and armored forces were at the same time outflanking enemy positions to the south. The British were well fortified and both sides took heavy losses over the following days. Rommel's attempt to surround Gazala ultimately failed with a loss of one third of his tanks. The British counterattacked after every assault and eventually forced Rommel to go on the defensive. The tide turned on June 2, when the 90th Light and the Trieste Divisions surrounded the British strongpoint at Bir Hakeim, 40 miles [65 km] south of Gazala, eventually capturing it on June 11. Rommel attacked to the north, forcing the British out of Gazala, who then began an all-out retreat eastward on June 14, nicknamed the "Gazala Gallop" to avoid being surrounded and destroyed.

Rommel's forces reached the coast east of Gazala on June 15, preventing the escape of Allied forces still in position in the area. Rommel then once again turned his attention toward Tobruk. The port city of Tobruk was all that stood between his army and Egypt and this time it was held primarily by the survivors of the battle of Gazala. Rommel pushed his men and, after a full assault on June 21, Tobruk's garrison of 33,000 men surrendered. For this victory, Hitler made Rommel a Field Marshal. Tobruk and Benghazi were the only ports between Tripoli and Alexandria, and now both of them were under German control.

The Royal Navy controlled the Mediterranean, however, and shelled the Germans in Tobruk and Bengazi at every opportunity. When Rommel captured Tobruk, his forces were not being resupplied through it, so the port did him little good. His supplies still had to make the long overland trip from Tripoli, over 1,000 miles [1,600 km] and they were often bombed by Allied aircraft. Hitler now approved Rommel's request to attack Mersa Matruh in Egypt in order to protect his hold on Libya, supply lines, protect Tobruk, which was being turned into a supply point, and be in position to move on Alexandria and Cairo.

Rommel's goal now was to exploit the damage he had inflicted on the British with a drive further into Egypt. Once again the Italians did not approve the plan but Rommel argued that the British could easily outflank his positions at Sollum on the Egypt-Libya border if he did not create a front further east. The loss of Sollum would require supplies to continue to come through Tripoli and be trucked to the front. Rommel desperately needed a secure supply route and an eastern depot established if he was to continue.

Rommel continued his eastward offensive on June 22, and made excellent progress with little resistance. On June 26, Mersa Matruh, containing four infantry divisions from the British X Corps, was surrounded. A majority of the defenders managed to escape to the east, but the city fell on June 29 with the loss of 7,000 prisoners and most of the supplies stockpiled there. The remains of Eighth Army continued to fall back toward Alexandria but halted at El Alamein, 50 miles [80 km] west of that major seaport city.

Rommel's men had been fighting and moving continuously for

more than a month and they needed rest, but Rommel felt the British were in worse shape. Both Rommel and Auchinleck knew the last defendable location before Alexandria was El Alamein, and both were determined to have it. Auchinleck had very little time to prepare and not much in the way of forces to defend it when on July 1, 1942 Rommel attacked what was left of Eighth Army. The resulting series of battles, called collectively the First Battle of El Alamein, lasted until July 22 with both sides maneuvering and attacking wherever they found a weak point. Rommel later admitted that Auchinleck was his equal when it came to fighting a battle. After 22 days of combat in the summer heat, both sides settled into lines with Auchinleck's Eighth Army holding a line of about 80 miles [129 km] long from the coast south to the Qattara Depression, an area impossible to maneuver through. Facing him in parallel lines was Rommel's Panzer Army Africa. Daily probes, artillery engagements and minor assaults took place for the next month while both sides prepared for the next engagement.

Rommel had to regroup and resupply and go on the offensive again before the Eighth Army could be resupplied. Rommel had his own supply problems with Allied naval and air forces based in Malta sinking his supply ships, and aircraft shooting up his supplies in Tobruk, Bardia, and Mersa Matruh. Most of the supplies were still coming through Benghazi and Tripoli, traveling slowly overland by truck where they were vulnerable to Allied air attacks.

The British also began resupplying their forces and changing commanders again. General Auchinleck was replaced as Commander-in-Chief Middle East Command by General Harold Alexander, and General Bernard L. Montgomery took over command of the Eighth Army from General Neil Ritchie. Rommel was well aware of the buildup of British forces and knew that the time for an offensive was rapidly running out. On August 30, Rommel attacked the Eighth Army with the 15th and 21st Panzer Divisions, the 90th Light, and the Italian 20th Motorized Corps. A breakthrough along the southern flank occurred, but Montgomery had arranged his defenses along the Alam Halfa ridge with a commanding view of the entire area. Rommel could not break the defenses at Alam Halfa, and fuel shortages prevented further attempts. Rommel withdrew back to his lines on

September 4 and dug in after losing over 3,000 men, 50 panzers and 400 other vehicles. The Battle of Alam Halfa was over and Rommel was running out of options.

For the next two months, Rommel continued to build up his forces and improve his defenses, but he could not even begin to approach the buildup of Montgomery's Eighth Army. By the time the Second Battle of El Alamein began (most people just call it El Alamein and lump it together with the battle in July), Eighth Army had over 195,000 men against 105,000 Axis troops (50,000 Germans and 55,000 Italians.) Montgomery had 1,300 tanks, 2,300 artillery pieces and 750 aircraft to overwhelm Rommel's 490 tanks, 1,200 artillery pieces and 675 aircraft. Rommel's chief advantage was that he was on the defense with entrenchments and fortifications several miles deep. It was not a great advantage, for if Montgomery ever broke through the defenses or Rommel ran out of supplies, it would be pretty much over for Rommel and Panzer Army Africa.

In late September, Rommel's health forced him to go to Germany for recuperation. Generalleutnant Georg Stumme was selected to temporarily replace him. Also around this time the Panzer Army Africa was renamed the Deutsch-Italienische Panzerarmee (*German-Italian Panzer Army*) since there were more Italian troops in Africa than there were German. The Second Battle of El Alamein began on the night of October 23 when Montgomery began a direct attack along the southern front following a 1,000-gun artillery barrage. Rommel was still in Germany when the attack began, and General Stumme died of a heart attack on the opening day and was replaced by General der Panzertruppe Wilhelm Ritter von Thoma. As soon as he heard of the attack, Rommel left for Africa but it took him two critical days to get to his headquarters. The best he could do by the time he arrived was to dig in and defend his line which was protected by mine fields, artillery and machine guns.

Rommel learned after his arrival that the fuel situation had not improved and had worsened to the point where he could not plan any sustained mobile operations. Counterattacks by the 15th and 21st Panzer Divisions earlier on October 24–25 had resulted in heavy tank losses. On October 26 Montgomery changed the focus of his attack to the northern front. In a week-long running battle, Eighth Army continued to wear down the Axis forces, while Montgomery continued to build up a mobile reserve to punch through Rommel's lines. Rommel also initiated a counterattack on the 26th, but it ran into the British attack and was repulsed.

On November 2, Montgomery launched his next attack and an attempt with his mobile reserve to punch through the Axis lines. Having very little armor and even less fuel, Rommel decided it was time to pull back. Panzer Army Africa was now reduced to a shell of its initial strength. There were only 35 useable tanks and very little fuel, but they had fought the British to a draw, inflicting staggering but replaceable losses. Some of Rommel's brigades being reduced to 25 percent of their initial strength. The next day Montgomery decided it was impossible to renew his attack before receiving more reinforcements. This was the break that Rommel needed so that he could begin the orderly withdrawal he had been planning for days. At noon on November 3, Rommel received an order from Hitler forbidding any retreat; his army had to fight until victory or death. Rommel could not justify disobeying a direct order from Hitler even though it might mean the total destruction of Panzer Army Africa.

Montgomery renewed the attack on November 4 after receiving substantial reinforcements. He had almost 500 tanks to send against Rommel's 35. The Italian 20th Motorized Corps was surrounded within the first few hours and fought bravely until they were completely destroyed. Motorized British units (with armor) streamed through the breach created and threatened to surround the entire Panzer Army Africa. Rommel ordered a general retreat in spite of the order from Hitler. General Thoma, appalled by the order from Hitler, mounted one of the few available tanks and drove into the battle, probably planning his own suicide, but he ended up getting himself captured. Rommel received permission from Hitler to retreat early on November 5, but after he had already begun to do so under his own initiative. Only a fraction of his once victorious army, those units that still had fuel, were able to escape. Most of his armor and all of his unpowered equipment, which made up the bulk of his army, was lost. Fortunately for Rommel, Montgomery failed to follow up his victory, allowing him to withdraw his remaining forces 1,000 miles [1600 km] back to El Agheila, south of Benghazi. Unfortunately for Rommel, on

November 8, 1942, three days after the end of the Battle of El Alamein, British and American forces landed on the north coast of Africa between Casablanca and Algiers. Rommel was now trapped between two much larger armies. German reinforcements from Italy on November 9 managed to establish a front in Tunisia that prevented eastward movement of the Allied forces and protected Rommel's rear.

On December 16, Montgomery, marching through the desert, outflanked Rommel, forcing him out of El Agheila, and chased him into Tripoli, which was captured on January 23, 1943. By February 18, Rommel had been forced into Tunisia where he set up a defensive position called the Mareth Line. Rommel now had Montgomery and the Eighth Army to his east and the Allied forces from the North Africa landings to his west. He was trapped in a pocket about 100 miles [160 km] long with overwhelming forces arranged against him. In mid-March, Rommel, by now a sick man, turned over command of Panzer Army Africa to Italian General Giovanni Messe. Now renamed the Army Group Africa (by this time it consisted of one German and three Italian corps), the remnants of three Panzer divisions, the 10th, the 15th, and the 21st, were all that were left of the German units in Africa.

Although Messe had replaced Rommel, the two jointly commanded the Axis forces until March 9, when Rommel departed Africa for the last time. Before he left, he handed over command of Army Group Africa to Generaloberst Hans-Jürgen von Arnim. His departure was not announced to his men for fear the news would completely demoralize the troops. Hitler also wanted the British to think that Rommel was still somewhere in Africa, waiting to attack unexpectedly. On May 1, General der Panzertruppen Hans Cramer was made the last commander of the DAK and two weeks later he would be captured by the British. On May 12, General Meese was promoted to Field Marshal and the next day he formally surrendered the remnants of Army Group Africa and the DAK to the Allies. German Major General Von Hulsen simultaneously surrendered the remnants of the 21st Panzer Division.

The 21st Panzer Division was reconstituted in France on July 15, two months after the original division had surrendered. The 21st remained in France until the Allied landings at Normandy in June 1944, when it became the only Panzer division to engage the Allies on D-Day. The division's commander now was Oberst Edgar Feuchtinger.

In this incarnation, the 21st Panzer Division was a fast moving force designed to counter the invading Allied army. It was comprised of tanks, halftracks, self-propelled artillery and troop carriers. The division, as was the original in North Africa, was once again under the command of Rommel, who was now commander of all German forces from the Netherlands to the Loire River in France. Rommel knew the invasion had to be stopped on the beaches, but Generals von Rundstedt and Heinz Guderian disagreed and wanted to wait until the invaders were further inland. Hitler compromised and placed the bulk of the German forces near the beach but not near enough to be of any immediate use. The only significant German organization available to counter the Normandy landings on June 6, 1944 was the 21st Panzer Division, near Caen in the area of the British landings.

The 21st Panzer operated alone on the first day of the Allied invasion and came under heavy air attacks, but did manage to delay the British advance at Caen. They succeeded in reaching the coast at Lion-sur-Mer and split the 3d British and 3d Canadian Divisions, inflicting damage on both. Rommel was away from the front for the first days of the Allied invasion but reassumed command on June 9. The division remained in combat in the Caen area during the next two months. The 21st Panzer Division was eventually trapped and largely destroyed in the Falaise Pocket in northern France in August 1944.

In September 1944, the 21st Panzer Division was again reconstituted and combined with the 112th Panzer Brigade and the 100th Panzer Regiment. The much smaller division took part in the retreat to the German border and fought notable defensive battles at Epinel, Metz and in the Saar area. It was eventually withdrawn from the front to be refitted in Kaiserslautern. Even as late as September, there were depots operating in Germany at reasonably full strength, and the 21st was quickly re-equipped. The lack of manpower, however, made it pointless to supply the division with equipment it could not utilize.

On January 25, 1945, the division was once again reformed, now as an independent division, comparable in size to the original 5th Light Africa Division. Its last commander was Oberst Helmut

Zollenkopf. The division contained a single battalion from the 22d Panzer Regiment. It contained one Flak platoon, two Panther tank companies and two additional Mk. IV tanks. The last reinforcements were sent to the division on February 9. It was then redeployed to the Eastern Front, where it fought the advancing Red Army at Goerlitz, Slatsk, and Cottbus, inflicting heavy losses on the enemy. It can be said that the 21st Panzer Division fought to the last tank before surrendering to the Soviets on April 29, the day before Adolf Hitler's death in the Chancellery bunker.

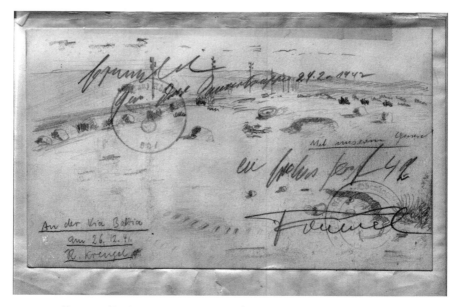

Rommel's signature on Krengel's War Diary (lower right).

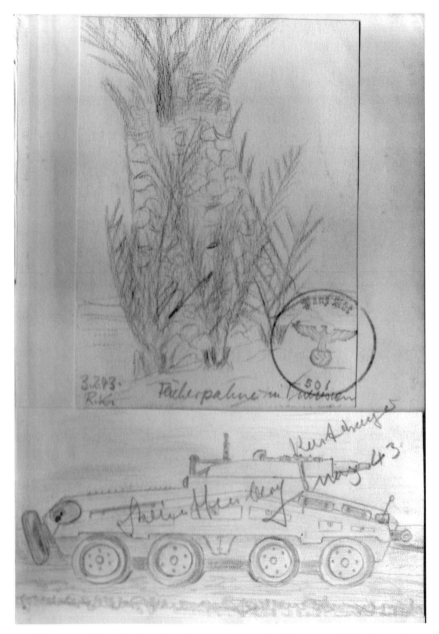

Claus von Stauffenberg's signature (on the drawing of the Puma).

[Translation]

"For months we have been suffering under the torture of a problem which the Versailles Diktat created – a problem which has deteriorated until it becomes intolerable for us. Danzig was and is a German city. The Corridor was and is German. Both these territories owe their cultural development exclusively to the German people. Danzig was separated from us, the Corridor was annexed by Poland. As in other German territories of the East, all German minorities living there have been ill-treated in the most distressing manner.

". . . proposals for mediation have failed because in the meantime, first of all, there came as an answer the sudden Polish general mobilization, followed by more Polish atrocities. These were again repeated last night. Recently in one night there were as many as twenty-one frontier incidents; last night there were fourteen, of which three were serious. I have, therefore, resolved to speak to Poland in the same language that Poland for months past has used toward us.

"This night, for the first time, Polish regular soldiers fired on our territory. Since 5:45 a.m. we have been returning fire, and from now on bombs will be met by bombs. Whoever fights with poison gas will be fought with poison gas."

—From an Address by
Chancellor Adolf Hitler to the Reichstag
1 September 1939

Chapter 1

CONSCRIPTION AND ON TO FRANCE ("CASE YELLOW"), 1939

27 August, 1939: I arrive at the Stahnsdorf barracks [12 miles, 20 km southwest of Berlin] at 6 PM to report as a conscript to the 3d Reconnaissance Reserve Battalion [of the 3d Panzer Division].

1 September: Start of the war against Poland. The Führer speaks on the radio to all German people. [The 3d Panzer Division was involved in the Polish campaign.]

3 September: England and France declare war on Germany and Italy.

6 September: My 21st birthday and I have a day off in Berlin.

18 September: The war with Poland is concluded. They have surrendered to our forces.

20 October: Today my training is over and I'm being transferred and permanently attached to the 3d [Panzer Division] Motorized Reconnaissance Battalion.

29 November: We get orders to move out, proceed with all our equipment to Magdeburg, and stay overnight.

30 November: We continue our journey to Bad Oeynhausen.

1 December: Today we travel to Schwege, where we stay in barracks and celebrate our first War Christmas on 24 December 1939.

1940

2 January, 1940: Today we leave Schwege behind, our orders are to proceed to Krefeld via the Autobahn; it's bitter cold, - 20° C. [-4 ° F]

3 January: Arrival in Krefeld; we have training and indoor duties. I also visit the family of Dr. Oehnke, friends of my family, who live in Krefeld; my parents come to visit me, otherwise no news.

9 April: News reaches us today of Germany's occupation of Denmark and Norway, and of battles around and in Oslo.

6 May: We're on alert and do some night exercises.

10 May: We leave our camp by the steel factory in Krefeld, move our whole unit via Jülich toward Koslar, and stay overnight on the way.

11 May: We advance past Koslar and Hongen and reach the Dutch frontier; here we have our first air alert but see no planes.

12 May: We travel through Bilzen and Houtheim and to the Belgian border.

13 May: First action at Waremont; we attack a French Divisional Headquarters and have our first comrade to be killed in action, KIA. Sargeant Maivaler was killed by a French counterattack with tanks.

14 May: We travel from Waremont to Undruge to Hauppauge.

15 May: We are now in St. Vincent, Belgium. As we secure the flank of our Division, we come under heavy fire; shrapnel hits my steel helmet – lucky me.

We pursue the enemy from St. Vincent to St. Paul, Genlines, and Nivelles.

16 May: At Chateau de la Rouge we secure a bridgehead over the Senelle Canal and lose 1st Lt. Vaato, KIA, 1st Lt. [Winrich] Behr was awarded the Iron Cross, 1st Class. We advance to Nivelles, then Perbais, and Ernage.

19 May: We reach the French border near Maubeuge and have a well deserved rest.

20 May: After reaching Presian we are assigned local reconnaissance duty, but then we are told to move out to Villiers-Pol. We arrive and then have a rest day there.

22 May: In the afternoon we suddenly receive incoming fire from French mortars that kills SSgt. Schwarz; one other comrade is wounded.

23 May–4 June: We advance through several French towns without enemy contact. At Les Mesnil we secure the crossing of Panzers across a small river.

5 June: We travel through Somme, Clery sur Somme, Herbecourt, Assevilliers, and Charelness.

6 June: We secure another bridgehead for the division in the Roye, St. Mard and Chaville area.

12 June: We participate in a big pursuit of the French near Chateau Thierry; lose PFC Alfred Puder (KIA) and reach Monomial. On 15 June we are in the Auxerre-Avalon area; so far we've taken 3000 French POW's.

16 June: Heavy engagement with enemy tanks who attempt a breakout; we lose Sgt. Reger (KIA).

24 June: We reach St. Etienne and receive the news of the cease fire so we all celebrate and have a deserved rest. [France formally surrendered to Germany on June 25.]

We stay in St Etienne until 2 July and then march via Verdun to Thionville and have one day of rest there. We cross into Germany on 4 July through the Westwall; travel through Saarbrücken, to Kusel. On 3 July, I receive the black wound badge for the scratch on my head during the French attack.

7 July: We leave Kusel and travel through Mainz, Frankfurt, and Nauheim to Schaaz. The following day we load onto train flat cars and proceed through Eisenach, Gotha, and Erfurt, to Weissenfels in Saxony.

9 July: We return to our home base at Stahnsdorf. Here I celebrate my 22d birthday on 16 September.

[There are no entries from 10 July, 1940 to 6 February, 1941. During this time period, the 3d Panzer Division was stationed at Stahnsdorf and saw no action.]

Chapter 2

MY NORTH AFRICA CAMPAIGN, 1941

6 February: We board a train at the railroad station in Potsdam. At 11 AM, we move out and travel through Berlin, Leipzig, Hof, and Regensburg.

7 February: We travel from Regensburg and Munich to Innsbruck, and reach the Brenner Pass at 10 PM. The next morning we go through Bolzano, Trento, Verona, and Vicenza to Padua; then on to Bologna, Rome, Naples, and Caserta. There we load our vehicles and armor,

10 February: In Caserta, visiting the old town.

11 February: We have breakfast at 5:30 AM and move out to Naples and at 8 AM the loading of our vehicles onto the transport D-Ruhr begins. From 4 PM to 6 PM we have time to stroll through Naples.

12 February: At 1 AM, action stations on all ships; we leave Naples in a convoy with D-Kypfels, D-Ruhr, Adana, and Ankara. We have an escort of 1 destroyer and a torpedo boat. In the afternoon, we are in sight of Sicily. As darkness sets in, we travel in a line with all lights out.

13 February: On board D-Ruhr, I have bridge duty for 2 hours. The African coast is soon in view (Tunis); we change course to the east.

The dock at Tripoli.

Axis officers in Benghazi, with "Viva la Duce" signs in the background.

14 February: We meet up with an Italian convoy. We are now escorted by German and Italian aircraft; lots of Ju-52's. The weather is foggy but very hot. We arrive in Tripoli at 8 PM and immediately start unloading.

15 February: At 4 AM we finish our unloading and sleep for a few hours on a bicycle race track. We are up at 8 AM and change into Africa uniforms. I'm assigned as a motorcycle messenger and we load up the side car. At noon, we parade through Tripoli where General Rommel addresses us and reviews our equipment. We then depart for Misurala.

16 February: By 3 PM we are in Misurala and at 7 PM we arrive in Sirte and occupy a position between some sand dunes. [Krengel's company was one of the first to arrive at Sirte.]

17 February: All day we have a sandstorm, called a ghibli. We have to dismantle and clean the carburetor on the bike. In the evening, General Rommel arrives at our position and congratulates us in the name of our Führer.

We have our first reconnaissance mission and move nearer the seashore. The next morning we load machine gun belts with bullets and in the afternoon, we have a swim in the Mediterranean.

19 February: We move out to Nufilia, very rocky terrain here. We are on security duty from 8 to10 PM and from 6 to 8 AM. [Nufilia was the site of the very first battle of British and German forces in North Africa; also referred to as En Nofilia or just Nofilia.]

20 February: Our Company is loaded onto trucks and is assigned to Battle Group Fallois Rastram.

21–22 February: Our Battle Group returns without enemy contact; we receive Italian rations for the first time: olive oil, Aniseed, tobacco, bread, and pasta.

23 February: At 3 PM, we depart with Battle Group [Winrich] Behr to

El Agheila. Our orders are to escort our Panzers and take prisoners. We leave with 2 platoons, one heavy 8-wheeled armored vehicle [Puma], our motorcycle infantry, and a radio group on a truck. At 7 PM, we are 10 miles from El Agheila. [El Agheila is located in far southwestern Cyrenaica and was the site of several battles. The British had taken it from the Italian Tenth Army during Operation Compass.] We stop here but the infantry continues on foot.

24 February: At 7 AM, we strike into El Agheila and surprise the British, capturing 8 armored cars and 3 POW's. We return to our positions near En Nofilia at 2 PM and rest. We listen via radio to a speech from our Führer.

25 February: We occupy a fort at En Nofilia. It has a triangular shape and contains a radio station. Our group has one big room. General Rommel arrives and brings us cigarettes, a box of oranges, and some Italian wine.

26 February: I have guard duty from 8:30 AM to noon. The radio mentions a report by the Army High Command in Berlin about our successful operation into El Agheila. My duty has been extended for another day; we are responsible for the watering point.

28 February: The new Commander of our Battle Group is 1st Lt. [Wolfgang-Dieter] Everth. We are moving out again toward El Agheila. We stop at noon in the desert and General Rommel arrives in a Fiesler Stork plane. His pilot gives me some cigarettes.

29 February: We receive some bad news: an Italian cruiser was sunk near Tripoli. Also, a tragic mistake happened today. PFC Reichelt returned from a walk in the dark and forgot the password. He was shot and killed by our guard. He is the first fatality of the DAK. He was buried with full honors.

3 March: At 9 AM we move out to a position 24 miles west of El Agheila and get a look at the assembled DAK. We are 6 miles behind the front line. We take a dip in the sea and rest.

7 March: Feel sick today and report to the medic. A headache and cold make me ill for two days.

10 March: Fit for duty finally. We are doing a reconnaissance to the south; to a mountain we call Tafelberg [Table Mountain]. In the early evening, after returning, the drivers of our Pumas receive the Panzer Battle Award.

12–14 March: Before noon I drive in a car to Bengahzi and arrive there at 9 PM to report to the doctor at the hospital; heavy ghibli [sandstorm] today. On the 14th, we are supposed to receive Volkswagen Kubelwagens so I hear.

15–18 March: We camouflage our vehicles and attend to our weapons. On the 17th, we do a short reconnaissance to the Table Mountain. On the 18th we are attacked by British fighters, "Hurricanes," and we shoot one down; no casualties in our unit.

19 March: Another Hurricane shot down. News reaches us that we are supposed to move back to make room for an Italian Division. Our 5th Panzer Regiment reaches the Via Balbia Archway. We have a strong ghibli on the 21st. [Hitler awarded Rommel the Oak Leaves to the Knight's Cross on this date.]

22 March: We are ready to attack in the general direction of El Agheila. At 2 PM on 23rd, we reach a point 8 miles west of El Agheila. We sit around for hours but then march along the seashore toward El Agheila.

24 March: We occupy the fort at 4:30 AM without a shot being fired, and by 5:30 the whole company has arrived. Two British trucks roll by not far off but nobody has given us permission to fire, and when permission is finally given the Tommies are out of range. We are then shot at by 40mm British AT [anti-tank] guns and this time we are allowed to return fire; no results seen. Later the whole Battle Group arrives for the major attack on El Agheila.

The leading Panzer hits a road mine and blows up; 2 dead. Lt.

Seidel is KIA during the attack but we take El Agheila by early evening.

25 March: We can see Hurricanes above us but they do not attack. We drive along the coastal highway to marker [kilometer marker] 14, where we are relieved by the 8th Machine Gun Battalion. We construct a defensive position with sand and tents; very hot today.

26–29 March: We are in our sand castle hunting fleas; we swim in the sea and wash our uniforms. In the evening Berlin Radio announces the capture of El Agheila.

30–31 March: Panzers are rolling by toward the east. We greet them with a hearty "Arriva." There is fighting around Mersa El Brega with both Stukas and Panzers involved. We move out of the sand castle on 1 April and 12 miles east of El Agheila we bivouac on the roadside.

2 April: At 6 AM we leave Mersa El Brega, but have several halts waiting for our artillery to push the British back toward Agedabia. Our Panzers are now in the action as well; we detour through knee deep sand dunes and at 5 PM we hear that Agedabia has been taken by our Panzers [5th Panzer Regiment]. We set up a defensive perimeter with PaK and armor just north of Agedabia.

3 April: At 1 PM, we advance to attack a group of enemy tanks that have been reported in our area but it was a false alarm. We return and come under command of the 3d Reconnaissance Battalion, Battle Group Wechmar [Oberst Irnfried Freiherr von Wechmar, Knight's Cross, 13 April, 1941; German Cross in Gold, 16 January, 1942].

At 6 PM, we advance toward Benghazi and encounter numerous destroyed Italian tanks along the road. We capture a whole British supply depot, but continue our march through the night.

4 April: By 3 AM, Benghazi is burning and the city is free of enemy. We roll through the town at 5 AM and stop for a rest in a palm grove to catch up on sleep. The civilian population is elated and treats us as liberators. We are given British rations captured the day before. Later we continue our advance. The target is Mechilli, 18 miles southeast of Benghazi.

In Mechilli we get into a firefight with an Australian Infantry Battalion. Sgt. Ruder is killed by a bullet to the head and two others are wounded. I receive some tiny bits of shrapnel in my hand but nothing serious. We are awake all night. It's very cold.

5 April: We are moving out early today. 3d Platoon is under the command of 1st Lt. Wangemann. We move into Regima and occupy the village without a fight. Tommie has disappeared somehow to the east. We advance along a camel route; to call it a road would be a real exaggeration. A halt is called after traveling about 40 miles to the east in the desert.

6 April: We send out an armed patrol that spots enemy tanks ahead. We retreat but capture 2 enemy soldiers in the process. We march throughout the night.

7 April: Before we reach Mechilli, a halt is called because the area ahead is well mined. 1st Lt. Everth's Puma trips a mine but the explosion causes no casualties. Sgt. Schuberth and a Pioneer Platoon clear a gap in the mine field. These are the new Thermos mines, which are very hard to detect. We accidentally fire on one of our own trucks that had lost its way in the desert; no casualties.

At 4 PM General Rommel arrives in his Fiesler Stork. He tells me that he was almost captured by a British desert patrol when he landed at one of our fuel depots that had been left unguarded.

8 April: We have another ghibli today that causes many breakdowns due to sand problems. We nevertheless advance with what we have past Mechilli and find much British war material; trucks, gasoline, rations, and other things.

We keep up the advance all night to the north and toward the city of Derna.

9 April: We reach the Derna airfield at 2 AM. We seem to be the only unit that has made it here in one piece. We have a short rest and at 11

AM we depart to the east. We have 2 mishaps with a Puma but we are still rolling. At 32 miles west of Tobruk we call a halt.

10 April: We are being transported on captured trucks now and go around Tobruk to the south. Our target is either Bardia or Sollum. Long-range artillery from Tobruk targets our advance. Karl Blum is severely wounded by artillery shrapnel. We can't stop and tend to him during the drive so we just do what we can for him. We call a halt well south of Tobruk to avoid their artillery.

11 April: Today is Good Friday and we have a few hours rest but the British have no intention of leaving us alone. We have 6 air raids with both bombers and fighter-bombers so we decide to move out at 2 PM. Two battle groups move out in the direction of Tobruk, under fighter-bomber attack. Two men, Schaeffer and Elden, are wounded. We arrive at the outskirts of Tobruk at midnight but orders come in to not attack and instead to move under darkness toward Bardia.

12 April: 1st Platoon on reconnaissance to Bardia; another ghibli storm and terribly high temperatures. We have no water except the reserve for the vehicles. Our company should catch up with us tonight.

13 April: Today is Easter Sunday and the British bombers arrive to bring us Easter eggs in the form of bombs; not much water or food today. What a Happy Easter. Finally, our Motorcycle Unit arrives.

14 April: We stay where we are but have several air attacks and our flak guns have no ammunition. We leave at 5 PM, travel 4 miles to the east, and find a wadi [ravine] to set up tents in. The wadi is marked on our maps as the "Valley of Peace." Ha ha ha.

15 April: We have several British attacks by air; Corporal Lange is wounded. One platoon is sent to an improvised airfield to mark a landing strip. We camouflage our trucks. The British attack Sollum and simultaneously attempt a breakout from Tobruk – without success. We hear that our commander [1st Lt. Behr] will be the first German in Africa to receive the Knight's Cross [awarded 15 May,

1941]. We secure Sollum airfield and place AT guns around the perimeter.

On 17 April we return to our camp at the Valley of Peace; motorcycle units at last bring us plenty of water. During the night of the 18th, we are bombarded by super heavy (380mm) artillery; probably from British battleships offshore. A radio message arrives; Yugoslavia has capitulated.

20 April: An alarm comes at 1:30 AM; British seaborne troops have landed at Bardia; our 1st and 2d Platoons form a security screen. 3d and 4th Platoons with flak move out to Bardia. They return with 60 POW's. In the evening, we assemble to congratulate our Führer on his birthday. Sepp Ziegler is promoted to Sergeant. The Iron Cross 1st Class is awarded to Lts. Napp and Wangemann and to SSgt. Gunther. My friend Eric Wolff receives the Iron Cross 2nd Class.

24 April: We attack British positions at Sollum, but we are beaten back by heavy fire from British battleships and cruisers offshore. On 24 April at 7 PM, we retreat.

25 April: This is a black day for us of the 3d Platoon. As we marched along Via Balbia, with some men riding on trucks, we were attacked by our own Luftwaffe, one heavy bomb exploded next to a truck, killing:

     Pvt. Otto Völskow
     Pvt. Walther Braun
     Pvt. Josef Schmidt
     Pvt. Johann Schmid
     Sgt. Ziegler
     Sgt. Kurt Lange

and wounding: Gunthmann, Mihl, Rieck, Roschka and Sgt. Lirka. 1st Platoon was detailed for burial and we buried them along Via Balbia between Ft. Capuzzo and Bardia.

26 April: At 1 PM we are told of a new operation, code named "Wendepunkt" ["Turning Point"] that is supposed to dislodge enemy artillery from Hill 206. We overrun the battery and 1st Lt. Behr, who commanded the operation gets mentioned in General Rommel's report.

27 April: We secure Hill 206 with PaK, flak and patrols. The British attempt to filter into our positions but they fail.

29 April: Hill 206 is quiet until 4 PM when a [British] Hurricane shows up to view our positions. We dig ourselves some holes for cover and watch the Tommies do the same thing in the distance. At 5 PM, the expected heavy artillery barrage on our position comes. There are several dead and wounded at the flak pit; one gun receives a direct hit and is totally destroyed. Lt. Napp is wounded; we retreat to Fort Capuzzo, where there are Panzer and assault gun reinforcements. We eventually return to the Valley of Peace.

30 April: Hill 206 is retaken by the Panzer Division and we have a bath in the harbor at Bardia. On May 3d we are still in Bardia and on May 4th we listen to a speech given by our Führer. We run our trucks around Sollum to stir up dust and make the British believe that we are getting reinforcements. On 6 May we get many false alarms that lead to unplanned night exercises.

7 May: A hunt for desert rats is in progress in our camp. At 5 PM we move out from Hill 206. We encounter the wire fence that divides Libya from Egypt and runs for hundreds of miles from the seashore to the Sahara Desert. We run into an ambush but manage to fight our way out. Eric has a high fever and gets transported back to the aid station.

AA guns pass us on the way to Sollum. We stop for the night by the wire fence.

9 May: Ghibli again–and very hot. Ten men have been ordered to fetch POW's from the front. Thermometer shows 47° C. [117° F] During the sandstorm a British artillery battery cruises into our lines; we capture the surprised unit and add four more guns to our arsenal – brand new 87mm's. Eric has returned and is fit again. On 11 May we undertake a short reconnaissance mission and engage a British Hussar

[tank] unit but no one inflicts or sustains any damage.

12 May: During the night, we pursue the enemy with Panzers, half tracks and mobile artillery. 3d Platoon has a truck breakdown; we take him in tow and turn around and go back to Bardia. Later Lt. Napp turns up with a broken axle on his Volkswagen Jeep.

13 May: Rumors are being circulated that our Deputy Führer Rudolf Hess has fled to England, but these are only rumors.

We're camped in another wadi; I've been in Africa 3 months now.

15 May: Heavy artillery fire is heard in the direction of Capuzzo. British tanks attack along the highway from Capuzzo to Sollum. One of our motorcycle units is reported missing. We're on alert but are relieved at noon by an Italian unit. We break camp in the evening and set off for Tobruk at 11 PM.

16 May: British tank attack on Bardia; we counterattack and Tommie retreats. We return to the Valley of Peace and find things the same as before when we were here. We do have one surprise, however; the very first German Me-109 fighters in the sky above us.

17 May: The Knight's Cross was indeed awarded to our Company Commander, 1st Lt. Behr. We are all very proud of him.

19 May: Ready to move out to Sidi Azeiz, since we have been relieved by an infantry battalion. At 1 AM we pack up and march off; we look like a gypsy caravan. We arrive at Sidi Azeiz late in the afternoon and set up camp. We are not far from Bardia, where we have to go for fresh drinking water and baths in the sea.

21 May: We're attacked by 5 Vickers Wellington bombers at 8:30 AM and about 20 bombs fall on our position. Werner Kubling and Heinz Georg were killed by a direct hit on their foxhole. Eric, Gille, Raff, and Flamy are wounded. Our flak has 3 dead. We bury our comrades at 6 PM north of the road. Hans has to drive the command car now that Werner is dead.

22 May: There is news that a British convoy was sunk in the Mediterranean. We are at camp to refit and repair equipment. We are also building a wooden shelter, as it is too hot in the tents. We get news that we have captured Crete [Unternehmen Merkur, or Operation Mercury], and that the British ship *Hood* was sunk by the *Bismarck*.

26 May: At 11.30 AM we have an assembly. We are being transferred and converted to Divisional Reserve with the 5th Motorcycle Group. A rumor is circulating that we have been selected for an attack on Halfaya Pass, but tonight we join a Panzer unit at Sidi Suleiman. We hear that the *Bismarck* is in a battle in the Atlantic.

27 May: We depart at 1 AM for Capuzzo, from there we move to an attack position. At 5 AM we start the attack on the pass. At 6.30 AM we dismount our vehicles and clamber up rocky hills, pushing the British back toward the coast. We capture several tanks and guns and 300 POW's. At 4 PM we return to our camp and get the news that the *Bismarck* has been sunk.

28 May: Our last day at Sidi Azeiz; we set off at 11:30 PM for Tobruk with all wheeled vehicles. I'm in the Jeep. Eighteen miles from Tobruk we stop for the night and gas up our vehicles at a supply depot during the night of the 29th.

30 May: Our unit departs, minus those of us in our Jeep. We mistakenly put diesel in our gasoline tank; took us half an hour to drain the stuff out and race after the Company. South of Tobruk we hit a mine but we are both okay. The front axle broke in half, so we wait for a tow. Two hours later we are still waiting. A truck finally arrives but he too runs over a mine. We search the area and find 4 more of the devices. It's dark now, so we sleep in a wadi nearby.

31 May: At 9 AM a recovery truck arrives and we are towed to the west of Tobruk. Our advance party has found a nice place to set up camp between dunes, right by the seashore.

1 June: We are sitting at the rest camp in the dunes. Eric will recuperate a few days in Derna. Things are quiet from 1 to 8 June, but on the 9th the British remind us that there is a war going on and attack with a few fighter bombers. Two of our Me-109's take up the challenge and shoot two of them down.

10 June: Inspection day–and it is a hot day. The inspection went something like this:

Sgt. Tapper to Pvt. Bolten: "You haven't got a towel, Bolten?"

Pvt. Bolten: "No, Sir"

Sgt. Tapper: "Then what do you use for drying?"

Pvt. Bolten: "The sun, Sir"

That was about it.

12 June: Today our vehicles get a new camouflage coat of paint, which dries in seconds in this heat. The next evening orders arrive for us to move out.

14 June: We're ready at 5 AM to depart this nice camp. We move out at 10 AM and immediately come under fighter-bomber attack. Gehrke is killed; Reschke and Heichen are wounded. We march south of Tobruk to our old haunts in Sidi Azeiz.

16 June: We have a flat tire on our Jeep and are under constant attack by British aircraft but they don't do much damage. We are told that the enemy has now lost 60 tanks at Halfaya Pass and that a British attempt to land by sea in our rear at Bardia has been repulsed.

17 June: We attack Sidi Omar but the enemy puts up heavy resistance. Two machine gun battalions attack and take the town finally, despite heavy losses. The enemy attacks with aircraft but without success. Our Italian Air Force "friends" have better luck, or maybe worse luck – they bombed our 39th Anti-Tank Regiment twice today, killing and wounding 50 of our troops. When they come around a third time we send an open radio message to their leader, "Please could you bomb the enemy by mistake for once. You are attacking the wrong side." They turn off this time but we take no chances and disperse our group.

18 June: Constant fighter-bomber attacks today. It is very hot, but by the 19th things are almost back to normal; we see only our own planes on the 20th and all is quiet on the 21st.

22 June: We hear the news of war beginning with Russia. One of our Pumas needs a replacement suspension so we drive to Bardia. We hear on the radio in Bardia that the battle cruiser [*Admiral*] *Scheer* is returning to Germany.

28 June: We're still in Bardia but we hear news of our victories in Russia; Brest Litowsk captured by our forces there. We return to our unit and set up a new camp at Cape Ras [at the entrance of the Gulf of Oman].

28 June–13 July: We're in camp, listening to news from Russia and killing time. A few of our men have been attached to a supply company under the command of Theilen. Bialistok [Poland] has been taken along with 160,000 Russian POW's. In Russia, German troops have reached the Dnieper River.

We receive 15 new replacements and salvage some lumber from a stranded freighter. A Hurricane was shot down near us. The latest news from the Atlantic is that the USA occupied Iceland on 8 July – and they're not even at war. On 9 July we practice firing our carbines. The Iron Cross has been awarded to Pvt. Kalies. In Russia, the Battle of Minsk brings us 375,000 POW's. On the evening of 12 July, we staged a soccer match against 2d Company and won 3 to 2. In Russia we take Witebsk.

14 July: 4th Company challenges us to a soccer match; we take them on but during the game 2 Hurricanes attack our Stukas and shoot down 2 of them, and our fighters down 2 of theirs. The score is 2:2. We continue our game and win 5:1. On the 15th another 5 Hurricanes are shot down.

19 July: In Russia, Smolensk has been taken. Here in camp, we have a film in the evening. General Rommel and staff arrive to watch the movie too. Nothing much is happening here; guard duty by the shore, one man taken to the hospital with malaria. I've been admitted to the field hospital with stomach pain but I'm able to watch a Karl May movie while there titled "Through the Desert."

3 August: Night guard duty in the desert north of Bardia. A Doctor inspects our medical facilities and we get more good news from Russia. On the 8th, enemy bombers fly over, searching for targets.

9 August: We are loading up finally, to relieve the 3d Reconnaissance Battalion near Sollum. 1st Lt. Behr has been transferred back to Germany. We move out on the 10th and arrive 10 miles north of Capuzzo at 9 AM. We do a short patrol toward Sidi Omar.

11 August: We return to Sidi Omar and tour the positions of the Italian "Savoy" Division. It is a very hot day again. We are staying here with the Savoy Division, resting, eating macaroni and fresh meat. In the evening we are relieved by the 4th Pioneer Co.

14 August: We move to Capuzzo but return to the Savoy Division on the 17th; same old routine, in out in out and then back to Sidi Omarch. It rained for a change – now our engines won't start.

27 August: Today I have been in the Wehrmacht for 2 years.

4 September: Now the nights are getting cooler. Ssgt. Gier has departed for a few days for Appolonia. On the 7th we move out at 3:45 AM to Sidi Omar and then we are sent from there to El Abitt for patrol duty.

8–9 September: We are still patrolling near El Abitt.

12 September: Rumors abound that we will be attacking somewhere soon. During the night many Panzers move east along the [Via Balbia] Coastal Road. I don't feel very well. The next night I'm in bad shape, no food and I'm constantly sick. I still feel bad on the 14th and 15th.

16 September: My 23d birthday and I'm spending it in Africa. We are relieved by a Pioneer Company. I still feel sick so I report to the medic and I am taken to Bardia Field Hospital. Yellow Jaundice is the finding and the cure is staying warm, extra salt, and a diet of rice, flour, oats, and fresh fruit, but I don't feel any better on the 18th or on the 19th. Feeling better on the 20th and on the 21st I'm able to go for a short walk.

23 September: At 11:45 PM, we have an air raid alert. We were all in bed and before we could reach the shelter several bombs detonated in and outside the hospital. It's a terrible tragedy; we don't know who's dead and who has survived. I'm slightly wounded on my left upper arm and my eyes hurt.

24 September: We count 6 dead and many wounded. The wounded are air lifted to Athens in Greece. I'm okay but outside I find an unexploded bomb right under my window. I was transported by road to Derna but the hospital there couldn't do much for my eyes. I need a new pair of glasses from a qualified optician, but the nearest one is in Benghazi.

26 September: Early morning I'm taken to Benghazi Military Hospital and have my eyes examined, then I'm allowed to visit the town. Tomorrow morning I will be taken by air to Tripoli to another military hospital. Another overall examination and my ear gets treated where bomb shrapnel hit me.

We have an air raid alert at 2 PM but no bombs fall in our vicinity. The hospital staff even gives me a bottle of German beer, the first I have had in months.

30 September: Another examination today, then I'm free to walk the city of Tripoli and visit the Wehrmacht cinema where the movie "Bismarck" is playing. After the movie, a film is shown of the latest speech of our Führer.

4 October: I'm suffering again from stomach cramps and jaundice and there was an air raid on the city. I'm now on the observation ward for several days and receive a new pair of glasses on the 9th.

11 October: I'm still in Tripoli. I walked into town and visited the Rialto Restaurant for a nice dinner. I'm getting restless here but have to stick it out. I had to pay 84 Lira for my new glasses. Listening to the radio I hear the news from Russia. Kalinin and Kaluga have been taken. Bryansk and Wjasma were taken along with 650,000 POW's.

20 October: Woke up early this morning to a loud "Boom." Apparently a buried bomb with a time fuse went off; window panes broken but no casualties.

30 October: Finally I am supposed to be released from the hospital today and leave at 2 PM. I am to report to the local Front supply office. The next morning I am taken by truck to Camp 5 and at 5 PM by air to the front. We stop overnight in Benghazi and the next day we stop 50 miles west of Derna. 3 November, we stop near Tobruk.

4 November: At noon I arrive at my company 6 miles west of Bardia and everyone greets me with a big hello. The Company had suffered two deaths during my away time; Mueller died of cholera and Lt. Krause of diptheria. Hans Römer, my driver, has been transferred to HQ. 1st Platoon is scheduled for a reconnaissance mission. I want to go too, but I am told to stay put. I have to go for recuperation to a Wehrmacht home.

7 November: At 5 AM, the platoon moves out without me. It's getting really cold now in North Africa. Also I got the news that my cousin died on the *Bismarck* in May. Our Commander lets me out with a platoon on a short patrol on the 8th. On the 9th I finally receive some much awaited Field Post mail from home and spend all day the 11th going through the letters. Lt. Napp tells me that I have to report to General Rommel on 12 November.

12 November: I leave for Derna and report with 14 other men to HQ. We are told that we have been selected for recuperation in Appolonia and we arrive there at noon. We have an evening out and visit a bar. This is supposed to be home leave away from home so we enjoy it. Appolonia is an old city near Cirene, directly by the sea. Our Camp has 3 buildings named after our German garrisons: Stahnsdorf, Krummhausen, and Krefeld. We have good meals, no duty, and we are allowed to purchase civilian clothing. We spend a lot of time strolling around town. We listen to radio broadcasts and hear that the [British] carrier *Ark Royal* has been sunk by U-boats. We get beer in the evenings.

17 November: The wet season has started and it rains for hours; the roads are flooded and we try in vain to keep the water out of our building. In the evening the weekly supply truck from Benghazi arrives. The driver knows all the latest news. The British have started a new offensive and there is much going on at the Sollum front. Trenches and sand dunes have collapsed. The evening radio news on the 20th mentions the British attack for the first time.

21 November: We hear that 260 tanks have been destroyed at the front. We are on light duty now and have been detailed to guard the local power station. On the 22d we get no news from the front at Sollum. I hope all is okay with my outfit. Rumors say that our main coastal highway is under heavy artillery fire.

24 November: A funny thing happened last night during our guard duty at the power plant. We heard someone approaching in the dark and cocked our rifles and asked for the password twice. The answer was I–AA. That was not the password so we fired and then investigated. We had killed a stray donkey. We titled the report, "Donkey Battle at the Power Station." Off duty I read a lot, write in my diary, listen to radio reports, drink beer, and get the front news from passing truck drivers. One report says that our supply convoy was ambushed by a New Zealand unit on the coastal road and that we lost many men as POW's.

It's still raining and we are still doing guard duty at the power plant.

27 November: Tonight the bar is full of men. We hear that we are supposed to go back to the front shortly to make room for new troops here. We don't hear much news from the front but watch a war movie about our African expedition. I'm still in Appolonia. On 2 Dec, I decide to write my Christmas letters home. On 3 Dec we get radio news that our cruiser *Kormoran* was sunk, but so was the Australian cruiser *Sydney*.

4 December: So now we hear it officially that our troops are fighting west of Bardia, near Sidi Omar and in the southern part of Cyreneica. If this is right, we seem to have lost Bardia and are retreating west. Two men from my company arrive on 5 December and tell us about Bardia being surrounded. The coastal highway cannot be used anymore.

8 December: I visit Walter Ludwig in the hospital and he tells me of the fighting at Bardia. My company has had 10 people KIA. They are driving around in circles in the desert and here I am, fit and can't do a thing to help them.

Last night Japan entered the war against the USA and sunk 6 battleships and 2 carriers somewhere in Hawaii.

9 December: What a way to fight a war. The world is upside down and we're sitting here putting on weight. On 10 December we get more news. The *Prince of Wales*, the *Repulse* and the *Langley* have been sunk by the Japanese off Sumatra. We get some fighting news regarding our front as well.

11 December 11: Two of our motorcycle messengers stop by, telling me that our supply column now is at Cirene. This means we have retreated further.

At 3 PM the Führer spoke over the radio. We have declared war on the USA. The carrier USS *Saratoga* is reported sunk in the Pacific.

12 December: Back to my unit finally. I arrive at 3 PM and find it camping in a wadi. Twelve men are reported KIA and 6 missing. We sleep in a cave full of lice and other vermin but otherwise it's quiet right now. Our driver can switch the radio on so we hear the news from the Far East. The American ship *Arizona* has been sunk and our Japanese allies now occupy Burma. Some mail arrives by motorcycle messenger. We're on alert to retreat to the west on short notice.

18 December: We depart this inhospitable place. Our target is 25 miles west of El Agheila, our old hunting grounds from last March. Eight of the men ride on the water carrier tank wagon, but a flat tire soon stops us. We stay overnight in a Casa along the road; much retreating traffic on the highway.

19 December: At 7 AM we are off and catch up with our group near Benghazi where they have stopped for a gasoline delivery. Nothing comes, so we try to scrounge gas ourselves. Meanwhile, Derna has been cleared by us. We just can't move on this totally blocked highway, so we stay overnight.

20 December: At 7 AM we get gas and try to reach the rest of our group that is a few miles west of Agadabia. At Agadabia the 90th Light Division has put up a defensive front but we drive further west anyway, until we reach a point 26 miles west of El Agheila. We set up a tent camp. The Führer speaks to us via radio. The next day we hear a speech on the radio from General Field Marshal von Brauchitsch. Since we are near the sea we take refreshing baths. There is fighting east of Benghazi now; British planes are constantly in the vicinity.

24 December: Christmas Eve but there is not much to remind us of Christmas. We sing "Holy Night Silent Night" and British bombers drop a few presents near our position.

25 December: We are divided into groups and assigned to other units, so we board trucks that take us 70 miles west of El Agheila. We arrive there on the 27th. We are being held in reserve right now. It is cold and wet so the new tents we receive have sun roofs of course. Where the Hell is the sun?

28 December: Our orders have been changed. We are moving back to our old unit; we even have to give the new equipment back. We sleep with the supply convoy and are supposed to be moved further west in a few days.

31 December: There are too many men without transport so 700 of us will be taken by 8 trucks to Tripoli for a work detail. We celebrate the New Year without a drop to drink.

Time to read a newspaper and get out of the heat.

Manning a PaK (anti-tank gun).

A captured British Bren Gun carrier.

Chapter 3

_____

CHASE AND BEING CHASED THROUGH THE DESERT, 1942

_____

1 January, 1942: At 7 AM we are off for Tripoli, reach Camp 5 and buy several crates of beer to celebrate a late new year.

We are detailed now as a Work Command, loading trucks, shoveling sand, clearing roads and such. News on 4 Jan tells us that Bardia has been captured by the British. We have dinner in the harbor on an Italian freighter. The Führer gives his New Year's speech to the troops via radio.

9 January: We unload supplies in the harbor day in and day out. In the evenings we watch movies in a warehouse; meals are taken on the ships we unload. At least the ships have warm showers that we are allowed to use.

10 January: We spend several days filling 5-gallon cans with gasoline for the front. The rumors that we are supposed to go to the front are not true. On the 13th we're back in camp to service our 55mm PaK and our Pumas – but we're still in Tripoli. On 22 January we are informed that finally our forces will counterattack in the Cyreneica desert. This attack was successful and the Tommies were beaten back to Agadabia. The duty goes on day by day, haircut in Tripoli, beer in bars at night, and work by day. On 9 February we hear of the death of Dr. Fritz Todt. The next day we visit the de-lousing station. A Yugoslavian destroyer enters the harbor.

12 February: We have an inspection by the Military Police who find that 8 men have taken things from ships during our work detail.

I am now in charge of 300 men.

14 February: One year in North Africa. Today our Company of the 33d Reconnaissance has a free day. We stroll through the harbor area and see a new Bloom & Voss 6-engine sea plane at anchor. It's a day for celebrations and we continue in camp. Later we hear news on the radio that the *Scharnhost, Gneisenau* and *Prince Eugen* broke through the British blockade and are back in Germany now. The weather is stormy. We even have a tornado that rips 2 roofs off hangars.

23 February 23: I meet Lt. Peters in town and he tells me that my old Battle Group has demanded my return. He tells me that Eric has been awarded the Italian Front medal. Several of our trucks have been lost to enemy bombing and Pvt. Rost was KIA. Lt. Napp has returned to the group.

I hope now to get back to my old outfit.

24 February: Yes, it's true; I am going back to the front. I leave at 10 AM and travel to a rest area near Tagiara, then via trucks to Misurata. It's 500 miles to the front so it will be a long drive through the desert. On 26 February we reach a point 40 miles west of Benghazi. I have a nasty cold.

28 February: In Benghazi we are reorganized into companies. My unit receives three 50mm PaK's, three 37mm PaK's, two British 6-wheeled armored cars, and a compliment of Motorcycle Infantry. Because I still suffer from a bad cold, I have to see the medic and have to go to the Field Hospital to rest. I stay there until 2 March.

3 March: At 8 AM I leave the hospital and set off on a truck. Traveling eastward, we reach a point 120 miles from Derna. On 4 March we see a signpost directing us to our battle group, and finally get there at 3 PM. We are roundly welcomed. Eric is going home to Germany on leave. I get a surprise in the evening; Major General [Georg] von Bismarck, our Divisional Commander arrives and talks to me.

5 March: It rains all day; everything is flooded out, but in the evening I go for a visit to the so called "GPU Cellar," a cave 200 meters underground with a nice bar and good beer.

6 March: Now I'm back and so is my cold, this time with a headache. I go to see the medic and I'm relieved of duty to cure my cold. On the 9th we hear tales that we are moving out soon. My cold is no better so an ambulance takes me to the Derna Field Hospital. I am sent from there by truck to Benghazi Hospital but my illness gets worse so I am put aboard a Ju-52 to the Base Hospital in Tripoli. I arrive there at 9 PM and I am admitted to the same room I had in October last year. According to the doctor I suffer from Trigenies Neuralgie [Trigeminal Neuralgia]. A new female nurse tends our ward; Suzi is her name.

During the next days I am X-rayed, examined by several doctors, take pills and medicines, but the headache is still very bad. For several days my head is treated with short wave radiation and by the 25th the pain is abating. I visit our Division Priest, Herr Heichen, and talk to him for an hour. One day, I think on the 29th, I lose consciousness and get a 4-day rest from the radiation treatment.

1 April: Still in the Tripoli Base Hospital but I expect to be fit in a day or so. I feel much better by the 4th. I report to the Wehrmacht Office in Tripoli to return for duty, visit the old friends from the work detail in the harbor, but stay for Easter in Tripoli with the work commando and visit Suzi in the Ward. She surprises me with 4 Easter eggs. I'm still in Tripoli on 8 April. From the Wehrmacht Office I hear that our group now is south of Timini. My last day in Tripoli is 13 April.

14 April: At 5 AM I board a truck and go in a convoy to Tanagra. The next day we have a heavy ghibli, but we manage to drive to a point 50 miles from Nufeila. On the 16th the ghibli is still raging as we set out for El Agheila, 40 miles west of Agenais.

17 April: We are now 13 miles east of our old town of Benghazi and continue to Derna. Here we call a halt; we are supposed to be reinforcements for the 21st Panzer Division. We finally find the division assembly area south of Termini.

20 April: I report to Division HQ and the first person I meet is ex-Lt. Napp, who has been promoted to Colonel and is a Staff Officer of General von Bismarck, who is now commanding the 21st Panzer Division. We shake hands and exchange wishes of good luck.

21 April: We wonder about the usual birthday speech by our Führer; nothing was mentioned about it last night. We get 2 days of new training in such things as, "how to overcome desert fatigue," as if we old African hands didn't know how to do that already.

New companies are formed; 3 heavy machine gun units to each company. On 24 April the companies report to the medics for check ups. We all suffer from stomach problems. It's the bad unclean food and the drinking water, combined with the lice and sand fleas.

26 April: Six days after the 20th we hear the Führer's birthday speech. We get our new sun roof tents back and its great fun setting them up.

29 April: We have an inspection tour of the division by General von Bismarck. We are training on our new anti-tank guns. On 4 May we read about Lt. Napp's promotion to Colonel.

6 May: At 6 AM we fall in line for details. Our company has 10 officers, 10 NCO's and 30 of lower ranks. We form 2 anti-tank platoons, 1 Pioneer platoon, and 1 Flak platoon with 2 Quads (20mm). We also receive 4 NSU tracked motorcycles plus a vintage French 25mm PaK. The next day we do training with the NSU's and Quads; still in training on 10 May. On 11 May we get 2 more Officers and 75 more men so we are full strength again.

14 May: We move to a wadi 2 miles from base; very hot today and lots of British air activity on the 15th and 16th. For several days we will train our newcomers on the weapons. Finally we move near the Derna airport after giving all our surplus items to the Quartermaster for keeping.

26 May: Today I get a lift into Derna to do some shopping and end up being cheated out of 400 lira by a filthy Jew or Arab; I don't see much difference in them myself. I report him to the Military Police and they take him in. From the front we hear that the Africa Corps is attacking Tobruk (again, like last year). Lt. Eigenbauer and several men are sent to Benghazi to fetch 2 more NSU tracked motorcycles. We get some news from Russia on the radio. Our forces have taken Charkov along with 165,000 POW's.

1 June: Today we received 8, yes 8, brand new NSU Ketten motorcycles, and we are supposed to get more. Our company is almost ready to move up, but bad news reaches us on the 2nd; our major was wounded during a fighter-bomber attack. But nevertheless, so far the Africa Corps has taken 2000 POW's, destroyed 350 tanks and 53 artillery pieces. Ten of our men are taking a truck to the front line to collect captured machine guns and rifles.

5 June: A sad day; a messenger from the line brought the news that Willi Orcher was KIA, so now I'm the only one left from our old group that fought in France. We regroup and I become leader of the 1st Machine Gun Platoon and continue my training. At Derna fighter base there is a lot of activity with Me-109's, Stukas, and Ju-88's.

11 June: We hear that our new guns have arrived in Benghazi. So far, we have 4 KIA and 27 wounded at the front.

13 June: We take our trucks and Pumas to Benghazi to fetch our new guns; some are the long-barrel ones with folding shields, a new suspension and synthetic rubber tires. On the 15th news from the front: the British Gazala garrison is surrounded. We are training on the new guns. We write a letter to the Führer thanking him for the new NSU tracked motorcycles. We go swimming in the sea near Derna. Up at the front, our battle group is fighting south of Tobruk while we build sand castles here in Derna.

19 June: Tobruk is now surrounded; 4 men have been wounded at the front. We have been assigned a new Field Post number: 42339.

Tobruk has been taken again by us. Our company now has 12 anti-tank guns. On the 25th we hear that we have retaken all the positions we lost last year: Halfaya, Sollum, Capuzzo, and Sidi Barani.

27 June: At last we are receiving ammunition. Could it be that we are moving up to the front? We hear now that our troops and the Italians are south of Mersa Matruh.

29 June: Our forces are now well into Egypt and we took Mersa Matruh today, capturing 6000 British, Australian and New Zealand troops, and even Indians and French Legionnaires. We are getting ready to move out, and by 1 July all is packed and loaded. We even built a few small trailers to hitch up to the NSU motorcycles. We will be quite a caravan once we get going.

3 July: We get a wake-up call at 4 AM. We move out and about 6 miles from Tobruk we reach the harbor area; lots of traffic as we get nearer. The harbor is littered with sunken freighters. We pick up one more 37mm cannon from a Wehrmacht arsenal and stay overnight in Tobruk. The next morning we move to Bardia, then on past Sollum, Capuzzo, Halfaya Pass, Sidi Barani, and stop 8 miles east of Mersa Matruh. Past Sidi Barani the roads are better. This is Egypt, not Libya. We have had no air alerts so far.

6 July: A 5 AM wake-up call and we move out at 6:30 AM via El Daba. 18 miles east of El Daba, the left suspension of the Puma breaks, but we can't stop. We got lost somehow and can't find our main group. We end up right at the front line and turn back for 12 miles and set up camp for the night. Soon our sleep comes to an end; enemy bombers spotted us with the help of parachute flares. They drop bombs all around us and onto the main highway. This circus goes on for 4 hours until daylight when the Tommies fly home. We finally find our group on the 7th, near the coast, unhitch our guns and settle down for a meal and a swim in the sea.

9 July: We move out at 7 AM, south toward the front. On 10 July we meet up with 33d Panzer Battalion, but the enemy plasters us with artillery before we can find a suitable position, so we seek shelter in a wadi. At mid-day enemy fighter-bombers join the fray and damage one of our cannons. We move to a deeper wadi and wait for daylight.

11 July: We're stuck in this wadi and can't even stick our noses out. A messenger arrives on a motorcycle, warning us that the enemy has broken through our lines north of us at El Alamein and that our troops will try to contain the breakthrough. We dig in and during the night a truck with supplies arrives.

12 July: We change position to the north and draw fire from concealed enemy light artillery. Just before 3 PM, General Rommel arrives right at the front line. His armored car stops beside the main highway and immediately comes under enemy PaK fire, and then heavier artillery joins in. The British must have an observer somewhere near us. Like a young boy, General Rommel jumps from one hole into the next, then crouches behind a PaK shield, looks with his binoculars, shouts orders and even directs a PaK to fire on an enemy tank in the distance. He even helps the crew pull the gun around. My group, being a heavy machine gun company, takes on enemy infantry walking behind oncoming tanks.

Just before dark, the General mounts an NSU and drives to the south, his armored car shot to bits by British tank gunners. The enemy mysteriously disappears in the smoke and dust and we move forward for about 2 miles. We settle in a wadi but we are still under sporadic artillery fire; no serious casualties occur.

13 July: All day we stay in the wadi and take much artillery fire and attacks by fighter-bombers but we see no enemy tanks. After mid-day the artillery fire eases up and increases to the south of us. Over the radio we are ordered to the south to join Battle Group Rommel. This sounds rather suspicious. Is this an enemy trap? We contact the battle group a few minutes later and they confirm the order. We shake our heads; a battle group is normally commanded by a 1st Lieutenant or maybe a Colonel. Now we have one under the command of a General!

We join Battle Group Rommel at 6 PM and are told that 1st Lt. Kiehl, the battle group leader was wounded and that the general just happened to be there at the time and immediately took temporary command of the group. We're in a narrow wadi and well sheltered for the time being. The artillery fire has moved to the north and west. The General decides to stay overnight and told us not to use the radio because that would alert the enemy, who listens in on our radio traffic. In a cave we brew some coffee. The General reads some of my diary and signs the front page. He and an aid sleep in the cave with us.

14 July: We move out at daybreak to our former position. General Rommel departs to the rear on a supply truck. At noon we are under heavy fire. A 76mm shell explodes near my hole and I receive another small shrapnel wound to my left ear. The artillery fire dies down a bit, but by 6 PM it starts all over again. We suffer a direct hit on one of our guns; Sgt. Wilbezon is killed immediately and Pvt. Frohn is wounded. The next round explodes by the trucks and disables two vehicles and wounds Lehmann, the driver. We move out of this unhealthy place to the south; heavy artillery fire on us but we manage to seal a gap in the front where the enemy broke through and surrounded one of our Pioneer battalions. We take 200 enemy POW's and rescue the Pioneers.

17 July: Yesterday we stayed all day under cover in the wadi, drawing light artillery fire, but today we are moving up to attack. Sgt. Hester has been severely wounded. Later I'm ordered to General Rommel's HQ to take over as temporary messenger so that we can stay in contact with an Italian division. I am told that this division lost 30 percent of its strength in the last enemy breakthrough. I am relieved as messenger in the evening and make my way back to my unit under heavy fire.

18 July: At 4:30 AM we are under fire once again. At 11 AM General Rommel arrives, and he and Major Eberle go on a reconnaissance patrol. When they return, we are ordered to move south along the telegraph road to the Taqua Plateau; no enemy activity. The next day, fighter-bomber attacks but we have no casualties. We move to the eastern end of the plateau to cover a Pioneer company that is on a mine laying detail.

20 July: We're still guarding the Pioneers, who are extending the mine field well into our front. By 7 PM the Pioneers are done and we all return to base camp. As soon as we arrive at camp, an enemy patrol vehicle runs into the field creating lots of fireworks.

21 July: We are still guarding the mine laying Pioneers. At 6 PM an accident occurs.

During fuse setting, a Pioneer sets off a mine and 60 of the devices explode, killing 9 Pioneers and 3 men of my company; several more are wounded. We have to leave the dead and retreat to the wadi.

22 July: Early in the morning the Pioneers recover the dead. We guard the recovery but are attacked by enemy infantry. We reply with Puma fire. They fire on us with AT guns and one Puma sustains a direct hit; Sgts. Riba and Rössler are both wounded. Sgt. Riba loses a leg. I attend to Riba and drive him hellbent to the field aid station. On my return we stage a counterattack, pushing the enemy off the plateau that has cost us many casualties. Another Puma gets hit by AT fire; one of my old comrades, Heinz Pahn, is KIA.

23 July: Things are quiet today. We receive water and ammunition and form a security screen on the plateau with AT guns and 2d and 3d Companies. Because of my constantly re-occurring tropical skin boils, I drive to the Field Hospital for treatment. Its 20 miles east of Daba near the railroad line from Kairo to Mersa Matruh. On the 26th I get my wounds and my skin boils treated and stay there until 3 Aug, assigned to indoor duty.

3 August: I get a truck and driver to fetch supplies from the 90th Division depot, but the truck breaks down. Next day I get a converted water carrier truck to take us 10 miles east of Marsa Matruh, but this time the steering column king pin breaks and there is no replacement. It's too dangerous to drive this wreck so I tromp back on foot for a replacement truck; no deal. The only other truck has a broken clutch. Ssgt. Kurz of the depot radios our battle group to send transport for me.

6 August: My replacement truck shows up finally and we set off for

Palling around in Mersa Matruh. Note the solemn fellow in foreground wearing a British helmet.

Mersa Matruh. Five miles down the road, the truck with the broken clutch catches up with us and stays with us. How does the driver manage???

7 August: We stopped for the night last night and slept in the back of the truck. This morning the clutch-troubled truck shows up again. This time I have had enough and order him back. I hope he makes it. There are enemy patrols in the area driving fast Austin Jeeps.

8 August: In the morning a NAG rescue truck arrives. We load one broken truck on the back of the recovery truck. My own vehicle, with 2 flat tires, gets hitched to the back. What a sight this must be to see on the highway; a German Büssing NAG truck, loaded with an English Scammel truck, towing an Italian Fiat Jeep. We do however finally reach our own battle group supply depot. I bet the General would love to have seen that convoy.

9 August: Two companies of our battle group arrive at the depot to search for enemy patrols. We move all of our supply trucks to Daba near the seashore. On the 10th we receive an urgent radio message instructing all units to return to their original position. WHY??? Orders are orders, so we move out to Mersa Matruh near the coast and are assigned to the Coastal Command. We don't understand; we're Army, not Navy.

12 August: We're under Coastal Command, but on the 13th, we move the main part of the group toward Sollum. I have to go ahead to the field aid station for bandages for my hand. Here I meet up with my friend Eric Wolff again, who has just returned from leave in Germany. I stay at the aid station on the 14th. My left hand has blood poisoning and goes into a sling; next day it's the other hand and I stay at the aid station until the 18th.

18 August: I return fit for duty, but I have to stay here in Sollum to wait for the arrival of my unit, which is searching for enemy long range desert patrols. They arrive on the 19th and we have a day of rest for the group.

20 August: We listen to news from home on the radio about the British landing attempt at Dieppe ["Operation Jubilee"]. Companies are being reorganized today. My job is to protect the Pioneer battalion. A few shots are fired on an enemy patrol by the shore.

21 August: At 5.30 AM we depart for Daba and reach the Moshee. We call a halt at 3 PM.

22 August: We're up and ready at 6 AM and move out to the El Taqua Plateau, but our truck gives up with an ignition problem. We try to push it but can't. We hitch up to another truck and advance just 3 miles when the wheel bearings run hot and seize. Luckily, we find an Italian unit to stay with for the rest of the night. It seems our vehicle problems are reaching a dangerous level.

23 August: In the morning an 88mm flak battery rolls by that is looking for our battle group and gives us a lift. We reach the group at 9 AM. No one bothers about our truck we had to leave behind.

Bomber attacks and sporadic artillery fire, but we have no casualties. On the 25th I'm taken back to where we left the truck. It's still there plus the gun. We find a British Commer truck and mount the gun on the back and return to our position. Nothing happens in the next few days, apart from the familiar enemy air raids. We are detailed to stake out a passage through a mine belt. At night we have the normal [British] artillery fire. On the 29th we watch a dogfight above us between our Me-109s and enemy fighters. Our flak joins in the fight and downs 2 planes. Rumors about a new attack are coming in.

30 August: At 3 PM there is a conference at General Rommel's forward HQ regarding the new attack. The General suggests a southern pincer movement to take El Alamein from the rear, then, once it is taken, we are to direct an assault toward Alexandria and Kairo [Cairo], 60 miles away along the coastal highway. My reconnaissance unit is on the right flank. The General's orders must be followed to the letter if we are to achieve success. We have very little gasoline to mess about in detours, and food is low too. We are living on enemy rations we captured.

At 7 PM we set out toward the east. Pioneers clear a passage through our own mine belt, then we go in convoy; 48 vehicles and gun carriers. We reach an enemy mine field and have to stop and wait for it to be cleared. Immediately the British open up on us, one truck bursts into flames, wounding the driver severely.

31 August: At daybreak we get through the first mine belt but at the second and third belt a traffic jam occurs. We draw heavy gunfire from enemy armored cars but we get through and pull 4 of our Panzer IVs with 75mm guns forward. The enemy retreats to the east. We stop in a wadi for the night. Eight hours of bombing during the night by 4-engined American bombers. About 2000 bombs fall in our vicinity. We have 3 men KIA, several wounded and we lose 3 guns from a battery of 4.

1 September: We move to the Djebel Rim for better cover and repair a radiator. We watched a single Me-109 shoot down 6 enemy bombers. We get bombed and shelled again at night but we have good cover now.

2 September: Sitting around here and wondering what the Hell is going on; surely along the coastal road things are going better. A water tanker arrives with 300 gallons of water while artillery fires on us. In the late afternoon we get orders to move out. After 5 miles the orders are rescinded because we don't have enough gasoline, so we do a 180 degree about turn and head back to our original position. I am assigned to guard the mine belt and keep the passage open for our retreating Army; day and night we have heavy air raids.

3 September: At daybreak we retreat back to the first enemy mine belt. The Pioneers are having trouble keeping a passage open; air raids with air torpedoes, really heavy stuff delivered by enemy artillery.

4 September: We stay behind and use the mine belt as a security screen. The enemy works us over with machine gun fire, artillery and PaK. A truck is hit and burns out, but no one is hurt. We have 6 Pumas guarding the belt and enemy night fighters above, but no attacks. Bad news reaches us from HQ. Our Commanding Divisional General, Georg von Bismarck, was killed in action a few days ago. Because of our own trouble, we had not heard the news until now. There is some good news too. Jochen Marseille [known as the "Star of Africa"] shot down 17 enemy aircraft on 1 September and his score now stands at 125. Hopefully, our 6 days of racing around in the desert has come to an end.

6 September: We stay put until 11 AM, then move for better protection to a small wadi a mile or so to the west. I quickly make a drawing of our position and leave to find a supply truck. Maybe the map is good enough for him to follow. Sgt. Eichorn goes with me as he has a bad tooth that needs to be seen to.

7 September: Have to see the doctor to get him to look at a bad boil on my lip. He treats me and I return to my unit. We lay low here until 12 Sept.

13 September: We are guarding the Pioneers who are mine laying today. Mail came from home today too. We have several air raids; Willy lost a leg, but we quickly got him to the medic so he might be okay. We leave here on the 14th headed toward Daba, along the coastal road and stop near Daba for the night.

16 September: By 6 AM we are on the road, in the direction of Oasis Siwah and when we reach Mersa Matruh we refuel our tanks, then head south. The road is in good shape. We stop near Siwah for the night.

Today is my 24th birthday. The next day at 6 AM, we are off again; we traverse the Quatarra Depression that is below sea level. At 5 PM we reach the first mine belt of Siwah. We get through the passage and stop south of Siwah in a palm grove.

18 September: We are near Siwah, eating dates and lemons and listening to radio news from home. We clean ourselves up as best we can and repair weapons. We are told on the 19th that General Rommel is coming for an inspection tour.

21 September: At 6 AM we're dressed and trying to clean up the place. At 11 AM, two Fiesler Storks land and 3 Stukas afterwards. Several other generals are with Rommel; we give them a precise salute. The Marshal surely is impressed with our accomplishments and talks to us for some time. At 1 PM it's time for them to take off. To show his appreciation, he orders the 3 Stukas to dive on our position with blaring sirens as a farewell greeting. We were even filmed by a camera crew. I would like to see that clip some day.

22 September: Today here in Siwa we are given instructions by the Pioneers on how to avoid, defuse, and find mines. Later we build a wooden shelter for the supply truck; it's very hot today. I hear a rumor that those who have been in Africa more than 12 months are going to be sent home.

23 September: We're still in Siwa the 24th and 25th. On the 26th we have a weapons inspection by the Regimental Commander. I have to write a letter home, its Dad's birthday tomorrow; he will be 59. On 28 September I apply for leave; whether it will be granted is another matter. On the 30th a parcel arrived from home. We are getting a new battalion commander today, Major [Hans-Ulrich] von Luck [und Witten]. On 1 Oct. I take the Staff Sergeant to Siwa market to buy fruit for the company. Adolf Hitler speaks to us over the radio at 3 PM. Marshal Rommel is in Berlin too, so we are told.

3 October: After morning inspection we are told that all those that have been in Africa since February 1941 will be relieved. Question: relieved for other duty – or sent home on leave?? No one has any answers. The next day, 4 Oct., all we hear is Göring's speech over the radio. Bernhard M. gets promoted to 1st Lieutenant. No other news, so we go for a swim in the sea.

8 October: The War Merit cross is awarded to Sgt. Geiger. I'm not feeling well; fever and shakes, so I go to see the doctor in Siwa. He says I have another cold. 1st Lt. Becker is off to Germany on leave and I get a few days official recovery in bed. I miss the visit of our Commanding Panzer General, Stumme, who took over after General

The diary's author, Rolf Krengel, with comrades in the desert (above)
and at an oasis (below).

von Bismarck was KIA. I'm feeling better on the 17th but stay in bed until the 20th.

20 October: I'm fit for duty, so I organize a machine gun shooting competition and we come in second. We also do a night march and cover 5 miles in 1 hour 28 minutes with full gear. The prize? A bar of chocolate.

Kurt Schulte gets promoted to Lieutenant and takes over 2d Company, including the Pioneer platoon.

October 24th: I hear rumors that I will finally be granted home leave. Will I????

26 October: At 5 AM we are getting ready to move out of Siwa and by 11 AM we are on the road to Mersa Matruh. We march all night. The suspension breaks on one of the Pumas. News comes in that the British have started another big drive at El Alamein. My leave, if it ever existed, is obviously cancelled now. We reach Mersa Matruh but march on to Darba and dig in by the sea to repel any attempted seaborne landing by the enemy.

28 October: We wake up because of a huge explosion. We are told later that one of our ammunition trains was blown up by saboteurs.

To date, the Africa Corps has destroyed 306 enemy tanks since March last year.

We have a ghibli on the 29th, so we can't do anything. Everyone looks for shelter in a sand storm.

We hear today that our most successful fighter pilot, Jochen Marseille, has died in a plane accident. [Marseille's plane went down near Abdel Rahman, 30 km west of El Alamein.] I think his total tally was 128 enemy planes shot down.

We adjust all the sights on our cannons. The heat distorts the alignment. A new Staff Sergeant arrives to take over a Pioneer Company; his name is Böhme.

2 November: There are a few attempts by enemy patrols to penetrate our lines, but they are repulsed. We can't do much patrolling because our gas tanks are half empty and we would need that gas in an emergency. At 5 AM we're ordered to move to an army reserve assembly point, near the sea. We watch a sea battle between 4 enemy corvettes and an Italian cruiser and a destroyer. All 4 enemy vessels were sunk and we took 100 sailors POW.

3 November: Another alert. We drive to El Darba along the Telegraph Road, which is littered with destroyed equipment and vehicles. We come under fighter attack but our Flak shoots down 2 Hurricanes. We break through to the 164th Infantry Division and get the men out of a pocket.

5 November: The 164th will stay with us until transport is found to take them back; then we will move out toward the west. We have radiator problems and try to repair it ourselves but it's no good, so we blow up the truck and try to catch up with rest of our battle group.

6 November: Heavy rain hampers further progress and we only have one truck left. The others are with the main group that we have not caught up with yet. During the night our one truck gets stuck in deep mud. We throw everything off but it doesn't help, so we throw a hand grenade into it to render it useless to the pursuing enemy. We're on foot now, marching 12 miles through heavy rain. It's everyone for himself now. A private and I stop an ambulance going west and hitch a ride so we can search for our battle group. On the 7th we make it to Bardia, no luck, so we go on to Tobruk. When we arrive, we thank the ambulance driver and report to the Wehrmacht HQ there.

8 November: During the wait outside the HQ I see a low loader truck and 3 NSU's with our regimental markings headed for the front. I jump aboard and we reach a point 10 miles west of Bardia to stay overnight.

9 November: I found our group at Mile Post #9. They have been here since 4 November searching for us. We move out toward Tobruk with me driving an NSU. The Coastal Road is a mess of hold-ups and abandoned vehicles. I found out that, since the attack on El Alamein by the enemy, we're in a headlong retreat west. On November 11th we are on the road south of the city, moving in a westerly direction on the Via della Asse Highway. Twelve miles down the road, the NSU breaks down. Pvt. Kruger and I get aboard the other NSU. A passing truck has a rope which we use to pull the broken NSU. We can't keep up with the others. Later we sleep in the open by the roadside.

12 November: We headed toward Derna and finally caught up with one of our trucks. We all slept on the back of it last night; constantly in fear of the fighter-bombers that circle above, searching for easy pickings. Today we continue along the road and come upon a burning supply truck. We manage to rescue cigarettes and rations from it before we blow it to bits. On the 14th we reach Derna and find gasoline to refuel, meet up with part of the group, and continue to Berta before calling a halt.

15 November: During the night the rear guard blew up the main road behind us. We are dangerously close to the enemy who is following at top speed. We can't seem to be able to get out of this jam. We are hemmed in by our own retreating 90th Division. On the 16th it rains and the going is hard. We pick up 4 guys from the 361st Infantry Regiment, then stop in Driana east of Benghazi and get drunk for a change. The 4 guys from the 361st had 12 bottles of wine in their haversacks.

16 November: Drive to Benghazi quartermaster store for new uniforms and rations; weather is bad, lots of rain. We drive on past the airfield of Bunia and stop for the night in a lousy Arab shack; next morning we move on toward Agadabia. On the highway, we are mixed in with the 21st Panzer Division. In the afternoon our PaK that we have been towing breaks down, no repair is possible so we smash the breach block to make the gun useless. We reach Agadabia and stop at a lone farm house.

20 November: We are near Mersa El Brega and stop in a Palm grove at a water hole (oasis), occupied by Italian Pioneers, to stay overnight. Being a nice day on the 21st, we stay an extra day to wash and eat good Italian food. On the 22d we reach El Agheila but cannot get any food so we carry on, ending up in the middle of a retreating column. Finally on the 23d we catch up with our unit and set up camp. We find out that Lt. Bachalle was KIA a few days earlier. I go to see the medic for new bandages for my boils on the 23d. The next day we move 6 miles west of Arco. We have no bread, a small can of water, and there is no depot anywhere near here to get anything.

28 November: At 8 AM we are off to the west and go 24 miles to Buerat [Libya] and refuel. In the town of Sirte, we fetch water for radiators, and find some cigarettes and even a tube of toothpaste. On the 29th we have a flat front left tire so we drag behind the group and lose sight of them. The tire eventually comes off completely so we drive on the metal rim, but reach our group at 6 PM near Stours, where we get new tires.

30 November: Today finds us near Tripoli with another flat tire. The roads are just stone and dirt. Twelve miles west of Tripoli we come upon a new Panzer Division in a rest area. We go to the motor pool in Tripoli and get a new truck, plus 5 new 1-ton Ford trucks. We still have our NSU's and we are issued, for the first time, the 75mm long barrel PaK.

We stay in Tripoli for de-lousing and a decent bath. When I get back to the unit, two brand new Pumas with 37mm cannons are parked in the yard – yes, they are ours, just issued to us. I take over command of one of them.

5 December: Today we lost one of the older Pumas. Somehow it caught on fire during refueling and burned to the ground. We are cleaning guns today and servicing the breaches; nothing is going on here. We stay in Tripoli until 22 December, servicing the guns and Pumas, going to the Wehrmacht movie house, and swimming in the harbor. I was sick a few days with a stomach ailment.

22 December: We moved out during the night to Misurata, along the Via Balbia once again because the enemy is closing up on us. We send out patrols under 1st Lt. Reinhold, but no enemy contact. We are near

Sedada at a small air strip and will shelter here for the night and stay here tomorrow until we find a wadi to celebrate Christmas in.

24 December: We are well sheltered here for Christmas. We get a few presents and mail. Each soldier receives a half bottle of brandy, a half bottle of sweet brandy, 3 gingerbread men, chocolate, and 50 cigarettes. We celebrate inside the Puma; it is quite comfortable in here.

25 December: Marshal Rommel lands in his Stork – Christmas greetings all round until 2 PM, when we move out to Buni 18 miles west and set up camp with a defensive screen. On the 26th, we're still here but we have now set up four more 75mm AT guns. The British are not far off to the east but leave us alone. We stay until 31 Dec., patrolling and doing reconnaissance with the Pumas. Pioneers lay mine belts up front. On the 30th our patrol goes a full 12 miles to the east but finds no enemy.

31 December: Our battle group is assembled and we celebrate New Year's Eve. Our last Puma arrives as well so we are a complete battle group now.

1 January, 1943: We don't get up until 9 AM and I drive to the supply depot to get them to bring us gasoline and ammunition. I also have to pick up 5 British POW's. I talked for 3 hours with the 1st Lt. at the depot. We are staying in camp Fatma for now, bringing our guns and Pumas up to date. We are not far from the British lines. On one patrol we surprise an enemy desert patrol that soon retreats after a few shots from our Pumas.

We keep guard over the Pioneers engaged in mine belt laying and build a few dummy guns to deceive the enemy reconnaissance planes. Occasionally enemy long range artillery plasters us with a few rounds. On 11 January we finally get our Christmas goose, three weeks overdue. We also got some bad news regarding our fuel supply. We heard that 16 tankers were sunk off Tripoli by enemy aircraft operating out of Malta.

13 January: We are ordered to accompany a panzer battalion in an attack on the British held position of Fort Fortino, but the order is cancelled shortly afterward.

15 January: At 7 AM all Hell broke loose; a surprise heavy attack with tanks by the enemy on our positions. We opened fire with 50mm and 75mm guns. Our Pumas guard our eventual retreat over the pass.

8:30 AM: there are several enemy tanks in front of our position; these are U.S. General Grant tanks and take a lot of punishment. I fire 15 rounds and the first Grant explodes but the others keep coming. Our orders are to stay put, no retreat. We go back 300 meters and engage the two other Grants. We score nine hits but they still keep coming. One of our Pumas is hit. SSgt. Böhme was killed, shot in the neck. Herbert Gröger was killed as he attempted to jump out of the turret hatch of the Puma he was in. The Puma is wrecked – two 40mm AT shells went straight in it and exploded. 1st Lt. Wille is wounded badly. A Kubelwagen comes up and takes him then races off to the rear. I escape with 5 nasty cuts from shrapnel. Now we are executing a fighting retreat. We cannot hold out but our 75mm PaK gives us time to get through the pass. The firing stopped once we got through.

I received a morphine injection from a medic then a field ambulance picked me up and took me for treatment to Fascia Field Hospital. Here Field Marshall Rommel sees me and congratulates me on the Grant killing, plus 15 other hits on enemy tanks. He said they were confirmed by 1st Lt. Wille who is also in the same hospital, badly wounded but not in immediate danger. I demand to return to my unit as I seem, to myself anyway, to be fit. The request is granted just as the morphine takes effect and I sort of fall into a half sleep.

16 January: I report back to my unit; a new replacement for 1st Lt. Wille is already there, a 1st Lt. Quandt. Since I am not in perfectly fit condition, I sit and ride in the back of the ammunition halftrack. Confirmation of the destroyed tank is given to me by the Group Commander. Again the British artillery fires at us and we retreat via Sedala to Benimidi, marching at night to avoid enemy fighter-bombers.

17 January: We retreat further but stop at several passes to hold back the enemy who is pursuing us relentlessly. Just before we reach Benimidi, one of our 75mm PaK's and the mobile flak on the HT run into one of our unguarded mine belts. No casualties, but the equipment is wrecked. We dash through Benimidi. I am suffering from terrible bowel cramps because of the morphine injections.

18 January: The road is very bad but we reach Tahuma. We see a lot of retreating traffic here as we march on to a point 6 miles east of Tahuma. The next morning we retreat to Castel Benito, south of Tripoli, with enemy aircraft attacking. There was one U.S. Tomahawk shot down by a lone Me-109. We arrive in Azizia on the 20th. The shrapnel wound in my leg is hurting so I am ordered back to the supply column and then on to the hospital for new bandages. I then return with a Panzer to our Battle Group. I sleep inside the tank. The roads are all one big traffic jam. Some of our group has left toward the west. I follow their route the next morning in a Puma to Zuara, about 60 km from the Tunisian border. A radio operator tries his best to make contact with my group but all he knows is that they were going to Gabes, west of the border.

I stay here all day; several attacks by U.S. and British aircraft. By the 23d I have rejoined my group and we cross the border. The jeep breaks down with engine problems. We hitch the thing to a Puma and reach a palm grove late afternoon. We are lucky because we have the radio in the jeep. We hear on the radio that our forces in Stalingrad are surrounded.

25 January: I have been at a field ambulance station for treatment of my shrapnel wounds then I was transferred to Staff Hospital. Two other men of my group are there. We receive flour, sugar, and eggs so we cook on our little gasoline stoves all day in the hospital tent. My leg is swollen and I cannot walk much. By the next day the swelling had gone down considerably.

30 January: Today is the 10th anniversary of the founding of the 3d Reich. We make omelets as the radio broadcasts Hermann Göring's sad speech about the Stalingrad situation. Later we listen to a proclamation by Dr, Göbbels. I stay in the hospital for treatment of my injuries until 5 February and leave the aid station at 5:00 PM and return to my unit.

6 February: Several of our men who had been captured by the enemy at Siwab and managed to escape from a POW camp return to the unit. I am staying in camp with the unit. There is no enemy activity except the normal air attacks with Stirling bombers and U.S. fighters. I received my second soldbuch and visit Eric Wolff in 2d Company. On the 13th my bandages are coming off.

14 February: Two years today I have been in Africa. At 1:00 we have an inspection and congratulations go all around to the "Old Africans" as they call us now. A small celebration is in order for tonight.

17 February: Nothing is going on so I made myself a nice metal badge of a Puma with AA-3 scratched on it [3d Panzer Reconnaissance Platoon]. On the 18th, two of our Pumas returned from the front line and on the 19th I returned to full-time duty.

20 February: The returning unit that was at the front has lost 3 men. Sgt. Rosenfeld was killed in action and Pvt's. Loechner and Lengaiker were wounded when they ran into an Italian mine field. We get news that 5 of us will be returning to the front shortly. The weather is cold and wet.

23 February: We are told today during an inspection that at the recent battle at Gafsa, 169 British tanks and vehicles were destroyed. Some of our group is still engaged at the front. Lt. Kurt Rosenthal has been KIA; Rudi Wechner and Willie Lengader are wounded.

21 February: We are supposed to go to the front, or so we hear but we are still at the camp on the 22d. On the 23d orders arrive to get ready. We set off in our Pumas on that date. The weather is very bad – rain and wind, and several times we get stuck on bad roads. By the late evening we are with the Battle Group. My orders are to protect Lt. Wille's Pioneer Company. I have trouble with my Puma; the engine keeps stalling.

25 February: I set off early to pull 1st Lt Wille's jeep out of a mud hole, but by doing so, the differential on the Puma breaks and we ourselves now need to be pulled back to base. On the 26th we finally have the Puma going again and head south with a rest stop at 11 AM. Group Commander Wangemann arrives and awards me the Iron Cross 2d Class for my tank kill on 15 January. The award comes with a temporary certificate signed by Rommel. At 6 PM I return to the unit and work on the vehicle. In a small Arab village we find a native who sells us 300 eggs, enough for the whole company. On the 28th we are still at the village, cleaning our weapons. I receive many congratulations for the Iron Cross. Later I see the field doctor for an examination.

1 March: In the morning, I visited the Aid Station and got an appointment to see the doctor at Base Hospital tomorrow. I set out on foot hoping to catch a lift on a truck. I got a lift in a Jeep, first to Gabes. A forward airfield was under attack there by fighter-bombers, but I managed to reach the Base Hospital at Sfax. I met Willy Langacker there. He had lost an eye so I wrote a few letters home for him.

3 March: An Italian artillery truck gives me a lift to Tunis. I am supposed to report to another Base Hospital (36) at Carthage for an eye examination. In the evening I go out in Tunis and walk around town.

5 March: I make it to Carthage Base Hospital 36 and get examined by Dr Eisenhardt who recognizes me from Tripoli. When I tell him that I have been in North Africa over 2 years, he promises to get me home to Germany immediately. In the evening I strolled around the harbor and met up with Franz Genk, [Claus von] Stauffenberg, and Horst P. Later, I get a farewell from the hospital staff. News from the front is scarce right now. I received news of my departure, scheduled for the day after tomorrow.

[A month later, on 7 April, von Stauffenberg was severely wounded when his vehicle was attacked by British fighter-bombers. He was sent back to Germany and spent 3 month in a Munich hospital.]

Two Italian soldiers and a German at Bardia.

Bath time for the troops at the Bardia beach.

Chapter 4

HOME TO GERMANY, 1943

---

6 March: Looks like my last day in Africa.

7 March: At 7 AM I reach the air base and finally I leave African soil at 8:55 AM. I was in North Africa exactly 752 days.

At 10:30 AM we land at Palermo, Sicily, then take a plane to Napoli and arrive there at 1:30 PM. It's raining. I go by Wehrmacht bus to the main hospital but I have the evening off so I stroll around Napoli. There are many shops but I don't have enough money to buy things.

8 March: We exchange 300 Francs for Liras to buy things in the Cantina. We hear that we are going to be transferred to Germany on 11 March. On the 9th I sell a few tins of meat for Liras. On the 10th at 2 AM we board a hospital train. I'm in compartment 17, bed # 44. We travel via Rome and Florence to Upper Italy. We receive many presents from people at station stops.

11 March: We travel through Upper Italy, Verona, Trento, and arrive at Bozen at 6 PM. We're in German territory now, Innsbruck. On the 12th we make it to Feldkirch, arriving at 9 PM. We go through a delousing, get new uniforms, have a good bath and get much rest.

13 March: I received my ration card for cigarettes and at 2 PM I phone

187

my parents who say they are all well. I'm still in the hospital in Feldkirch on the 17th.

18 March: My parents arrive in Feldkirch for a visit and I stay with them until 9:30 PM. The next morning they visit again and Dad does a drawing of me. After the evening meal, we stroll around Feldkirch.

21 March: This is the last day of my parents visit and we listened on the radio to our Führer's speech. In the evening my parents depart; I hope for not too long. News comes over the radio that the British have started a new attack in southern Tunisia. I stay in Feldkirch Base Hospital until April 2d.

2 April: I have been released from the hospital. I get a train permit to Nuremberg and arrive there on the 3d with a 14 day leave pass and go home to work on my library and go shopping with Mother. I get a high fever on the 6th and go to Dr. Kläver for an examination. It's my malaria with fever and cold chills; must go to bed. On April 12th I am admitted to the Bamberg Wehrmacht Hospital. The doctor says it is indeed malaria and calls an ambulance that takes me to the Barenschanze Hospital in Bamberg. There are 34 other malaria cases here, all in room 6.

14 April: I still have a fever. They are doing blood tests. On my 4th day in the hospital, my parents come for a short visit.

25 April, Easter Sunday: I'm well enough to walk around Bamberg and see my parents and my brother Karl, who tells me he is getting married. We visit the Old Castle. My parents go back to Nuremberg. I still have not recovered. I have a visit from Sigmund who is taking a training course near here. On the 29th mother comes for a short visit, and, since I have a short leave pass for Nuremberg, I go home with her. I have to be back at the hospital on 3 May.

9 May: Today is my last day in Bamberg. I still have my 14-day leave pass to use yet. I'm going back to Nuremberg.

13 May: Still on leave in Nuremberg; met Karl's future in-laws, Mr. & Mrs. Schmiedel. I go by train to Munich on the 14th and arrive in the evening. On the 15th I meet a girl named Elisabeth, visit Frau Mair, see a show with Elisabeth, and have dinner at Mrs. Mair's.

18 May: I stay in Nuremberg until 26 May. I must get back to Berlin now and report to the Company at Klein-Machnow. The next morning, in Berlin, I report for examination to a doctor who orders more convalescence leave for me. I stay in Berlin until 3 June, then travel by train back to Nuremberg.

18 June: Four weeks at home have come to an end; sorting out my library, visiting relatives and friends. Today I return to Berlin to report for duty. I have evenings off and go into the city. Some of the shrapnel left in my leg starts to hurt so I visit the Berlin Schöneberg Military Hospital and one piece of shrapnel is removed on the 23d. I visited two girls, Grete and Erika, while I was out.

I got new bandages on my leg but the wound has gone septic so I've been taken to the Tempelhof Hospital.

2 August: All hospitals in Berlin have been closed for an unspecified time??? I'm still in the Convalescents Company but I am allowed to go out at night. I met a girl named Monika. She is a hospital nurse and is scheduled to leave Berlin on 5 August.

11 August: Last night there was a heavy air raid on Nuremberg and I have not heard from my parents. I tried to phone on the 12th but there are no open lines to Nuremberg. Finally on the 16th a letter arrived. Three fire bombs hit our house. The top floor is burned out. The house next door is a total loss. I'm allowed to go home on the 18th to evaluate the damage to our house.

20 August: I'm home until the 23d. In the evening I took Monika out and during the night we had a very heavy air raid on Berlin; 60 bombers were shot down. [This was the beginning of the first heavy night raids on Berlin by British bombers.]

1 September: Again there are heavy air raids on Berlin. It is Elisabeth's birthday. I go to see Herr Meissner on the 3d.

On the 6th I report to barracks, as Panzerführer of 1st Company, with 1st Lt. Schwalbe.

16 September: Today is my birthday; I'm 25, and celebrate with Karl-Heinz and Frau Meissner.

18 September: In the morning we load our vehicles and 7.5 PaK's onto a train at Berlin Grunewald to depart for Wandern proving ground. After arriving in camp, I visit the village of Tweezing and return to camp at midnight.

20 September: On the first day of shooting at paper targets, I hit the target 3 times with 7 shots – very good, same score the next day. Several days pass with target practice. We do patrols with a 7.5 half-track and finish up our training on the 24th with a nice get together in the evening. On the 25th we are transferred to HQ Company. We load up on the 26th and finish by 1 PM. After that I have a good-bye visit to the village. We return to Berlin on the 27th and unload our equipment from the train. Dad's birthday is today; he is 60. On the 28th I get promoted to Panzer Leader and we have an inspection by Commander Schwalbe. I get some bad news; Erika is in the hospital for an operation.

1 October: I get promoted to Chief of the training group for the 75mm PaK. I report to the commander and find out that 20 of us are to be transferred to the "Hermann Göring" Division [1st Paratroop Panzer Division, Hermann Göring]. On the 2d I get instructions on how to train recruits on the 75mm.

15 October: I am still in instructor training but it is supposed to end tomorrow. I have been assigned to Lt. Steindorff who has another group of new recruits. Monika arrives in Berlin on the 20th and on the 27th I get a short leave to Nuremberg.

I visit Dad's workplace and in the afternoon work in my Library. I also visit the town hall to hear the damage report on my parents' house from fire bombs. I was told that the top floor will be repaired and Mr. & Mrs. Luthard will live there. I return to Berlin on the 29th and visit Karl-Heinz.

4 November: Finally I am totally fit for front line duty, or so the doctor tells me. All I can do now is just sit around and wait, go into the city, see friends and relatives, and go to the cinemas. I do have air raid patrol duty, however. We listen to the Führer's speech on 8 November. I met Willi who has recently been promoted to Lt. Colonel. We celebrate on the evening of the 10th in a beer hall.

11 November: I'm in Zossen today for practice shooting; 46 rounds fired, 26 hits scored, 13 of them bull's eyes. Later I return to Berlin. Dad visits me. He's staying in the Magdeburg Hof Hotel. More air raids at night on Berlin. I will be taking Dad back to the railroad station on the 18th. On 22 November we have really heavy air raids on Berlin. I'm on alert all night; heavy damage. I catch an S train to Innsbruck Square in Berlin, and then have to walk through the burning streets. At 3 PM I reach Bellevue to see Mrs. Growitz's daughter. Mrs. Growitz just sits in her burned out house – dazed. I took her to Lankowitz to her relatives. We expect another heavy raid tonight.

24 November: We have several more air raids. Karl-Heinz lost everything in the fire. I take my family to Lichterfelde. We have to walk because Anhalter Station is in ruins. I return to my barracks late.

25 November: We are detailed to help in the rescue and relocation of Berliners. I take the company Kubelwagen jeep and tell all my men to move out with the people's furniture to Pankow on the outskirts of Berlin. On the 26th we again have a heavy air raid on Berlin. I am ordered to B-Nikolasee. I found out in a letter from her that Erika has a baby but she will not marry the father. We're on clearing rubble duty at Lützow square.

I request and get a leave pass to go by train to Eger to visit Erika. She looks well and the baby is wonderful. I am not really sure what I came for but I wanted to see her. On 3 December I say goodbye to Erika and get a train to Berlin. During the night, there is an unusually heavy air raid on Leipzig. I reach our barracks at 11 AM on 4 December. I am on duty in Berlin, assisting in clearing debris with my company until 20 December. On the 21st I get Christmas leave to Nuremberg. I'm home for Christmas for the first time since 1940 and we celebrate. I received many good books for my library. On the 25th I work in my library. Maria is visiting and we have an excellent dinner of goose with Knödel [potato dumplings].

26 December: I have lunch at the Schmiedel's, without father who stays at home. He's not very well. We hear the radio news that our battleship *Scharnhorst* was sunk. I have been seeing operas and on 29th I will return to Berlin. As soon as I arrive, we have another air raid. I'm 6 hours late. On the 30th, a new group is formed; I'm now Chief of Group 208.

31 December: We are celebrating the New Year in our barracks; much drinking and plenty of toasts to 1944. I finally get to bed at 2 AM.

3 January 1944: I am training 15 new recruits on the PaK 75mm. We are also learning how to retreat in a bad situation. I managed to visit Willi in Wilmersdorf; twice he's been bombed out now. Traveled to Zossen for new training and was able to buy several books in Berlin on my return.

19 January: Not much has happened except that we went to Zossen to practice cannon firing. On 30 January there was a heavy air raid on Berlin. We were sent to Kaiser Alley to rescue people trapped under rubble. It looks like this will be our assignment for a while. I met a new lady friend named Lore on 8 February and by chance, I saw Monika in Wannsee the next day, but I am spending my free time with Lore. Nothing to report of importance, except air raids continue on Berlin

15 February: Nothing of importance has happened lately. Today Karl-Heinz came to visit me in our quarters and we had a unit inspection, which went very well. On the 17th I visited our company's winter garden that we made and Lore came for a visit. I did have a minor accident on the 18th and almost broke my arm; had a tooth extraction on the bottom left on the 21st.

24 February: We are training at a re-created Russian village with me in charge of 2d company.

25 February: We are still in training at the Russian village. Nothing of importance is happening, but Lore visits me often here.

4 March: During our training, the first full-scale daylight air raid on Berlin takes place.

6 March: There is a massive air raid on Berlin at noon, several fire bombs fall in our area. [This was the first very large scale U.S. Air Force bombing of Berlin.] The Metro Train line to Wannsee is totally blocked.

Lore arrives on 10 March. She lost everything in the last air raid but she is otherwise well. On 16 March I received a message that Dieter Goeschen is KIA – my best friend for over 10 years.

17 March: Our new Battle Group commander arrived today and new recruits were sworn in to our Führer. I visited with Lore's relatives (Frau Meissner).

19 March: Today is Wehrmacht Day [Tag der Wehrmacht, a Winter War Aid fundraising and propaganda holiday]. I have 14 days of leave coming so I take Lore on a short trip to Pomerania. The first few days I spend with Lore in Berlin, going to the opera and visiting relatives, but on the 30th, Lore has to leave. I board a train to Nuremberg and the train runs into a heavy air raid at Fürth. I arrive home at 7 PM; all are well.

1–7 April: On leave in Nuremberg, nothing important happening, but my throat is swollen and I have a fever. I manage to get up and visit the local Wehrmacht Medical Officer, who orders me to the hospital. He suspects diphtheria and gives me injections of calcium. I have several bad nights.

9 April, Easter Sunday: I spent my Easter in the hospital but got to feeling much better by the 10th. My mother brought my belongings to the hospital as I have been transferred to Herzogenauchach Hospital. I stay there until June 14th, then I am released for several weeks of convalescence treatment.

4 July: I returned to Berlin and met a new girl named Kathy B. I reported to my unit and got detailed to 1st Company as a "Not fit for Duty" person. I'm on light duty most of the time.

20 July: There was an attempt on our Führer's life today. He is slightly injured. In Berlin, all government buildings are out of bounds today; otherwise, things are quiet.

30 July: We get a little more background news regarding the attempt on our Führer's life. Reichsführer Himmler has now been promoted to Commander of the Replacement Army and Guderian is now Chief of the General Staff.

6 August: Today I met Inge Strudthoff and have fallen in love with her.

21 August: I request to be transferred to a combat unit. On the 25th I get a short leave to attend the wedding of my brother and Maria in Nuremberg. The wedding is in the Moritz Chapel. The reception is at the Schmiedels' house.

27 August: The Schmiedels visit our house for dinner.
     Today is the 5th anniversary of me being in the Wehrmacht.
     I return to Berlin on the 28th and the next day I get transferred to a new front unit. Inge visits me in the evening.

2 September: Today I reported to 1st Lt. Noding regarding my transfer. He offered me a post as an instructor but I declined his offer. I have 2 days leave to sort out my future university matters. On the 6th my request for front line duty is denied, so now I'm in training with the Panzerfaust and Panzerschreck weapons. I get 2 days leave on the 23d and go with Inge to the theater and help Karl-Heinz move his furniture into his new home in Lichterfelde. On the 25th I go to see the medic for bad stomach problem. On my own request, he discharges me on the 29th. I see Inge in the evenings.

1 October: I went to see Karl-Heinz and Maria and had lunch with them. Inge and I are visiting Nikolasee. Lore telephoned but I only spoke briefly with her as she is helping build the East Wall fortifications. Inge returned home to Althagen on the 3d. I find time to visit a dentist. I'm in charge of guard duty until 6 PM. I wrote a long letter to my parents.

8 October: Inge is in Berlin and we visit relatives, local restaurants and friends. My request for transfer to front line duty is being reconsidered, so I get a short leave pass and depart for Nuremberg on the 13th. Write letters to Inge. Willi visits with family. I get a nice letter from Inge on the 16th.

19 October: There is another heavy air raid on Nuremberg. I volunteer for rescue operations.

20 October: A telegram arrives with orders for me to report to my Commanding Officer immediately, so I leave home and return to Berlin, but was told nothing when I arrived. There are rumors that we are to form a new front unit. I met Inge a few times in Berlin. I get new uniforms on the 24th but so far, I have no orders.

26 October: I finally get some news. I have been transferred to the front, so I say goodbye to Inge and others and depart by train from Anhalter Station at 11 PM. On the 27th I am still on the train and pass through Halle, Bebra, and Fulda. I finally arrive at training PaK range Wildflecken on the 28th at 3 PM. My new commander is Major Geiser. I'm detailed to be the commander of a 7.5cm PaK Unit of Headquarters Company.

30 October: Today I received the arm band "Feldherrnhalle" [SA-Standarte Feldherrnhalle was formed in 1935 and renamed Feldherrnhalle in 1936. Its headquarters was in Berlin, with battalions of the unit stationed in Berlin, Hannover, Hattingen, Krefeld, Munich, Ruhr, Stetten and Stuttgart], and got 8 days home leave. I choose to stay in Berlin with Inge and we visit Karl-Heinz and Maria.

4 November: Today is probably the last time I will see Inge. On the 5th I go by train to Nuremberg, buy writing paper for our company and stay home until the 7th.

8 November: I depart Nuremberg and travel through Fulda and Schmalnau and arrive in Valwerda at 3 PM. Its only November the 8th but I start writing my Christmas letters to Inge. We have a memorial service on the 9th [anniversary of the November 9th, 1923 Beer Hall Putsch] and march to the Feldherrnhalle. Our training continues on AT guns and radio communications. On 13 November we get a new vehicle, a diesel Tatra Sd Kfz., 220 horsepower, 234/3 with a 75mm L/24 cannon.

[There are no further entries in the diary until the following month.]

7 December: We are ordered to get ready to move out.

15 December: We arrive in Prague early and travel on to Uschtinietz. On the 16th we take quarters in private houses until our camp is ready.

18 December: We are in northern camp Milowitz in an Anti-Tank group. In the evening, the radio reports on the Ardennes battle.

23 December: We have our Christmas party with the Commander included. My Christmas mail brings a long letter from Inge with a photo. The rest of Christmas was the usual guard duty and Duty Officer's work. On the 31st we celebrated New Year's Eve.

Chapter 5

THE END OF THE WAR, 1945

---

1 January, 1945: Went to bed at 3 AM. At 2 PM we had our first inspection of the New Year. We hear that 579 enemy aircraft were shot down during a raid on Nuremberg. I'm still on guard duty on the 13th. I visit a friend in Prague, Herr Meindl.

17 January: I'm still in Prague. We hear of a new Russian offensive in the east. We are doing intensive AT training now and our unit has the highest score in practice firing. On the 22d we score 16 direct hits out of 20 rounds fired. We hear of another air raid on Nuremberg over the radio. I am granted home leave and race to the railroad station before my leave gets cancelled. On the 27th I am on a train to Pilsen and arrive in Nuremberg at 7 PM.

28 January: I talk to Dad for a long time. My library now contains 1011 books – very impressive. I am home until the 31st and take a train back to Prague.

1 February: We are training in camp with AT and Panzerfaust. SSgt. Kurt Irmer was killed when a warhead on a Panzerfaust exploded prematurely. I was only a few feet away but I'm okay.

I received a letter from Inge saying that she is now a doctor. We continue our AT training.

17 March: I attended a Court Martial for a guy named Janz in Prague. On the 19th we get re-named Tank Reconnaissance Unit Feldherrn-halle and are now on Corps status.

22 March: My new Fieldpost Number is 67739A.

28 March: We fall in for departure, pack our bags and drive to the railroad station on the 29th. We reach Vienna on the 30th, and on the 31st we reach Pressburg [Bratislava]. We march through Kuty and then 12 miles to the east.

1 April, Easter Sunday: Easter once again but we have no time to celebrate. We unload our gear near Cazoo and see German tanks returning from the front, some badly shot up.

3 April: We patrol along a Russian breakthrough. One of our half tracks gets hit by Russian PaK; Hans Mill is killed, so is Kurt Pieger, and Paul Schreiber is severely wounded. We retreat to Garstin.

5 April: We retreat through Rustay, Holic, Lanzhof, and Hindenburg to Eisengrub. SSgt. Flotte is wounded. Nuremberg had another heavy air raid last night.

7 April: Today is just not our day. We set off at 6 PM but shortly the air compressor fails and after we repair it, the suspension breaks in half on one wheel. Nevertheless, we continue on 7 wheels. [The Puma had 8 wheels.] We reached a repair depot but they moved out before we had time to work on our Puma. We are under Russian air attack but we receive no hits.

9 April: We get a new Puma and a 5-man crew and drive to Nikolsburg. We are attached to a night patrol on April 11th and with one more Puma we do reconnaissance toward Zitzersdorf and Gross-Inzersdorf.

10 April: At 7 AM we do reconnaissance toward Absdorf and repel an enemy attack with our 75mm AT guns. Then we begin to receive mortar fire. SSgt. Klasenbusch is KIA with shrapnel to his head. Six of our wheels are flat. We retreat and use the 2 spare wheels for repair. On 4 good wheels and 4 flats, we reach our line at Mistelbach.

13 April: At 3 PM we get new attack orders for the Hindenburg area. My 20mm command vehicle has radio problems so I'm on my own in Hindenburg. When everyone started to retreat, I followed. The town is not safe to stay in alone. On the 14th we are ordered to patrol north of Hindenburg. We encounter an enemy infantry unit on the 15th and attack it. We destroy 2 heavy mortars.

16 April: We patrol a dense forest area near Thaya. Russian tanks are reported on our front. On the 17th we patrol Selowitz. The sugar refinery is in flames, which lights up the area but the town is free of enemy except for an enemy patrol on horseback that is quickly destroyed.

18 April: I do a lone patrol and find 50-60 enemy tanks assembled nearby, but some of our Tiger and Hetzer units keep them at bay; lots of air activity by our Luftwaffe. We get new orders to proceed to Brünn.

19 April: I refuel at a gas depot, then patrol the area around Schwarzkirchen and observe 40 heavy Stalin tanks. On patrol, we met Lt. Menke who was MIA. We pick him up and retreat toward Mohelo but we run into a partisan unit at 10 PM. Several members of our group are wounded. In retaliation we destroy the village. A partisan truck and one of their commanders were taken prisoner.

20 April: At 4 PM we return to our Battle Group and drive to Brünn to fill up with fuel. I write a long letter to Inge.

21 April: We are ordered to retreat to Poysdorf. Commanding General Klamann is with us. We are in Germany proper now, just over the border. We do a few patrols on the 22d, then I am ordered to Corps HQ at 4 PM. I stay with Corps HQ until the 26th then transfer to Lechwitz. Messages arrive from the front where part of my unit is fighting. Sgt. Muller has been badly wounded. They are still fighting partisans just over the border in the Protectorate.

1 May: I am still at Corps HQ. We receive the unbelievable news that our Führer has fallen KIA. We cry like little puppies.

2 May: With Corps HQ, the situation is uncertain. What are we going to do? On May the 4th we set off toward the west but have a breakdown on the 5th. We're stuck in a ditch with no way to get out. We sleep inside the vehicle. On the 6th I can wait no longer and march on foot to find a towing unit. With Scholl's towing unit we manage to get back on the road and head west to capitulate. We reach Winterberg and that's where we lay down our arms to U.S. forces.

Chapter 6

AFTER THE END

---

9 May: We are transported as POW's by truck to Freying. Jan Schmidt is with me in the same truck. We decide to make a break for it but we get deposited in a huge POW compound. We manage to break out of the compound at night and hide in a small forest. We find civilian clothes in an empty house and change out of our uniforms. We reach Ellenberg in the Bavarian Forest on foot on the 10th.

12 May: We leave Ellenberg and walk on the road through Zwiesel, Zell, Deggendorf, and Offenberg. We avoid control and checkpoints near Cham and have our first bath in a creek. On May 15th we walk 10 km and stop at a farm. We are welcomed. The next day we are off again, reaching north of Regensburg before stopping for the night in a house off the main road.

17 May: We bypass Regensburg and a truck gives us a lift to Seubersdorf. Jan knows a girl there that he wants to visit. We stop for the day and get a good meal. We help bury an SS man that was found dead in a roadside ditch.

19 May: We travel on foot to Neumarkt, then get another lift on a truck to Nuremberg. I reach my parents home at 1:30 PM.

6 June: Today I begin a trip to Berlin. I stop in Koburg to see Aunt

Gusti. I travel through the Thuringian forest on the 9th and reach Eckardsberg on the 10th.

11 June: I have made it to Nobitz and reach the American border zone at Rochlitz. Here I survey the opposite side of the Mulde River, which is in the Russian zone of occupation. I cross the Mulde River on the 14th and a farmer with an oxcart takes me to Kiebitz and gives me a bicycle.

16 June: I pedal to Riesa, where a bunch of Pollacks steal my bicycle but leave the rucksack behind. So I'm on foot again.

17 June: I traveled through Wittenberg and Jüterbock today. On the 18th I reached Berlin and arrived at Inge's house at noon. We spent the next few days going out, watching stupid Russian films, and visiting old friends in Wannsee. On the 24th I stayed the night with Inge. We went swimming the next day.

I organized trips to farms to get food and managed to get several pounds of potatoes on 11 July.

15 July: I leave Berlin to return to Nuremberg. I avoid the zone control points and swim across the Mulde River at night to reach Nuremberg on 19 July.

Here my war diary ends. I'm not legal yet so on 27 July, 1945 I drive to Ansbach to be interrogated at 1 PM. By 7 PM I'm cleared and can go home. I reach home at night.

Therefore, I was a soldier from:
    27 August 1939
    to
    27 July 1945
    5 Years and 11 months.

This diary now ends.

[There is one final entry added three years later.]

7 July 1948: With a U.S. travel permit, I travel by air from the University of Munich via Frankfurt to Tempelhof airport in Berlin on an official U.S. plane with the staff of U.S. General Lucius Clay, who is preparing to organize the Berlin Airlift.

Two aspects of the German experience in North Africa:
bundled up in the desert during winter (above) and relaxing in
dress uniform at an oasis (below).

Epilogue

THE FALL OF BERLIN AND THE AIRLIFT

The end of the war came most dramatically in the capital of the Reich. No major city in the interior of Germany was prepared for a ground assault; Berlin certainly was not. This was to have been an offensive war with defense preparedness a secondary concern. Berlin was probably the least well fortified against an invasion because, to Germans, it was inconceivable that ground defenses would ever be needed for any German city–certainly not for the capital of the Reich. There were anti-aircraft guns and air raid shelters because bombings were expected, but there were few man-made fortifications around the city even as late as 1945. Life basically went on in the capital, where the concentration of propaganda was greatest, right up until the Russians were literally at the city limits.

Strategic misinformation originating with Stalin had convinced the Allies that Berlin was not the top priority of the Soviet government. The United States would be part of a well planned and drawn out division and occupation of Germany. As for the fate of Berlin, the Soviets wanted no competition in deciding its fate and the Western Allies seemed perfectly content to let the Russians have it. No one doubted that Germany would fight to the last man. The battle of Berlin or as the Soviets called it, the "Berlin Strategic Offensive Operation," began in late April 1945 and was over by early May. Berlin surrendered on May 2, but fighting continued in other parts of Germany until the formal surrender on May 8. This was in reality a delaying tactic so that more German forces could surrender to the Western Allies instead of being captured by the Russians.

On January 12, 1945, the Russians began the Vistula-Oder offensive across the Narew River and simultaneously launched a massive drive from Warsaw, gaining upwards of 25 miles a day. After taking Gdansk (Dänzig), most of East Prussia, and Poznan, the Russians collected themselves along a broad front some 40 miles east of Berlin, along the Oder River. A counterattack by Himmler's Army Group Vistula failed on February 24, which opened the door for the Russians all the way to Pomerania and into Silesia. Things were equally bad in the south. Budapest fell on February 13 and the Russians entered Austria on March 30, taking Vienna on April 13. The final chapter was being written on the history of the Third Reich and events were happening too quickly for the German bureaucracy to respond.

Military commanders and most civilians knew that the end of the war was near and that it could come perhaps as soon as May. The real lack of war fighting materiel and the firsthand reports of the Russian advances could no longer be covered up by propaganda. Everyone in Berlin also knew that the fight for the capital would be the most determined battle of the war and many citizens escaped as soon as the fight for the city began. Berlin was never a strong center of National Socialism, even after Hitler became Chancellor. Most Berliners knew that Hitler was still in Berlin somewhere and that he had announced that he would not leave the city. This only added to the belief that the battle would be to the end. The insistence of an unconditional surrender by the Allies probably did more to prolong the war than anything Göbbels or Hitler could have manufactured. The years of propaganda had convinced the ordinary Germany that surrender to the Russians and the subsequent occupation by them would be far worse than death. The Wehrmacht fought bravely, not because they believed in the cause any longer nor because they thought they could still win, but to buy time for their loved ones to flee the Russians. The death of U.S. president Roosevelt on April 12 was used by Göbbels to promote hope that there would finally be real dissension among the Allies so that a separate peace could be attained with the British and Americans while they continued the fight against the Russians.

There were plans for an airborne drop on Berlin to end the war but Eisenhower was against such an idea. Eisenhower knew that Berlin would be jointly controlled by the Russians and the Western Allies after the war per the agreement reached between Stalin, Roosevelt, and Churchill at Yalta. The major contribution made by the U.S. and Britain were the bombing raids on Berlin which reduced the city to ruins by April 20 when the Russians entered the city. Stalin's objective was to have his armies advance as far west as they could in order to occupy as much of Germany as possible before the official cessation of hostilities. He had doubts that the Western Allies would give up any portion of Germany they had occupied prior to the end of the war. The only thing that was of more importance to Stalin was the capture of Berlin itself, because it was the seat of the National Socialist government. Stalin also believed Berlin was the site of the German "wonder weapons" he had heard so much about, which he intended to capture for post-war use.

Militarily, Hitler replaced General Ritter von Hausenschild with General Helmuth Reymann as the commander of Berlin defenses on March 6. On March 20 Hitler ordered General Gotthard Heinrici to replace Heinrich Himmler as commander of Army Group Vistula. Heinrici immediately set about reinforcing the Seelow Heights east of Berlin in anticipation of a Soviet crossing of the Oder River. He also had the flood gates on the dams on the upper Oder opened to flood the lower plains.

Ultimately, there were three rings of defense-in-depth set up around Berlin. They included anti-tank ditches and fortified bunkers all along the lines. The problem was, they also needed manpower to construct and occupy the bunkers and defense lines, and that was sorely lacking. In the first few weeks of April, Russian Marshalls Zhukov and Konev concentrated three Fronts, comprising two and a half million men for the assault on Berlin from the east, northeast and the south. The amount of materiel was staggering. Thousands of tanks, aircraft, artillery pieces and rocket launchers were pointed toward Berlin.

The battle for the Seelow Heights began on April 16 and lasted four days. The Russians committed one million troops and 20,000 tanks and artillery pieces to the battle. The Heights were defended by about 100,000 Germans with 1,200 tanks. On April 19, the 1st

Belorussian Front broke through the last line of defense on the Seelow Heights and raced for Berlin. Other Russian armies set out toward the U.S. front line southwest of Berlin on the Elbe River. This separated German Army Group Vistula in the north from Army Group Center in the south. By April 19 the German front lines around Seelow and to the south around Forst was destroyed. The entire German Ninth Army was surrounded west of Frankfurt with no hope of rescue or orders to retreat.

On Hitler's birthday, April 20, the Russian 1st Belorussian Front began to shell the center of Berlin and advance east and northeast of the city. The Russians planned to surround Berlin first, and then destroy the Ninth Army. The 1st Ukrainian Front drove through the northern end of Army Group Center, halfway to the U.S. front lines on the Elbe River at Magdeburg. The 2d Belorussian Front charged the northernmost flank of Army Group Vistula, which was being supported by Manteuffel's Third Panzer Army. Impossible orders from Hitler confounded the German command in the field to the point that Heinrici was called to the Führerbunker where he made it clear that unless the Ninth Army retreated west, it would be destroyed. If Hitler would not approve of the withdrawal, Heinrici was prepared to resign his command. In a rage, on April 22 Hitler admitted that the war was lost and blamed the generals for not carrying out his orders. He also reaffirmed his intention of staying in Berlin to the end, and then he would commit suicide. Hitler was given a bit of encouragement by General Alfred Jodl when he mentioned that General Walther Wenck was uncommitted and could move toward Berlin to assist in the defense of the city. The Germans were convinced that the Americans had permanently stopped at the Elbe River, so there was no point in Wenck defending it. Wenck was ordered to move the Twelfth Army northeast to support Berlin. It was pointed out that this would be a perfect opportunity for Heinrici to move his Ninth Army west to join Wenck. Heinrici was given permission to link up with Wenck. This was the opportunity Henrici was waiting for to move the Ninth Army.

In the meantime, Soviet forces were advancing on all fronts. A Soviet tank army was at the Havel River east of Berlin and another had penetrated the innermost defensive ring of the city. The center of Berlin was under continuous artillery attack. The Russian 1st

Belorussian Front and the 1st Ukrainian Front were tightening the circle around Berlin. On April 23, the last ground connection between Berlin and the German Ninth Army was cut. The 1st Ukrainian Front advanced west and engaged the Twelfth Army of Wenck, slowing his progress toward Berlin. On the 23d, Hitler replaced General Reymann as the commander of the Defense of Berlin with General Helmut (Karl) Weidling. History records that Weidling said he would rather be shot than command the army. Probably he was not the only commander to make that observation.

On April 24, the encirclement of Berlin was complete. Weidling had at his command a few decimated Wehrmacht and SS divisions, maybe 45,000 men, 40,000 Volksturm volunteers and a few thousand Hitler Youth, and SS Brigadeführer Wilhelm Mohnke. Mohnke was the commander of the Berlin Central District and had about 2,000 men of his own. Weidling organized his forces into eight sectors. The defenders ranged from infantry to paratrooper personnel and foreign Wehrmacht and SS battalions. His reserve was the 18th Panzergrenadier Division, which he stationed in Berlin's central district. However, the battle for Berlin was being lost outside the city proper with Soviet forces systematically destroying or scattering German forces on all fronts. On the 24th, elements of the Soviet Fifth Shock Army and the First Guards Tank Army reached the Berlin S-Bahn railway on the north side of the Teltow Canal. The citizens of Berlin knew they would be overrun by the Russians, and panic spread as Berliners realized there was no practical way out of the city.

The Soviet advance into the center of Berlin was along four main approaches: from the southeast along the Frankfurter Allee, from the south along Sonnen Allee, from the south ending near Potsdamerplatz, and from the north ending near the Reichstag. Fighting was heaviest, often house to house, near the Reichstag, the Moltke Bridge, Alexanderplatz, and the Havel bridges. Early on April 29, the Russian Third Shock Army crossed the Moltke Bridge and began clearing the surrounding area. The capture and occupation of government buildings began with the Ministry of the Interior. Heavy artillery was brought up and directed on any government building within range. In the very early hours of the 30th, in the Führerbunker, Hitler signed his last will and testament and married Eva Braun. The Soviets continued the attack in the southeast part of the city at dawn and captured the German Gestapo headquarters temporarily as the Soviet Eighth Guards Army attacked the southwest part of the city, northward across the Landwehr Canal, into the Tiergarten.

At 6 AM on April 30, the Russians began an assault on the Reichstag but were repelled several times by German 88mm guns located on the Berlin Zoo flak tower. The Russians eventually began to enter the building by nightfall. German forces had not evacuated the building and held off the Russians in hand to hand fighting for another two days. Weidling informed Hitler in person on the morning of April 30 that Berlin's defenders only had enough ammunition for another day. Hitler gave him and his forces permission to attempt a breakout from the city through the Russian lines. That afternoon, Hitler and Eva Braun committed suicide and their bodies were burned just outside the Führerbunker. In accordance with Hitler's last will and testament, upon his death, Admiral Karl Dönitz became Reichspräsident of Germany and Dr. Joseph Göbbels became the new Chancellor. It is interesting that Hitler chose the title "Reichspräsident" and not Führer for his successor. Perhaps he thought that Reichspräsident would be more accepted by the victors or perhaps he thought that no one other than himself could ever be the German Führer.

The surviving Berlin defenders fell back as the Soviets advanced, until the German forces were concentrated in a small area in the center of the city. There were about 10,000 German soldiers in the area facing attack from all sides. A few massive Tiger tanks from the Hermann von Salza Battalion took up positions east of the Tiergarten to defend the center of the city, but the possible escape routes were slowly being cut off by the sheer number of Russians in the area.

In the pre-dawn of May 1, General Krebs left the Führerbunker with orders from Göbbels to attempt negotiations with Soviet General Chuikov, commander of the Soviet Eighth Guards Army. Krebs told Chuikov of Hitler's death and the intention of the remaining National Socialist leaders to agree to a city-wide surrender. General Chuikov insisted on an unconditional surrender and Krebs returned to the Führerbunker with the message. Later in the day, Dr. Göbbels' wife Magda assisted in the murder of their six children. Both she and her husband committed suicide soon afterward. Göbbels' suicide allowed Weidling to accept the terms of unconditional surrender of his forces, but he delayed the surrender until the next morning to allow a breakout by those who wanted to attempt it. Most of Weidling's men chose to attempt to escape but only a few made it to the lines of the Western Allies.

Early in the morning of May 2, the Soviets captured the Reich Chancellery without much resistance because most of the German defenders had left in the breakout the night before. General Weidling surrendered his staff at 6 AM and he was taken to see General Chuikov shortly thereafter. Weidling ordered all of the city's defenders to cease fire and surrender. The Soviets arrested anyone suspected of either being in the German military or supporting the military, and placed them all in temporary prison camps before shipping them off to Russia as slave labor. Many were never seen or heard from again.

Wenck's Twelfth Army never did break through to relieve Berlin. It eventually made a fighting retreat back toward the Elbe River and the American lines. They left the Ninth Army survivors their extra supplies and vehicles to aide in their escape attempt. By May 6, many German Army units and individuals had made it across the Elbe River where they surrendered to the U.S. Ninth Army. The German Ninth Army was subsequently encircled in an area near Schönhausen. General Hasso von Manteuffel, commander of the Third Panzer Army, and General Kurt von Tippelskirch, commander of the Eleventh Army, surrendered to U.S. Army forces on the night of May 2. Von Saucken's Second Army, which had been fighting northeast of Berlin in the Vistula Delta area, surrendered to the Russians on May 9. Early on May 7, General Wenck's Twelfth Army's bridgehead on the Elbe River began to collapse, and rather than risk more of his men's lives and the lives of the civilians mixed in among them, he crossed the river that afternoon and surrendered to the American Ninth Army.

Berliners' initial contacts with Russian soldiers were generally positive. The front line troops were mostly well trained and well behaved, only shooting into houses containing soldiers that were firing on them. Professional soldiers of the Soviet Army even made an initial effort to feed the residents of Berlin – while warning the citizenry to beware the soldiers who would follow them. Rear guard conscripts, howeverk, raped, looted, and murdered. A conservative estimate puts the number of rapes by revenge-seeking Russians at more than 100,000 in the months following the surrender. Russian officers found guilty of such crimes were often punished by their commanders, but those commanders rarely punished their subordinates. The total breakdown of authority directly after the collapse of Berlin led to widespread atrocities, but by the late summer of 1945 some control was exerted on the troops, and common soldiers caught raping were punished more frequently. The rapes continued for three years, when finally the Russian occupation authorities started confining troops to military installations. Berlin had been suffering food shortages for many months before the end of the war. The final assault on the city and the subsequent looting and destruction had left the residents of Berlin starving.

The Soviet capture of Berlin was anticipated as soon as the attack began but few believed it would end so quickly. The Russians outnumbered the Germans in men five-to-one, guns 15-to-one, tanks five-to-one, and planes three-to-one. Inside the city, hope remained with the masses as long as Hitler lived, even if he was directing armies that no longer existed. Hitler had convinced himself that the fragile coalition between the Allies would come undone at five minutes to midnight. Stalin had no thought of coalitions: he wanted the Soviet Union to be the first to declare victory over the Germans and to claim sole ownership of that victory. The Soviet Army paid in blood for Stalin's single mindedness. The casualty rate for the Russian Army during the battle for Berlin was astronomical: four Russians died for every German.

On June 12, 1948 the Soviet Union declared that the Autobahn leading into Berlin from West Germany would be closed. The excuse given was that repairs had to be made because of bomb damage from the war. All ground traffic between the sectors ceased completely three days later, and on June 21 all shipping traffic into the city was stopped by the Soviets. All rail traffic into and out of Berlin was halted on June 24. The following day, the Soviet government announced that the Soviet sector would not supply food to Berlin's western (United States, British, and French) sectors and neither could food be brought through the Soviet sector into West Berlin. The aim of this blockade was to quickly force West Berlin to become completely dependent on the Soviet government for food and fuel.

There was no written agreement among the Allied victors for transportation through sectors governed by other nations, and the Soviets were not swayed by arguments that the routes had been open for the past three years. This was a blatant attempt by the Soviets to bring West Berlin to its knees and make it more vulnerable to Communist influence. There was talk in Washington about using force to supply the trapped Germans in Berlin but it was felt that the American people would not support action that could lead to an outbreak of hostilities with the Soviets. Diplomatic solutions were proposed and promptly rejected by the Soviets. There was nothing in the joint operating agreements developed before the end of the war that covered this type of behavior by one of the Allied nations. This was the first major conflict with the Soviets after the war.

Berlin had enough food for thirty-five days and coal for forty-five days. Something had to be resolved before winter or there would be widespread starvation and death in West Berlin. Estimates were that upward of 5,000 tons of fuel and food would have to be delivered every day to keep the population fed and warm. Militarily, the Americans and British were greatly outnumbered due to the post-war reduction of their armies, and personnel were not readily available for such a feat. The Soviets had not appreciably reduced the size of their standing army because Stalin was not at all certain there would be long-term peace. It is likely that if a military conflict had started over Berlin, the city would have been overrun by the Soviets. General Lucius Clay, the military commander of the United States' zone in Germany, was not optimistic about being able to defend West Berlin in the event of a Russian offensive, and that opinion was shared by most high-ranking officers who had been on the ground in Berlin at the end of the war. Berlin would quickly be lost if it came to a shooting war with the Russians. Clay went on to say that Berlin had come to be a symbol of the American intent to preserve and protect Europe from future Communist threat and that Berlin was essential to America's prestige in the eyes of the rest of the world.

General Clay also knew that the Soviets would not want to be the identifiable cause of another world war. He proposed testing the Soviets by sending an armored convoy along the autobahn from West

Germany to West Berlin – just to see how far they would go. President Truman vetoed this idea with the consensus of Congress. Neither one wanted to risk war with the Russians over Berlin if it could be avoided. Everyone felt there had to be another way – and indeed a loophole was found in the pre- and postwar agreements. The rail and ground access had not been negotiated – but the air access had. The Soviets could not claim that aircraft loaded with food was any kind of military threat, but would they nonetheless shoot down an unarmed aircraft that refused to change course away from Berlin? The Russians were placed in the awkward position of violating their own negotiated agreement regarding airspace, or backing down and allowing flights into and out of West Berlin. The Soviets backed down and did not attack Allied aircraft bringing supplies into the city.

The Berlin airlift was completely successful and by the spring of 1949 it was providing more cargo than had previously been delivered by rail or truck; in fact, more supplies than were needed. All of this was completely humiliating to the Soviets who had claimed, after the airlift started, that it would be impossible to supply Berlin by air with enough food and fuel to survive. The Soviets had no choice but to lift the blockade in May of 1949. It was evident, even to them, that the Allies could and would keep the airlift going indefinitely, if need be.

HISTORICAL TIMELINE
"To North Africa and Back"

1939

September 1, 1939: Germany invades Poland, unprovoked and without a declaration of war, despite Hitler's proclamation.

September 3: Great Britain, France, Australia, and New Zealand declare war on Germany.

September 5: The United States declares its neutrality.

September 17: The Soviet Union joins the war as Germany's partner and invades Poland.

September 27: Warsaw surrenders to German forces.

September 29: Germany and the Soviet Union agree on a plan for dividing up Poland.

November 30: The Soviet Union attacks Finland.

1940

March 12: Finland signs a peace treaty with the Soviet Union.

April 9, 1940: Germany invades Denmark and Norway.

May 10, 1940: Germany invades France, Belgium, Luxembourg, and Holland. Winston Churchill becomes Prime Minister of Great Britain.

May 15: Holland surrenders to Germany.

May 26: The evacuation of the British Expeditionary Force from France at the port of Dunkirk begins.

May 28: Belgium surrenders to Germany.

June 4: Dunkirk falls to the Germans, although over 300,000 Allied troops, without their vehicles and heavy weapons, have escaped.

June 10: Norway surrenders. Italy declares war on England and France.

June 16: Marshall Petain becomes Prime Minister of France.

June 22: France signs armistice with Germany.

June 28: In Great Britain, General Charles de Gaulle is recognized as the leader of Free France.

July 5: The Vichy government in France breaks off relations with the British government.

July 10: The air Battle of Britain begins.

July 23: The Soviet Union invades Latvia, Estonia, and Lithuania.

August 3, 1940: Italian troops occupy Somaliland.

August 19: Mussolini orders Marshall Graziani to invade Egypt.

August 25: First British air raid on Berlin.

September 3, 1940: Hitler announces plans for Operation Sealion, the invasion of England.

September 7: The beginning of the German blitz against England.

September 13: Marshall Graziani, with five divisions, crosses the Libyan border from Cyrenaica and advances toward Sidi Barrani in Egypt. The 4th Indian Division and the British 7th Armored Division retreat to Mersa Matruh.

September 16: Italian forces capture Sidi Barrani and build strong defensive positions.

September 27: Germany, Italy, and Japan sign the Tripartite agreement, creating the Axis coalition.

October 9: Neville Chamberlain resigns from the House of Commons, Winston Churchill replaces him as head of the Conservative Party.

October 12: Hitler postpones Operation Sealion, supposedly until the spring of 1941.

October 28: Italy invades Greece through Albania.

November 10: In a prelude to Pearl Harbor, carrier-borne British aircraft cripple the Italian fleet in Taranto.

November 20: Hungary joins the Axis Powers.

November 22: Greece defeats the Italian army and pushes Italy out of Greece.

November 23: Romania joins the Axis Powers.

November 26: The British Western Desert Force, commanded by General Richard O'Connor, begins planning for Operation Compass, the goal of which is to evict all Italian forces from Egypt.

December 9, 1940: Operation Compass begins under the direction of British Field Marshal Archibald Wavell. Over 30,000 British, Australian and Indian troops are involved. Allied units overrun most of the Italian camps around Sidi Barrani.

December 10: Sidi Barrani is encircled. Italian troops retreat westward to avoid being surrounded.

December 11: Sidi Barrani falls to Allied forces, and over 30,000 Italians are captured.

December 17: Allied forces pursue the retreating Italians, overrun Sollum and Fort Capuzzo and rout several other Italian positions.

December 18: Hitler orders directive to begin planning for Operation Barbarossa, the invasion of the Soviet Union.

December 19: Mussolini requests Hitler's assistance in Cyrenaica (northern Libya) to avoid having his forces destroyed by the British during Operation Compass.

December 21: Italian-occupied Bardia, Libya, is surrounded by the Allies. This time the Italians put up more than token resistance.

December 29–30: The Luftwaffe conducts a massive air raid on London.

1941

January 1, 1941: The Western Desert Force is renamed the British XIII Corps.

January 2–4: The British Royal Navy shells Bardia for 48 hours.

January 5: At Bardia, the Italians surrender to the Allies. Over 45,000 Italian prisoners and all of their supplies and equipment are taken. Allied losses are less than 400.

January 6: British XIII Corps pushes on toward Tobruk. Churchill is convinced that German forces will attack Greece and demands that troops be released from Wavell's offensive and sent there instead.

January 9: Tobruk is surrounded by British forces.

January 21: British and Australian forces mount major attack on Tobruk.

January 22: Tobruk surrenders to Allied troops and 25,000 more Italians are taken prisoner. The next British target is Benghazi and O'Connor's XIII Corps moves west to capture it.

January 24: At Derna, the Australians are temporarily delayed by Italian forces.

January 30: Australian troops capture Derna and the Italians withdraw toward Benghazi.

February 5, 1941: Italian forces begin to retreat toward El Agheila on the coast south of Benghazi. The British 7th Armoured Division starts to move across the unmapped Libyan desert to cut off the Italian forces.

February 6: The Australians capture Benghazi and 20,000 Italian troops. The 7th Armoured Division arrives at Beda Fomm ahead of the Italians, who make an unsuccessful counterattack to break through British lines.

February 7: The remainder of the Italian Army surrenders at Beda Fomm. Operation Compass is a success. In ten weeks, Allied forces have advanced 500 miles [800 km], captured 130,000 prisoners with their equipment and over 400 tanks, all at a cost of 500 dead and 1,200 wounded.

February 9: Elements of XIII Corps capture El Agheila. Churchill orders the advance to halt and troops to be sent to defend Greece, thus allowing the Germans time to form their new army with the eight Italian divisions in western Libya and Tunisia. British XIII Corps is deactivated and reverts to the Western Desert Force with General O'Connor in command.

February 12: Generalleutnant Erwin Rommel, former commander of the 7th Panzer Division, arrives in Tripoli with advance elements of the Deutsches Afrikakorps (DAK).

February 14: Units of the German 5th Light Africa Division arrive at Tripoli and are immediately moved up to Sirte to block a future British advance.

February 20–24: Near El Agheila, units of the 5th Light Africa Division tangle with British forces. This is the first engagement between German and British forces in North Africa.

March 4, 1941: With German intervention in Greece imminent, the British begin pulling out additional forces from Egypt and transferring them to Greece.

March 11: The last components of the 5th Light Africa Division arrive in Libya and plans are made for an attack on El Agheila. Hitler orders Rommel back to Germany for a series of meetings. His orders are that when the 15th Panzer Division arrives in Libya in May, he is to recapture Benghazi.

March 24: Rommel conducts a limited offensive with 5th Light Africa Division and recaptures El Agheila with few losses, and proceeds toward Mersa Brega.

March 31: The British 2d Armoured Division comes under attack by the 5th Light Africa Division near Mersa Brega and is forced to retreat toward Benghazi.

April 2, 1941: The 5th Light Africa Division recaptures Agedabia and then splits into three columns which continue to advance. One column speeds up the coast road toward Benghazi and the other two chase the retreating British that had formerly occupied Agedabia.

April 4: German and Italian forces re-enter Benghazi without resistance.

April 6: 5th Light Africa Division units capture Mechili and attempt to cut off the Australian 9th Division retreating toward Tobruk along the coast road. Germany invades Greece and Yugoslavia. Italy declares war on Yugoslavia.

April 7: The 5th Light Africa Division takes Derna and captures British Generals O'Connor and Philip Neame, the Military Governor of Cyrenaica.

April 10: The Australian 9th Division retreats into Tobruk, and Rommel encircles the city, laying siege. Hungarian forces invade Yugoslavia.

April 11: 5th Light Africa Division attacks Tobruk but the Australian Division holds onto the city. Other German forces capture Bardia.

April 14: Rommel attacks Tobruk but is forced to call off the assault. German advance forces take Sollum. Rommel also receives orders from Berlin to consolidate his forces on the Egyptian frontier after he captures Tobruk.

April 17: Yugoslavia surrenders to Germany.

April 22: The British begin to evacuate troops from Greece and send them to Crete and Egypt.

April 27: German troops cross the Egyptian border and capture Halfaya Pass, a major defensive position between Tobruk and Alexandria. The British fall back to defensive a line further east. Other British forces begin creating a permanent defensive line in front of Mersa Matruh, 80 miles [128 km] to the east. Greece surrenders to Germany.

German troops near Mersa Metruh, Egypt. Note the sign giving distances to Mannheim and Hamburg as well as Alexandria.

A view of Tunis.

April 30: A third attempt by Rommel to take Tobruk is beaten back by the Australian defenders. Rommel is ordered to suspend all attacks on Tobruk.

May 15, 1941: The British launch Operation Brevity against Rommel's forces and recapture Halfaya Pass, Sollum and Capuzzo.

May 16: Rommel counterattacks and retakes Sollum and Capuzzo, but not the strategic Halfaya Pass. Berlin orders Rommel to let the Italians deal with Tobruk while he concentrates his German forces on the Egyptian border.

May 24: The German battleship *Bismarck* sinks the British battle-cruiser *Hood*.

May 27: Rommel, reinforced with the 15th Panzer Division, retakes Halfaya Pass. Royal Navy capital ships and carrier aircraft sink the *Bismarck*.

May 28: After failing to repel a German paratrooper invasion, British troops begin to evacuate Crete.

June 4, 1941: The Luftwaffe bombs Alexandria, Egypt.

June 15: British forces begin Operation Battleaxe to relieve Australian forces holding Tobruk.

June 17: The British call off Operation Battleaxe with the loss of 1,000 British casualties and almost 100 tanks.

June 22: Operation Barbarossa, the German invasion of Russia begins. More than four million men, 4,000 tanks and almost 5,000 aircraft are involved in the largest German military operation of the war. The front is more than 1800 miles [2900 km] wide. The Soviets are caught unprepared. Germany, Italy, Romania, and Bulgaria declare war on the Soviet Union.

July 5, 1941: British General Wavell is replaced as Commander-in-Chief of the Middle East Command by General Claude Auchinleck.

July 6: The Luftwaffe bombs Tobruk and Sidi Barrani.

July 11: The German Army closes to within 10 miles [16 km] of Kiev in the Ukraine.

July 12: The Luftwaffe begins the first bombing raid on Moscow. Great Britain and Russia sign a mutual assistance agreement.

July 26: General Auchinleck travels to London for planning meetings regarding future operations to relieve Allied forces in Tobruk.

August 14, 1941: Churchill and Roosevelt sign the Atlantic Charter.

August 19: Part of the Australian troops trapped in Tobruk are evacuated by sea and replaced by Polish troops.

September 2, 1941: General Auchinleck issues orders for planning Operation Crusader for the relief of Tobruk and the retaking of Cyrenaica.

September 8: The three-year siege of Leningrad begins.

September 14: Rommel leads the 21st Panzer Division (formerly the 5th Light Africa Division) toward Sidi Barrani. British forces retreat. September 24: Rommel withdraws the 21st Panzer Division to the Libyan-Egyptian border after finding no fuel in Sidi Barrani to resupply his tanks.

September 26: The British Western Task Force and other units are organized into the Eighth Army, which includes the XIII and XXX Corps.

October 2, 1941: Hitler plans Operation Typhoon to capture Moscow. Army Group Center will lead the operation while Army

Group South simultaneously advances toward Kursk and Kharkov.

October 3: British Eighth Army commander General Alan Cunningham's plans for Operation Crusader, to begin on November 11, are approved by General Auchinleck. It is a complicated plan to destroy as much of the 15th and 21st Panzer Divisions as possible while providing an opportunity for the British forces trapped in Tobruk to escape.

October 10: Army Group South captures an additional 100,000 Soviet prisoners in battles along the Sea of Azov.

October 16: Soviet government officials evacuate Moscow, creating panic in the city. The Black Sea port of Odessa is captured by Romanian forces.

October 20: Army Group Center captures another 650,000 Soviet prisoners in Vyazma and Briansk. German forces approach within 40 miles [64 km] from Moscow.

October 24: The German Sixth Army occupies Kharkov after several days of heavy fighting.

October 27: The German Eleventh Army reaches Sevastopol.

November 3, 1941: Auchinleck is forced to delay Operation Crusader for one week to allow for the arrival of a South African Division.

November 18: The first phase of Operation Crusader begins with the British Eighth Army's drive to relieve Tobruk. The British XXX Corps advances over 50 miles [80 km] south of Sidi Rezegh. Rommel arrives from Rome and finds that his forces have been caught unaware. The DAK is sent to Bardia to prevent the British from encircling the town. November 20: British forces in Tobruk are ordered to break out and join with XXX Corps. Rommel sends the DAK to attack XXX Corps.

November 22: Army Group South captures the important city of

Rostov-on-Don. The German offensive on Moscow continues with the capture of Klin, 35 miles [56 km] away. A sustained battle rages around Sidi Rezegh which forces the British XXX Corps to halt its advance towards Tobruk after the loss of a large number of its tanks. The British XIII Corps, however, captures Sidi Omar and Capuzzo.

November 24: Rommel attempts to cut off British supply lines with a "dash to the wire" toward Egypt which completely confuses the British Eighth Army.

November 26: British General Cunningham requests permission to halt the Crusader offensive and strategically retreat to the open frontier. This request gets Cunningham fired. He is replaced by General Neil Ritchie.

November 27: Elements of German forces reach the Volga Canal, some 60 miles [95 km] northwest of Moscow. In North Africa, the trapped British forces in Tobruk break out and join up with the New Zealand Division of the Eighth Army.

November 29: Extreme weather conditions, a lack of supplies, and continuous attacks by Soviet defenders force Army Group Center to halt all operations less than 50 miles [80 km] from Moscow.

December 1, 1941: Rommel forces the balance of the New Zealand troops in Sidi Rezegh to retreat. His forces are becoming extremely fatigued and they aren't getting many supplies.

December 2: Isolated elements of German forces actually reach Moscow and are within sight of the Kremlin tower.

December 5: Rommel orders troops east of Tobruk to assist the attack on British forces around Bir el Gubi, but the attack stalls. His forces still hold Halfaya Pass.

December 6: The Soviets mount a major counteroffensive along 500 miles [800 km] of the Moscow front. The objective is to attack on two ends of the front to entrap Army Group Center in a pincer.

December 7: The Japanese bomb the U.S. naval base at Pearl Harbor, Hawaii. Japan declares war on the United States, Britain, Australia, Canada and New Zealand.

December 8: The United States, Britain, the Netherlands, New Zealand and others declare war on Japan. Japan launches attacks on the Philippines, Wake Island, Hong Kong and Malaysia. The Russian counteroffensive at Moscow breaks through the German lines in many places. Rommel decides to quit the fight around Tobruk.

December 9: China declares war on Germany, Italy and Japan.

December 10: British Eighth Army raises the siege of Tobruk. In the South China Sea, the British battleships *Prince of Wales* and Repulse are sunk by Japanese aircraft.

December 11: Germany and Italy declare war on the United States and the U.S. responds in kind. Soviet forces continue to make significant headway against German armies around Moscow. In North Africa, most of the remaining German forces have regrouped around Gazala.

December 13: The British Eighth Army attacks German and Italian positions at Gazala. Rommel decides he can't remain there, so he starts a long retreat back to El Agheila, the next defensible position.

December 18: Three Italian midget submarines penetrate the British fleet anchorage at Alexandria and sink two battleships.

December 19: With disaster looming in the Russian winter, Generalfeldmarschall Walter von Brauchitsch resigns as head of OKH. Hitler personally assumes command of the entire German Army. The British retake Derna, Libya.

December 23: Wake Island in the Pacific surrenders. Rommel starts the evacuation of Benghazi.

December 25: Soviet forces continue to push German units back on the Moscow front. German strength is less than 75 percent of June levels. Soviet losses, however, are tremendous. Since the beginning of Operation Barbarossa, Soviet losses exceed five million casualties. In North Africa, the British retake Benghazi.

1942

January 2: British forces capture Bardia and 8,000 German and Italian prisoners.

January 6: Rommel's forces escape from British pursuit and arrive in El Agheila.

January 12: The British capture Sollum in North Africa.

January 17: The last of the Germans at the Halfaya Pass, surrounded since the beginning of Operation Crusader, surrender; the British take more than 5,000 prisoners.

January 20: British troops capture Benghazi and seize a large amount of equipment.

January 21: Without approval, Rommel launches a counteroffensive against the British Eighth Army. The 21st Panzer Division seizes Mersa Brega.

January 22: Rommel's command is re-designated Panzer Army Africa. German panzers continue their push toward the east.

January 23: The Italian (and German) High Commands want Rommel to end his offensive and withdraw to his start line. Rommel refuses, so the Italians refuse to allow their troops to advance any further east with him. Rommel continues the advance with only German forces.

January 25: The Germans capture Msus and largely destroy the British 2d Armoured Brigade.

January 29: The Germans capture Benghazi.

February 1, 1942: General Ritchie orders his units to withdraw to the Gazala line.

February 4: The Germans recapture Derna.

February 7: Rommel halts his counteroffensive near Gazala. His short campaign has recaptured almost all of the ground Eighth Army had taken at the end of 1941. Eighth Army's morale is severely damaged.

April 18: In the Pacific, 16 B-25 bombers under the command of Colonel James Doolittle, flying off the aircraft carrier *Hornet*, conduct a bombing raid on Tokyo. Causing little physical damage, it provides a morale boost for Americans and a slap to the Japanese military.

May 2–8: In the Pacific, the Battle of the Coral Sea is is the first time in history two fleets have fought without ever sighting one another. The battle, resulting in the loss of the carrier USS *Lexington*, is fought entirely by aircraft.

May 26: Rommel begins Operation Venezia, an assault on the Gazala Line. More than 500 tanks drive south to outflank and encircle the British defenses, then drive directly for Tobruk. They are held up by British units in the "Cauldron," which requires all of Rommel's armor and several days to reduce. For days the two sides conduct a series of running battles.

May 28: Rommel's army begins to run out of fuel, requiring a direct run at the heavily defended Gazala line in an attempt to break through and thus shorten his supply lines.

May 30: First 1,000 plane Royal Air Force raid on Cologne. Rommel continues to try to eliminate the Cauldron.

May 31–June 1: The attack to puncture the Gazala line begins. Italian forces attack from the west and units of the DAK from the east.

Meanwhile, the "Cauldron" falls and Rommel now moves into the "Cauldron" area to await British counterattack. This frees up his supply route so fuel can once again reach his tanks.

June 2, 1942: Rommel sends the German 90th Light Division and an Italian armored division to Bir Hacheim to deal with the French forces there and to protect his flank.

June 4–7: In what is considered the turning point of the naval war in the Pacific, U.S. Navy pilots sink four Japanese aircraft carriers in the Battle of Midway. The U.S. loses the carrier *Yorktown*, but the Japanese naval air force has been gutted.

June 5: The British Eighth Army begins Operation Aberdeen, designed to encircle Rommel's forces that are now fortifying the "Cauldron." This is a bloody operation for the British, who lose 6,000 troops and 150 tanks.

June 10: German and Italian forces capture Bir Hacheim after a two-week series of attacks, although most of the defenders are successfully evacuated.

June 12: A resupplied Rommel breaks out of the Cauldron and attacks and traps British units between Knightsbridge and El Adem. Since he holds so much of the widespread battlefield, Rommel is able to retrieve and repair most of his lost armor.

June 13: British and South African units begin to evacuate the Gazala Line.

June 14: The British Eighth Army defends a line in front of Tobruk.

June 15: Rommel launches an attack against the Tobruk line but it is unsuccessful. The 15th Panzer Division blocks the main road west of Tobruk too late to trap the South African units retreating from Gazala. The 21st Panzer Division reaches Sidi Rezegh and is close to surrounding Tobruk.

June 16: Richie orders British XXX Corps to withdraw past Tobruk all the way to Mersa Matruh, Egypt, while ordering XIII Corps to take up positions at Halfaya Pass to buy time for XXX Corps.

June 17: There are over 30,000 mostly South African troops left in Tobruk. The Eighth Army abandons Sidi Rezegh and El Adem, thus subjecting Tobruk to another siege or surrender.

June 20: Rommel launches a massive air and ground attack on Tobruk, which is not nearly as well supplied as when the Australians held it the previous year.

June 21: Tobruk falls to the Germans. Over 32,000 prisoners, a half million gallons of fuel, 5,000 tons of food and 2,000 vehicles are taken. Rommel is promoted to Generalfeldmarschall.

June 23: Now fully resupplied, Rommel's forces reach the Egyptian border, while British XIII Corps falls back on Marsa Matruh.

June 24: The Germans cross into Egypt meeting no resistance. The British Eighth Army abandons Sollum and Sidi Barrani.

June 25: Rommel captures Sidi Barrani, Sollum and the Halfaya Pass in Egypt as the British Eighth Army retreats to Mersa Matruh. Auchinleck sacks Richie and takes command of Eighth Army to control the battle.

June 27: British forces begin to retreat from Mersa Matruh toward El Alamein.

June 28: The German "Case Blue" summer offensive in Russia begins. After heavy fighting, Rommel's forces capture Mersa Matruh and another large quantity of stores. Eighth Army makes a headlong rush back to El Alamein where Auchinleck has to make a stand.

July 1, 1942: Advance units of Rommel's army reach El Alamein. The British prepare to destroy the port at Alexandria to keep the Germans from using it. British staff and headquarters units in Cairo prepare to evacuate to Palestine.

July 2: Rommel continues to attack the British around El Alamein with little success. His army is now down to 26 operating tanks.

July 3: Rommel orders his German and Italian forces to cease all attacks on El Alamein while awaiting supplies and equipment.

July 4: Convoy PQ-17 to Murmansk is nearly destroyed in a long running attack by German aircraft and submarines. Twenty-five out of 36 ships are sunk, and 3,350 trucks, 200 aircraft, 430 tanks and 110,000 tons of freight are lost. On the Eastern Front, the Germans capture Sevastopol in the Crimea.

July 6–26: Eighth Army launches a series of probing attacks on Rommel around El Alamein, to be remembered as the First Battle of Alamein.

July 13: Hitler designates Stalingrad as the major objective for the summer campaign.

July 17: Rommel's supply situation worsens. He suggests that he should retreat back across Libya.

July 21: Auchinleck launches a major attack on Rommel, but little progress is made. British infantry morale is growing increasingly poor because of continued failures.

July 22: Auchinleck calls off the assaults, ending the First Battle of El Alamein. Both sides go on the defensive, Rommel building a defense-in-depth and Auchinleck building up his mobile reserves.

August 5: Churchill visits the Eighth Army at El Alamein.

August 6: American General Dwight D. Eisenhower is appointed commander of Allied forces preparing to invade North Africa.

August 7: In the Pacific, American landings on Guadalcanal begin.

August 13: Lieutenant General Harold Alexander replaces Auchinleck as Commander-in-Chief of the Middle East Command. Lieutenant General Bernard L. Montgomery takes command of the British Eighth Army.

August 19: On the northern coast of France, Allied forces, primarily Canadian, conduct a major amphibious raid on Dieppe, but it is quickly crushed by the Germans—an ominous warning for future attempts to invade France from England.

August 23–24: In the Pacific, the naval battle of the Eastern Solomons. German troops reach the Volga River in Russia.

August 31: Rommel begins his last attempt to break through the defenses at El Alamein and clear the Allies out of Egypt. The Battle of Alam Halfa goes badly for Rommel, who decides at 8:00 a.m. to call off the attack. He is, however, persuaded to continue the attack on the Alam Halfa Ridge.

September 1: German forces arrive at the outskirts of Stalingrad. The Battle of Alam Halfa continues.

September 2: Rommel gives orders to withdraw back to his defenses at El Alamein. It will take several days to carry out his orders.

September 6: Rommel has withdrawn back to where he started at the end of August. His losses are not critical, but he knows not to expect much in the way of support, whereas Montgomery is constantly being resupplied.

September 12: German forces completely encircle Stalingrad.

September 13: Small British units raid Benghazi and Barce. A combined British air and ground attack on Tobruk is conducted but is beaten off.

September 23: Rommel takes medical leave and returns to Germany, transferring command to Lieutenant General Georg Stumme.

October 10: Montgomery issues his final plan for the upcoming assault on German lines in what will be called the Second battle of El Alamein.

October 21–27: On Guadalcanal, a major Japanese attack on U.S. forces costs the Japanese twenty-five percent of their strength and gains little.

October 23–24: The Second Battle of El Alamein begins with a massive overnight artillery bombardment. The Eighth Army moves out on a six-mile wide front on the south end of Rommel's defenses. British units make some gains but don't keep to their timetable. During a visit to the front, General Stumme dies of a heart attack.

October 25: Montgomery intervenes directly in the push to break through the German lines. Rommel cuts short his sick leave to fly back to North Africa. By the time he arrives, a new British attack on the northern end of the German lines has begun.

October 26: Making little progress, Montgomery calls a halt to his attacks to regroup. Churchill feels the battle is being given up too soon, but Montgomery is consolidating his divisions at El Alamein for a planned final breakthrough.

October 27: The 21st Panzer Division attempts what is a major counterattack on the British forces, but it is beaten back by a smaller British force.

October 28–29: Montgomery has attacked the southern end and then the northern end of the Axis lines at El Alamein, which consist mainly of German troops. Now he makes plans to attack the Italians in the center.

November 1–2, 1942: Montgomery's breakout at El Alamein gets underway. British losses are heavy, but can be replaced. Rommel can not replace his, and by the end of the day he has only about 35 operational tanks.

November 3: Rommel starts to withdraw from El Alamein but Hitler orders him to stop. The Italians, however, can't be stopped. Montgomery doesn't pursue immediately because his units are stuck in a huge traffic jam trying to work their way through the minefields.

November 4: The British reach open ground and there is heavy fighting all around the El Alamein area. An Italian Motorized Corps is destroyed. Rommel orders the retreat to continue with his dozen or so remaining tanks in spite of Hitler's admonition to stand and fight. The British capture over 30,000 men, several German generals, over 1,000 artillery pieces and the remains of over 400 tanks that are damaged or out of service due to lack of fuel.

November 5: The British attack Rommel's rear guard, almost 100 miles [160 km] west of El Alamein, but most of the pursuit is held up because of an old British minefield for which they have lost the maps.

November 6: Working its way through the minefield, the British advance is held up now because their fuel is stuck in the traffic jam back in El Alamein. It also starts to rain, limiting the advance to the hard coastal road.

November 8: Operation Torch, the Allied invasion of French North Africa begins. British and American forces under General Eisenhower land in Morocco and Algeria. This puts a major Allied force deep in Rommel's rear area, placing his army between two larger ones. They meet little resistance. Mersa Matruh is retaken by the British.

November 9: German paratroopers land in Tunisia without incident. Their orders are to stop the new Allied forces in French North Africa. In Egypt, Sidi Barrani falls to advance elements of Eighth Army.

November 11: In Stalingrad, the last major German attack to capture the city begins. In Africa, Eighth Army takes Halfaya Pass and occupies Bardia without opposition.

November 12: British Eighth Army recaptures Tobruk.

November 19: The massive Soviet counterattack to encircle the German Sixth Army at Stalingrad begins. Eighth Army captures Benghazi.

November 23: The Soviet pincers movement around Sixth Army closes tight and encircles Sixth Army which, in turn, has encircled Stalingrad. Rommel's units reach El Agheila, a 600 mile [965 km] retreat in 14 days.

November 27: With German forces now occupying Vichy France in order to protect its Mediterranean coastline, the French scuttle their fleet in Toulon to prevent it from falling into German hands.

December 4: Reinforced German forces facing the Allies in French North Africa capture Tebourba in Tunisia. It is apparent that Hitler intends to fight for all of North Africa.

December 8: German troops occupy the port of Bizerte, Tunisia. Fifth Panzer Army is created to defend against Allied forces landing in French North Africa. General Hans-Jürgen von Arnim is appointed as its commander.

December 12: Operation Winter Storm, the attempted rescue of General Paulus' Sixth Army trapped in Stalingrad begins.

December 13: Rommel begins to retreat from El Agheila; the Eighth Army captures Mersa Brega.

1943

January 5, 1943: The Soviet Caucasus offensive is well under way, pushing the Germans back toward Soviet forces already surrounding the Sixth Army at Stalingrad. Meanwhile, the Luftwaffe can not resupply the Stalingrad garrison with sufficient supplies.

January 14–24: Roosevelt and Churchill meet in Casablanca. Rommel's 21st Panzer Division is withdrawn westward to Tunisia to regroup and defend Tunisia from attack from allied forces to the west.

January 15: The British Eighth Army begins a new offensive in Libya.

January 18: The Germans counterattack in Tunisia but ultimately gain nothing for their effort.

January 23: Eighth Army enters Tripoli, thus liberating all of Libya.

January 24: Churchill and Roosevelt conclude the Casablanca Conference with a demand for the unconditional surrender of Germany, Italy and Japan.

January 29: Eighth Army's advance units approach the Tunisian frontier.

January 31: In Stalingrad, Paulus, 16 generals and two-thirds of the German Sixth Army surrender.

February 2, 1943: The final organized German hold-outs in Stalingrad surrender.

February 4: The first elements of British Eighth Army cross the Tunisian border.

February 9: The Japanese evacuate Guadalcanal.

February 14: Rommel's 10th and 21st Panzer Divisions begin a counterattack against the U.S. II Corps in central Tunisia. The Soviets capture Rostov-on-Don in the Ukraine.

February 15: Around the Kasserine Pass in Tunisia, Fifth Panzer Army

An entrenched 75mm PaK (anti-tank gun).

Troops and wire below sea level in the Quatarra Depression.

forces the retreat of the U.S. II Corps, inflicting heavy losses.

February 16: The British Eighth Army captures Medenine in southern Tunisia.

February 17: Rommel and von Arnim's units have destroyed most of the U.S. 1st Armored Division around Kasserine.

February 19–25: Fierce fighting in central Tunisia after the German Fifth Panzer Army breaks through Kasserine Pass and causes significant damage to the U.S. troops holding it.

February 22: Soviet offensives in central and southern Russia have been very successful, but now supply issues are starting to slow them down while their German opponents are building up strength for a counterattack.

February 24: Rommel is appointed commander of Army Group Africa.

March 6: Rommel mounts a major attack on Medenine but is driven off. British troops are amazed by the inept performance of their opponents. Most of the German combat veterans are by now killed, wounded or captured.

March 9: Rommel returns to Germany at Hitler's insistence. Von Arnim replaces him as commander of all Axis forces in Tunisia.

March 19–26: The British Eighth Army begins a week-long attack on the Mareth line.

March 26: Axis troops abandon the Mareth line.

March 29: British Eighth Army units race 100 miles [160 km] into Tunisia and break through Gabes Pass.

April 5–6, 1943: British and American forces attack the Fifth Panzer

Army in Tunisia from two directions. Allied air superiority is all but eliminating Axis resupply across the Mediterranean.

April 7: British and American forces meet in Tunisia.

April 14: Axis forces occupy their final defensive positions of the North African campaign, stretching from Tunis to Bizerta.

April 18: An Axis resupply run by air is ambushed and half the 100 aircraft are shot down.

April 22: British First and Eighth Armies, along with the U.S. II Corps and Free French forces begin an offensive to destroy the German and Italian forces at the bridgehead in Tunisia.

May 3, 1943: American forces capture Mateur, some 50 miles [80 km] northwest of Tunis.

May 6: British V Corps destroys what is left of 15th Panzer Division. American forces move toward Bizerta.

May 7: Tunis and Bizarte are both captured by the Allies.

May 10: The last organized Axis resistance in North Africa collapses. With no hope of evacuation, German and Italian troops begin a wholesale surrender.

May 12: Formal surrender of all German forces in Tunisia. This is the end of campaign in North Africa and the DAK. More than 250,000 Axis prisoners are taken, along with two dozen generals.

May 13: The Italian Commander, Marshal Messe, surrenders the balance of Axis forces, mostly Italian troops, in North Africa. All German and Italian operations come to an end.

May 16–17: The Dambuster Raid in Germany destroys two dams and floods much of the Ruhr River valley.

July 5–17, 1943: Operation Citadel, the German offensive against the Kursk salient begins. This will be the last major German offensive on the Eastern Front and will result in the largest tank battle in history.

July 9–10: Nighttime airborne landings inaugurate the Allied seaborne invasion of Sicily.

July 10: Operation Husky, the main Allied landings on Sicily, begins.

July 12: Hitler orders a halt to operations at Kursk and has forever given up the strategic initiative to the Soviets. Aircraft losses are severe and the Luftwaffe no longer dominates the skies. Hitler orders German units transferred to Italy because of the invasion of Sicily.

July 15: As the Germans at Kursk pull back to their start-lines, the Soviets launch a major counteroffensive.

July 19: Hitler and Mussolini meet in northern Italy for the last time before Italy surrenders. Mussolini knows Italy cannot hold out much longer. American units on Sicily advance with little resistance.

July 24–August 2: British RAF and American USAF units bomb Hamburg over 10 nights, causing massive firestorms that kill 50,000 civilians and make another 800,000 homeless. Allied forces led by General Patton capture Palermo, Sicily.

July 25: Mussolini is relieved of his office and arrested. Marshall Pietro Badoglio forms a new government.

August 17, 1943: American troops enter Messina, Sicily shortly before the British. Before Messina falls, the Germans are able to evacuate over 40,000 troops and a large amount of equipment across the strait to Italy. The campaign for Sicily is over.

September 3, 1943: General Castellano signs the Italian surrender in Sicily. It is not announced yet to prevent German takeover of Italy. The first units of Montgomery's Eighth Army land in Italy.

September 8: The surrender of Italy is finally announced. The Italian fleet departs Italy and surrenders to the Allies.

September 9: Allied forces land at Salerno, Italy and are met by ferocious German resistance.

September 12: German commandos led by Otto Skorzeny rescue Mussolini from captivity on top of the Gran Sasso in Italy.

September 16: The Battle of Salerno is over but it is a close thing. Allied forces start moving north up the Italian boot.

September 22: Two British midget submarines are able to attack the German battleship *Tirpitz* in Norway and put it out of commission for over a year.

September 23: Mussolini announces the formation of the Italian Social Republic.

September 25: Soviet forces capture Smolensk, their most important success since Kursk.

September 27: German troops take control of the island of Corfu after killing all of the Italian defenders.

September 29: Italians sign a full armistice agreement.

October 1, 1943: Allied forces enter Naples, Italy.

November 20: U.S. Marines land on Tarawa Atoll in the Gilbert Islands.

November 28–December 1: Roosevelt, Churchill and Stalin meet for the Teheran Conference.

December 24–29: General Dwight D. Eisenhower is announced as the Supreme Allied Commander for the invasion of Europe. Most of the other senior commanders of the invasion are also announced: Tedder, Ramsay, Leigh Mallory and Montgomery among others.

December 26: The German battlecruiser *Scharnhorst*, which has been attacking Arctic convoys for two years, is sunk by the Royal Navy. Only 36 of her crew of over 2,000 are saved.

1944

January 14, 1944: Soviet offensive at Leningrad begins.

January 15: Allied troops have advanced as far as the heavily defended Gustav Line that runs across Italy.

January 20: The first of many American attacks on Monte Cassino, a key defensive unit of the Gustav Line.

January 22: The U.S. Fifth Army's VI Corps lands at Anzio, Italy in an amphibious attack that meets little initial resistance.

January 23: Allied troops continue to pour ashore at Anzio, casualties are minimal, however, the Allied commanders fail to take advantage of the situation and don't move far beyond the bridgehead.

January 27: The 30-month Siege of Leningrad ends when German forces withdraw.

February 3, 1944: German forces begin a series of counterattacks on the Allied bridgehead at Anzio.

February 15: The monastery on Monte Cassino is completely destroyed during a massive Allied bombing raid.

February 16: The Germans begin a massive counterattack against the Anzio beachhead.

March 15: Another major attack on Monte Cassino. Destruction of the monastery has created an almost impregnable defensive position.

March 19: Soviet forces have reached and crossed the Dniepr River, another major obstacle on their relentless westward movement toward Germany.

March 22–23: Allied forces make another unsuccessful attack on Cassino, and then call off future attacks. All offensive action will halt for two months so the Allied forces can be reorganized and re-supplied.

April 2, 1944: The Soviets enter Romania.

April 19: Soviet attacks on Sevastopol continue. On the rest of the Eastern Front Soviet activity starts to slow down due to overstretched supply lines. Both sides welcome the respite.

April 28: On the south coast of England at Slapton Sands, a mock invasion to prepare for the upcoming Normandy invasion is attacked by German E-boats. At least 638 servicemen are killed, about three times the number that would die at Utah Beach on June 6.

May 9: Sevastopol surrenders to the Soviets.

May 11–12: after several weeks of general inactivity, four Allied corps begin a general advance against Monte Cassino and the Gustav Line.

May 15: German positions on the Gustav Line are beginning to collapse.

May 18: Hitler announces that Field Marshal von Rundstedt will become Commander-in-Chief West. His primary subordinates will be Rommel and Blaskowitz. In Italy, Monte Cassino is finally captured by Allied forces.

May 23: The Anzio beachhead comes alive as American forces stage large attacks on the German defenders.

May 28: With Allied offensives all along the front from Anzio, Monte Cassino and the Gustav Line, German troops start to pull back to the next significant defensive position on the Caesar Line.

June 4: Rome falls to U.S. forces.

June 6: Operation Overlord, the Allied invasion of Europe over the beaches of Normandy begins.

June 12: Another wave of Allied forces comes ashore in France. Over 326,000 men, 54,000 vehicles and 110,000 tons of supplies have been landed.

June 13: The first V-1 flying bomb lands in England.

June 15: The first B-29 Superfortress raid on the Japanese mainland. U.S. Marines land on Saipan in the Marianas.

June 19: Air combat during the Battle of the Philippine Sea. Called "The Great Marianas Turkey Shoot" by American airmen, over 450 Japanese aircraft are destroyed and two aircraft carriers sunk.

June 22: Operation Bagration begins. Four Soviet "Fronts" totaling over 2.5 million men advance along the entire Eastern Front and steamroll over 800,000 defending German soldiers. In two months the Soviets advance hundreds of miles, destroy German Army Group Center and inflict 540,000 casualties, the greatest defeat of the German armies during the war.

June 27: American forces take Cherbourg, France, the first major seaport on the continent to be captured.

July 9: British and Canadian forces finally capture Caen, France, an objective that was supposed to be captured on D-Day, June 6.

July 17: Field Marshal Rommel is severely injured in an attack by Allied aircraft.

July 20: Hitler is seriously wounded by a bomb blast in an attempt to assassinate him. Several thousand German military personnel and civilians are executed for taking part or knowing about the plot. Most are innocent.

July 25: Operation Cobra, the breakout from St. Lo in Normandy begins. Soviet troops enter Lvov in the Ukraine.

August 1: In France, Patton's Third Army becomes operational. In Poland, the Warsaw Uprising of the civilian Home Army begins. Soviet armies are only 12 miles away, but refuse to help the citizens of Warsaw, preferring to let the Germans do the job since most of the Home Army is anti-communist.

August 12: The city of Florence, Italy is captured by Allied forces.

August 15: The Falaise pocket in France is created by Allied troops, trapping parts of three German armies inside it. Operation Anvil/Dragoon, the Allied invasion of southern France, begins. In Italy, Allied troops reach the Gothic Line, the next major German strategic position in northern Italy.

August 17: In northern France, American troops under Patton quickly advance into the interior, capturing Orleans and Dreux. The Allies are in danger of scattering their spearheads. Hitler dismisses Field Marshal Kluge, who commits suicide the following day.

August 20: The last of the German forces to escape from the Falaise pocket do so. Over 50,000 troops are captured, but a greater number have escaped.

August 23: Romania surrenders to the Soviet Union and declares war on Germany.

August 25: French troops from Patton's army enter Paris.

August 26: Soviet forces reach the Danube River.

August 29: Soviet forces and Polish communist units announce that the Germans have killed around 1.5 million people in the former Majdanek concentration camp, the first one to have been captured. In France, Third Army captures Reims. In Warsaw, the fighting continues with the Home Army being slowly destroyed.

August 30: Allied troops start their advance on the Gothic Line in Italy.

September 2, 1944: British forces enter Brussels. American troops enter Mons. French forces capture Lyons.

September 8, 1944: The first German V-2 rocket lands in England.

September 17: Operation Market Garden begins. The objective is the capture of Arnhem and to vault the lower Rhine River. Three Allied airborne divisions drop to capture a series of bridges British ground forces will need to advance. In planning, German resistance is underestimated and the presence of two SS Panzer Divisions is unexpected.

September 25: The remaining British forces in Arnhem, about 25 percent of those who entered the town, are evacuated. The rest are killed or captured. It is a bloody, ineptly run disaster.

September 27: Patton's Third Army reaches Metz.

October 2, 1944: The Warsaw Uprising ends as German troops put down the last of the resistance. Over 200,000 Poles have died and Warsaw is destroyed.

October 3: U.S. forces puncture the Siegfried Line around Aachen.

October 14: Rommel, suspected of complicity in the plot to kill Hitler, is offered the choice of a public trial or suicide with a state funeral and safety of his family. He commits suicide.

October 16: Aachen is surrounded by American forces.

October 20: U.S. landings on the east coast of Leyte. General MacArthur lands and proclaims "I have returned." The Japanese navy initiates its last ditch plan to repel the invasion.

October 24–26: The Battle of Leyte Gulf. Several large clashes around the Philippines constitute the largest sea battle in history and a shattering defeat for the Japanese. When it is over, 1,500 American sailors, three small aircraft carriers and three destroyers are lost. Japanese losses exceed 10,000 sailors, one large and three small aircraft carriers, three battleships, eight cruisers and 12 destroyers. The Japanese now rely on suicide or "Kamikaze" attacks against American ships.

November 12: After several unsuccessful attempts to sink her, British aircraft manage to score several hits and the German battleship *Tirpitz*, sister of the *Bismarck*, is sunk in Norway. Troops of the U.S. Third Army cross the Moselle River south of Metz.

December 16: The Germans begin a major counteroffensive in the Ardennes region. Twenty-four German divisions pour through the front as poor weather grounds the Allied air forces. The German plan is to split the Allied forces and push toward Antwerp. The weather prevents Allied air operations in the area. The resulting month-long battle will be called "The Battle of the Bulge."

December 24: German forces in the Ardennes make their farthest advance and now go on the defensive.

December 26: The besieged town of Bastogne is relieved by Patton's Third Army. In Hungary, Budapest is surrounded by Soviet troops.

1945

January 12: Twenty-one Soviet armies launch a major offensive along the entire Eastern Front. The defending Germans are outnumbered five to one in troops and equipment.

January 27: The remaining Germans in the Ardennes are forced back to their start-lines. Hitler has already transferred much of their armor to face the new Soviet onslaught.

February 1, 1945: Soviet forces reach the Oder River on the outskirts of Berlin.

February 4–11: Roosevelt, Churchill and Stalin meet in Yalta. Stalin agrees to declare war on Japan two months after Germany's surrender. Postwar borders of Eastern Europe are determined as is the division of Germany into four zones of occupation.

February 13: Budapest surrenders to Soviet forces.

February 13–15: British and U.S. aircraft bomb Dresden, causing a horrific fire storm that kills up to 70,000 civilians.

February 19: U.S. Marines land on Iwo Jima.

March 7, 1945: Leading units of the U.S. Army's III Corps find a bridge across the Rhine River at Remagen and secure a bridgehead on the opposite shore. Hitler is livid and sacks General Rundstedt.

March 9: Bonn, Germany is captured by U.S. forces. In a devastating attack by B-29's, Tokyo is firebombed. Somewhere between 80,000 and 120,000 are killed.

March 19: Off Japan, the aircraft carrier USS *Franklin* is struck by two bombs from a Japanese aircraft. The resulting explosions and fire kill 832 crewmembers, the largest loss of life on a U.S. ship save the Arizona at Pearl Harbor.

March 27: Iwo Jima is finally secured after 23,300 American casualties. Of the 20,800 Japanese defenders only 200 survive. In Britain, the last V-2 rocket lands in London. Over 9,300 civilians have been killed or injured during the V2 campaign.

April, 1945: As an indication of how ineffective the German submarine war has become, during the month of April 13 Allied ships are sunk at the cost of 27 submarines.

April 1: U.S. forces land on Okinawa, the last stop before the land invasion of Japan itself. Over 450,000 soldiers and marines are embarked in the largest amphibious operation ever conducted. Opposing them are over 130,000 Japanese soldiers. At sea, the U.S. fleet has become the target of constant Kamikaze raids. In Germany, the U.S. First and Ninth Armies join up, trapping 325,000 German soldiers in the Ruhr pocket.

April 7: The Japanese battleship Yamato, largest battleship ever built, is sent on a suicide mission to Okinawa. With only enough fuel for a one-way trip to the Okinawa beaches, she is found by American aircraft. After several hours and attacks by over 300 aircraft, Yamato is sunk.

April 9: The Allied spring offensive in Italy begins.

April 12: President Roosevelt dies in Warm Springs, Georgia. Vice-President Harry S. Truman becomes President.

April 13: U.S. and British forces begin overrunning German concentration camps and the full horror of their existence become clear.

April 16: The final massive ground assault by Soviet forces to capture Berlin begins. Over two million men, 6,000 tanks and 16,000 cannon burst forth on the one million German defenders who have fewer than 1,200 tanks and about half that number of aircraft.

April 25: Soviet forces encircle Berlin.

April 28: Mussolini and his mistress are captured by partisans and shot and then hung by their heels in the main square at Milan. In Berlin, Soviet troops have penetrated to within one mile of Hitler's bunker.

April 29: Hitler marries Eva Braun. He then appoints Admiral Karl Dönitz his successor. In Italy, all German forces surrender.

April 30: Hitler and Eva Braun commit suicide in Hitler's bunker. Their bodies are carried outside and burned.

May 2: Berlin falls to Soviet forces.

May 3: Soviet and Allied forces meet for the first time.

May 7: Germany signs an unconditional surrender at General Eisenhower's headquarters. Hostilities will end at 23:01 (11:01 p.m.) the next day.

May 8: VE (Victory in Europe) Day.

May 23: Churchill resigns as Prime Minister when the Labour Party decides not to maintain a coalition government.

Chapter 6: After the End

June 22, 1945: Organized Japanese resistance on Okinawa comes to an end. U.S. forces have suffered 48,000 casualties. There are 120,000 Japanese military and 45,000 civilian dead.

August 6, 1945: An atomic bomb is dropped on the Japanese city of Hiroshima. Sixty percent of the city is destroyed and 80,000 people die in the resulting firestorm.

August 8: The Soviet Union declares war on Japan.

August 9: A second atomic bomb is dropped on Nagasaki. About 40,000 people are killed.

August 14: Emperor Hirohito decides it is time the war should end. He announces this in a radio message.

August 15: VJ (Victory over Japan) Day.

September 2, 1945: Japan formally surrenders in a ceremony on the USS *Missouri* in Tokyo Bay.

Appendix 1

BIOGRAPHY OF LUDWIG BLOOS

Knight's Cross winner Ludwig Bloos was originally thought to be the author of "Felzug in Russland," as his signature appears in the book. Further research revealed that while he fought in that campaign, and may have had contact with the true (anonymous) author, he never served in the 201st Panzer Regiment. For the following information on Bloos the authors are indebted to www. ritterkreuztraeger-1939-45.de and have translated it from the German.

Ludwig Bloos was born on March 7, 1915 in Oberweiler / Franconia, joined the 11th Panzer Regiment on October 1, 1938, and participated in the campaigns against Poland and France.

On June 9 1943, as a member of the 11th Panzer Regiment, he was promoted to platoon commander in the 8th Company and was wounded on March 5, 1944 by an AT (anti-tank) gun. On March 2, 1944, the 6th Panzer Division received orders to assemble east of Belgorodka, and the 11th Panzer Regiment was ordered to follow.

During a patrol prior to the attack on

the village of Gulewzy, the commander of the 8th Company, Captain Schmidt, was wounded, and Lieutenant Horn took over command of the 8th Company.

The initial attack on Ssosenowka was a success and the town was taken, so the main attack on Gulewzy was ordered in conjunction with the II Panzer Grenadier Rgt. 114. The order was given to eliminate a Russian bridgehead east of the Horyn River. This bridgehead was created by the Russians after the 2d SS Panzer Division retreated from the area on March 3. At 5 AM the attack began and reached Hill 273.4 to join up with an infantry unit, but the attack stalled and the Germans drew heavy fire from anti-tank guns.

The Panzers retreated and the infantry was unable to hold the hill and they retreated as well. Russian forces meanwhile almost encircled the division and the Germans were receiving fire from behind. By this time, only three Panzers were left and they were ordered to hold the hill at all costs. Lieutenant Horn's Panzer received a direct hit and the other two tanks retreated.

The fighting then became concentrated on the village of Bissowka, where Ludwig Bloos destroyed two Russian tanks and the other five turned back. Bissowka was now surrounded on two sides by the Russians, so a battlegroup under the command of 1st Lieutenant Bieling moved to Staro-Konstantinow in the rear with orders to hold that position. On March 5, all intact Panzers of the regiment were put under Bloos' command and they created a holding position outside the town of Kamenka. Here Bloos decided to execute a flanking attack with the three surviving tanks of his platoon so that the Panzer Grenadiers could retreat to a new holding position. He succeeded in destroying seven Russian tanks and the grenadiers were able to retreat to safety. Bloos received the Knight's Cross for this heroic action.

After the war, Bloos served in the newly created Bundeswehr and advanced to Staff Sergeant. He died on February 18, 1991 in Markt-beroldheim-Franconia.

CASUALTIES INCURRED BY THE
2D BATTALION/201ST PANZER REGIMENT
DURING ITS 1942–43 CAMPAIGN IN RUSSIA

Unseren Gefallenen!

Oblt.	Christian Goerdeler	Stab	gef. am	15. 5. 42
"	Arnold Völzke	5. Kp.	" "	31. 5. 42
"	Ludwig Ott	8. Kp.	" "	30. 6. 42
"	Joachim Gleim	6. Kp.	" "	26. 10. 42
"	Karl Crämer	5. Kp.	" "	29. 10. 42
"	Rolf Peitzner	6. Kp.	" "	6. 11. 42
"	Günther Korte	6. Kp.	" "	26. 12. 42
Lt.	Grubo von Viereck	8. Kp.	" "	17. 9. 42
Stabsarzt	Dr. Paul Feldweg	Stab	" "	15. 5. 42
Obfeldw.	Hermann Ziege	8. Kp.	" "	14. 5. 42
"	Ludwig Koch	6. Kp.	" "	15. 5. 42
"	Kurt Winkelmann	6. Kp.	" "	15. 5. 42
Obfunkm.	Herbert Fischer	6. Kp.	" "	15. 5. 42
Feldw.	Hans-Joachim Beese	Stabskp.	" "	14. 5. 42
"	Hans Elfert	5. Kp.	" "	30. 6. 42
"	Günther Schlage	6. Kp.	" "	30. 6. 42
"	Fritz Wulsch	8. Kp.	" "	11. 7. 42
"	Richard Böttcher	8. Kp.	" "	14. 9. 42
"	Walter Engelmann	5. Kp.	" "	9. 10. 42
"	Kurt Zieschang	8. Kp.	" "	31. 10. 42
Funkm.	Horst Müller	8. Kp.	" "	30. 6. 42
Uffz.	Herbert Arndt	6. Kp.	" "	15. 5. 42
"	Wilhelm Bommer	6. Kp.	" "	15. 5. 42
"	Herbert Fuhrich	8. Kp.	" "	16. 5. 42
"	Otto Krohn	5. Kp.	" "	17. 5. 42
"	Hans Neumann	5. Kp.	" "	17. 5. 42
"	Fritz Dickow	Stabsk.	" "	21. 5. 42
"	Wilhelm Scholz	5. Kp.	" "	30. 6. 42
"	Hans Schimmel	5. Kp.	" "	30. 6. 42
"	Kurt Zeitz	8. Kp.	" "	30. 6. 42
"	Franz Feder	8. Kp.	" "	30. 6. 42
"	Alfred Richter	5. Kp.	" "	29. 7. 42

Uffz.	Friedrich Wegner	6. Kp.	gef. am	14. 9. 42
"	Helmut Fischer	8. Kp.	" "	14. 9. 42
"	Heinz Müller	6. Kp.	" "	26. 10. 42
"	Fritz Schwarz	5. Kp.	" "	29. 10. 42
"	Theodor Heder	8. Kp.	" "	3. 11. 42
"	Franz Bauer	8. Kp	" "	8. 1. 43
"	Hermann Eisenmann	Stabskp.	" "	21. 1. 43
"	Franz Hapke	5. Kp.	" "	2. 2. 43
Obgefr.	Hubert Bleske	Stabskp.	" "	17. 5. 42
"	Helmut Bauer	6. Kp.	" "	20. 5. 42
"	Günther Baschin	6. Kp.	" "	17. 12. 42
Gefr.	Andreas Auteneder	8. Kp.	" "	14. 5. 42
"	Dietrich Wildt	Stabskp.	" "	17. 5. 42
"	Helmut Hirche	5. Kp.	" "	17. 5. 42
"	Helmut Drevermann	5. Kp.	" "	17. 5. 42
"	Johann Hirt	Stabskp.	" "	21. 5. 42
"	Richard Kissner	Stabskp.	" "	21. 5. 42
"	Heinrich von Lübke	5. Kp.	" "	30. 6. 42
"	Richard Käsow	6. Kp.	" "	30. 6. 42
"	Robert Sigismund	6. Kp.	" "	30. 6. 42
"	Bernhard Kloep	8. Kp.	" "	30. 6. 42
"	Josef Schneid	8. Kp.	" "	30. 6. 42
"	Hans Brenner	5. Kp.	" "	30. 6. 42
"	Paul Klotke	Stabskp.	" "	3. 8. 42
"	Raymund Michels	8. Kp.	" "	22. 8. 42
"	Günther Matthias	Stabskp.	" "	23. 8. 42
"	Heinrich Kaffine	8. Kp.	" "	4. 9. 42
"	Max Fuchs	Stabskp.	" "	8. 9. 42
"	Kurt Eck	Stabskp.	" "	11. 10. 42
"	Baptist Dotterweich	5. Kp.	" "	29. 10. 42
"	Ludwig Simon	5. Kp.	" "	29. 10. 42
"	Arnold Herms	5. Kp.	" "	29. 10. 42
"	Kurt Schönberger	5. Kp.	" "	3. 11. 42
"	Peter Seuter	5. Kp.	" "	3. 11. 42
"	Wolfgang Döttinger	6. Kp.	" "	3. 11. 42
"	Wilhelm Ruckaberle	Stabskp.	" "	25. 11. 42
"	Josef Strack	6. Kp.	" "	17. 12. 42
"	Bernhard Weber	6. Kp.	" "	17. 12. 42
"	Albert Kern	8. Kp.	" "	20. 12. 42
"	Alois Franske	Stabskp.	" "	21. 1. 43

Pz. Obschtz.	Alfred Say	Stabskp.	gef. am	27. 5. 42
"	Walter Jurczik	Stabskp.	" "	1. 2. 43
"	Werner Krohn	8. Kp.	" "	10. 2. 43
Pz. Schtz.	Günther Thieser	8. Kp.	" "	14. 5. 42
"	Richard Höger	8. Kp.	" "	14. 5. 42
"	Kurt Müller	6. Kp.	" "	15. 5. 42
"	Rudolf Kreibisch	6. Kp.	" "	15. 5. 42
"	Helmut Dietrich	6. Kp.	" "	15. 5. 42
"	Hermann Wolf	6. Kp.	" "	15. 5. 42
"	Edgar Muthesius	6. Kp.	" "	15. 5. 42
"	Helmut Schlenger	5. Kp.	" "	15. 5. 42
"	Walter Bartels	5. Kp.	" "	17. 5. 42
"	Helmut Schnell	5. Kp.	" "	17. 5. 42
"	Christian Lichtenberg	5. Kp.	" "	17. 5. 42
"	Wilhelm Schlösser	8. Kp.	" "	17. 5. 42
"	Emil Marquardt	Stabskp.	" "	21. 5. 42
"	Karl Beringer	6. Kp.	" "	22. 6. 42
"	Erich Höper	8. Kp.	" "	30. 6. 42
"	Paul Theuser	5. Kp.	" "	30. 6. 42
"	Emil Feix	6. Kp.	" "	30 6. 42
"	Anton Meyer	6. Kp.	" "	30. 6. 42
"	Heinz Hofmann	6. Kp.	" "	30. 6. 42
"	Albert Hammer	8. Kp.	" "	11. 7. 42
"	Friedrich Buhl	6. Kp.	" "	17. 9. 42
"	Alwin Neeb	6. Kp.	" "	17. 12. 42
"	Lothar Schäfer	5. Kp.	" "	25. 12. 42
"	Karl Frick	5. Kp.	" "	26. 12. 42

Appendix 2
_____

OBITUARY OF PROFESSOR ROLF KRENGEL
_____

The following obituary of Rolf Krengel was published by the Deutsches Institut für Wirtschaftsforschung (DIW), and has been translated from the German by the authors.

The German Institute for Economic Research mourns the loss of its former Senior Director: Professor Dr. Rolf Krengel

Professor Krengel passed away on December 9, 2002 at age 84 with 35 years of loyal service to the Institute. He played a significant role in the development of DIW Berlin and we thank him for that.

During his time at the Institute, Rolf Krengel reformed important fields of work through the DIW and presented the results in public forums. His revolutionary scientific work in the fields of production, investment and accounting, his activity in the field of public economic accounting and the input-output analysis and his engagement with modeling processes and applying the model to answer economic and political questions are to be mentioned. His first publication was about industrial accounting for the Federal Republic of Germany in 1956 and his DIR special booklet about the public economic input-output analysis social by produce, employment and productivity [unclear statement], income distribution and hierarchy in West Berlin goes back as far as 1953.

As a leader in the industry department, Krengel cherished a close contact with the economy. In 1961 he was the founder of the bi-annual industry conference in West Berlin. There more than 100 representatives from German industry discussed the economic development with DIW experts. Rolf Krengel's scientific activities were utilized many times. He was not only a member of many German consulting committees (for example, he was a member in the working group for the Secretary of State and the committee for the Department of Statistics), but international institutions such as the OECD (Organization For Economic Co-operation and Development,) the EU (European Union) and the academy of sciences in Moscow appreciated his invaluable guidance. In 1968, he became honorary professor in the economic science department of the University of Berlin and in September, 1978, he was awarded the Federal Cross for achievement for the following:

"The Enterprise Generation: How Science and Science Fiction
    Influence Each Other"
International MBA Day
How Environmental Researchers Strengthen a Pollution Free Market
Work with marketing guru Jagdip Singh
The RUB study: Preventing asthma in children with neurodermitis
Thueringer University Library Committee organization
City of Brandenburg award
Balancing and controlling skills for management
Polkoerper Biopsy Studies
Berlin's cultural wealth and life
Aid to Youth with Disabilities
Picture media knowledge
"Hanover looks to the year 2015"

Hypnosis used for treating chronic pain at Goettingen
RUB study: When tree roots penetrate water lines
"Ethics in Medicine" Award
Elected vice president of GDCh at the University of Jena
"Right to Teach" advocate

Rolf Krengel's Post-War Activities

On January 2, 1950, the first Weekly Report on the post-war economy was released, which included information current as of the end of
1949.

A committee was formed by the Berlin Senate, called the "Enquete
Commission," comprised of Rudolf Meimberg from the Berlin Central
Bank, Karl C, Thalheim of IHK and Ferdinand Grunig and Rolf
Krengel of the DIW. The task of the commission was to determine how
much investment capital would be required to employ another
200,000 people in commerce in the western sector of Berlin [which
would become West Berlin]. In the summer of 1950, Rolf Krengel
composed the quarterly public economic accounting report for West
Berlin. On the basis of this report, the western region of Berlin was
included in the European Recovery Program.

BIBLIOGRAPHY AND SOURCES

For the supplementary material in this work surrounding the translated diaries, the authors would like to acknowledge the assistance of several expert organizations and websites in addition to previous books. These include:

www.lexikon-der-wehrmacht.de/Gliederungen/Panzerregimenter/PR201.htm for background into the 201st Panzer Regiment and its commanders.

www.historynet.com/battle-of-stalingrad-operation-winter-tempest.htm for background on the Stalingrad rescue attempt.

Informationsdienst Wissenschaft, Germany, 9 January 2003, for the obituary of Rolf Krengel.

www.ritterkreuztraeger-1939-45.de for the biography of Ludwig Bloos.

www.historyindex.com (Lee Merideth) for assistance with the timelines and other historical information.

BOOKS

Carrell, Paul. *Hitler Moves East, 1941–1943*. Winnipeg, Canada: J.J. Fedorowicz Publishing, 1991.

Craig, William. *Enemy at the Gates: The Battle for Stalingrad.* New York: E.P. Dutton, 1973.

Hastings, Max. *Armageddon: The Battle for Germany, 1944–45.* New York: Vintage Books, 2004.

Heckmann, Wolf. *Rommel's War in Africa.* New York: Doubleday, 1981.

Hoyt, Edwin. *199 Days: The Battle for Stalingrad.* New York: Forge Books, 1999.

Irving, David. *The Trail of the Fox. New York:* E.P. Dutton & Co., 1977.

Jones, Michael K. *Stalingrad: How the Red Army Survived the German Onslaught.* Philadelphia: Casemate Publishers, 2007.

Liddell Hart, Basil. *The Rommel Papers.* New York: Da Capo Press, 1982.

Manstein, Field-Marshal Erich. *Lost Victories.* Novato, CA: Presidio Press, 1982.

Ryan, Cornelius. *The Last Battle.* New York: Simon and Schuster, 1966.

Schmidt, Heinz W. *With Rommel in the Desert.* London: Harrap & Co., 1951.

Toland, John. *The Last 100 Days: The Final Days of World War II in Europe.* New York: Random House, 1966.

Windrow, Martin. *Rommel's Desert Army,* Oxford, UK: Osprey Publishing, 1976.